CONFRONTING
ITALY

CONFRONTING ITALY

Mediterranean Surface Actions in 1940

Exploding the Myth of Mussolini's 'Mare Nostrum'

BRITANNIA NAVAL HISTORIES OF WORLD WAR II

University of Plymouth Press

This edition first published in the United Kingdom in 2019 by
University of Plymouth Press, Roland Levinsky Building, University of Plymouth,
Plymouth, Devon, PL4 8AA, United Kingdom.

Paperback ISBN: 978-1-84102-439-4

A CIP catalogue record of this book is available from the British Library.

Publisher: Paul Honeywill
Volume Editor: Charlotte Pett
Series Editors: G. H. Bennett, J. E. Harrold, R. Porter and M. J. Pearce
Editorial Assistants: Joss Plowman and Tasmin Dodson

Historical content courtesy of Britannia Museum, Britannia Royal Naval College,
Dartmouth, TQ6 0HJ.

Cover image © Edward Stables 2019

Every effort has been made to obtain rights providence of *Bartolomeo Colleoni*.

Typeset by University of Plymouth Press in Adobe Garamond Pro 9/14pt.
Printed and bound by Short Run Press, Exeter, United Kingdom.

The historical documents reproduced here appear as unedited text, apart from
minor changes made to date formats and corrections to typing errors found in the
original. www.royalnavy.mod.uk/The-Fleet/Shore-Establishments/BRNC-Dartmouth

> Victory Gulph of Palma
> Dec.r 14th 1803
>
> Dear Sir
>
> As Mr. Lutwidge sends me word that you have admired some of my Naval battles, I think that you will like to receive from me, a medal which was struck (by the partiality of my friends) in remembrance of one of them, at least it will serve to remind you that on the 13th Dec.r 1803 I had first the pleasure of being known to you, the wish to imitate successful battles is the sure road by exertion to surpass them which that you may do for your own honor and the advantage of your Country is the sincere wish of
>
> Dear Sir your much obliged faithful
> Nelson & Bronte

Letter from Admiral Lord Nelson, to Midshipman James Dalton, HMS Renown. Offering him encouragement

Britannia Royal Naval College

A majestic landmark, which towers above the harbour town of Dartmouth in Devon, Britannia Royal Naval College was designed by royal architect Sir Aston Webb to project an image of British sea power. A fine example of Edwardian architecture, the College has prepared future generations of officers for the challenges of service and leadership since 1905.

The Britannia Museum opened in 1999 to safeguard the College's rich collection of historic artefacts, art and archives and promote greater public understanding of Britain's naval and maritime heritage, as a key element in the development of British history and culture. It also aims to instil a sense of identity and ethos in the Officer Cadets that pass through the same walls as their forbears, from great admirals to national heroes to royalty.

Contents

Foreword

Admiral Sir Jock Slater

This volume of the Britannia Naval Histories of World War II, covering three surface actions in the Mediterranean in 1940, must not be read in isolation. The Navy Records Society Cunningham Papers [Volume 1] and accompanying biography of Andrew Cunningham by Michael Simpson are strongly recommended – as are the Commander-in-Chief's own autobiography: "A Sailor's Odyssey"; and other accounts and biographies, not least that by John Winton: "Cunningham: The Greatest Admiral Since Nelson".

In the spring and summer of 1940, the War Cabinet was preoccupied, inter alia, with the Norwegian Campaign, the Invasion of France, Dunkirk and the Battle of Britain. Despite Mussolini's bellicose pronouncements and subsequent declaration of war on Britain and France, the Joint Planning Committee in London had considered it "most unlikely that any Allied Fleet which could be concentrated in the Mediterranean would be strong enough to undertake an offensive naval policy"; and that was before the French Fleet was removed from the equation.

Cunningham, with his Flag in HMS *Warspite*, thought otherwise, supported indeed by the First Lord of the Admiralty, Winston Churchill, who was convinced of the strategic importance of the Mediterranean – so the Mediterranean Fleet was gradually reassembled. That said, with one or two exceptions, not least the modernised Flagship, the ships were old and slow and suffered considerable material deficiencies in main armament, armoured protection and anti-aircraft capability. Furthermore, although modern and well armed, the destroyers were in insufficient numbers. Nevertheless, the Fleet had been relentlessly trained and operational efficiency, confidence and morale were high.

The Commander-in-Chief was therefore set on testing the enemy's strength and resolve at the first opportunity, hence these early surface actions and the historic Fleet Air Arm attack from HMS *Illustrious* at Taranto; leaving the Italians in no doubt about the Mediterranean Fleet's absolute determination to succeed even against the odds.

On my desk as I write this foreword, is a small wooden plaque engraved with the immortal words of James Graham, Marquis of Mentrose (1612-1650):

He either fears his fate too much
Or his deserts are small
Who dare not put it to the touch
To win or lose it all.

This very same plaque sat on my Great-Uncle's desk in HMS *Warspite*, in 1940. It epitomises the fighting spirit, stamina, supreme courage and decisive action which so inspired his Fleet in all that they achieved, leading up to the victory off Cape Matapan in March 1941.

I commend these Britannia Naval Histories which articulate admirably for a wider audience the key and illustrious role that the Royal Navy has played in the history of Great Britain.

Jock Slater

Introduction

Michael Pearce

Italy declared war on Great Britain and France on 10th June 1940, six days after the Dunkirk evacuation ended and only twelve days before France signed an armistice to end her hostilities with Germany. Mussolini had long steered Italy towards the deceptive glories of war but the unseemly haste of his final decision was a direct consequence of Germany's astonishingly rapid defeat of France. The Italian dictator was confident that Britain would follow France's inevitable surrender by accepting unfavourable terms for peace and he determined that fascist Italy should share the spoils of victory. But the British resolved to fight on, come what may, and loudly ascribed Mussolini's opportunistic action to squalid self-aggrandisement; a view shared by many in Germany, albeit sotto voce.

Mussolini craved national prestige and personal glorification but he also coveted the French fleet and harboured expansionist territorial ambitions to annex Nice and the Cote d'Azur, Corsica and the French African territories of Tunisia and Djibouti. He also had aspirations to link the Italian colony of Libya with the newly conquered territory of Abyssinia (now Ethiopia) by taking control of British-dominated Egypt and the Sudan, thereby threatening British East Africa. Nevertheless, Italy could also cite a genuine and long-standing concern that gave Il Duce a less dishonourable pretext to join the winning side in a short sharp war against Britain, especially when France was no longer part of the strategic balance. On several occasions after the unification of Italy in 1861, she had felt vulnerable to potential diplomatic coercion by Britain, exercised through the threat of blockade made possible by the Royal Navy's control of the Mediterranean. This was re-emphasised in March 1940 when the British instituted a naval blockade of Italy's coal imports, a measure aimed at Germany as the source, rather than Italy but, even so, one that exposed as empty bombast Mussolini's claim to the Mediterranean as 'mare nostrum'.

Perhaps Italy could have gained from a brief victorious war but she was certainly in no position to engage in lengthy conflict, as the country lacked indispensable natural resources, particularly oil and coal, while having limited industrial capacity and infrastructure compared with Great Britain, France and Germany. As Britain's defiant attitude became clear, Italy found herself in the unenviable position of having to fight with what she had, which was even less than it might have been, because of Mussolini's failure to build up adequate stockpiles of oil and other strategic war materials. In addition, his enthusiastic championing of Franco's Nationalists during the Spanish Civil War had been excessively generous, given Italy's historical economic fragility: he had provided the Spanish fascists with significant support that his country could ill-afford, together with weaponry and armaments that should have been retained for Italy's own army and air force. These were a pale shadow of Il Duce's boasts, particularly in the case of the army, where many formations were poorly equipped, inadequately trained and badly led.

Mussolini felt that he could reasonably look to Hitler for supplies of war material but this confidence in his ally was misplaced, owing to the Führer's natural focus on Germany's own shortages. Even at the nadir of British fortunes in WW2, the Royal Navy's blockade strangled German trade very effectively, restricting the Reich's imports to whatever could be wrung from the subjugated territories of occupied Europe and a handful of shaky allies – together with limited quantities of iron ore and specialised commodities bought from Sweden and the unenthusiastic Portuguese and Spanish. These resources were never sufficient and the need to acquire raw materials, especially oil, became an obsession of Hitler's throughout the war, driving – and warping – his strategic priorities. Unsurprisingly, he put the insatiable demands of the German war machine before the needs of his Italian ally, for whose military prowess he had little regard. As a consequence, fuel shortages compelled the Regia Marina to curtail drastically its operational sorties by 1942-43 and take several ships, including two battleships, out of service.

Mussolini's declaration of war came on Italy's Navy Day, but the Regia Marina was far from ready, even though a European war had been widely anticipated since the middle 1930s, prompting world-wide rearmament. Large-scale programmes to build new warships and modernise existing fleets had been adopted by all major naval powers, including Italy, but the design and construction of large warships was a necessarily lengthy process, particularly the production of heavy guns and armour plate. Hitler planned to expand the German Kriegsmarine to be ready for his envisaged war with Great Britain in 1944 but Italy set 1942 as the date by which she would have a fleet of four powerful new battleships and four others comprehensively modernised. But in June 1940, only two modernised battleships were in commission: *Conti di Cavour* and *Giulio Cesare*. These had entered service during WW1 but both were completely reconstructed between 1933 and 1937, emerging almost as new ships, with lengthened hulls, modernised main armament of ten long-range 32cm (12.6-inch) guns, new secondary armament, increased armour and underwater protection, and entirely new machinery that enabled both ships to reach over 28 knots on trials, albeit that these were run lightly loaded.

Supporting these two thoroughly battle-worthy sister-ships, the Regia Marina went to war with a force of 19 fast and well-armed modern cruisers, some of which were among the most handsome warships ever built, although many were lightly constructed, sacrificing protection for speed. In June 1940 it could also deploy 130 fleet destroyers and light destroyers (the latter known in Italy as torpedo boats), together with 115 submarines – a larger number than any other nation at that time, except the Soviet Union. Aircraft carriers were a notable omission from the inventory, following the Regia Aeronautica being given control of all military aviation; the resulting lack of an integral naval air arm would seriously handicap the Italian fleet throughout hostilities. Of the other Italian battleships, two *Duilio* class ships were completing similar modernisation to their near sisters of the *Cavour* class but did not recommission until later in 1940, while the first two battleships of the formidable new *Littorio* class were ready for service only in August. The third ship of the class, *Roma*, joined the fleet in June 1942 but the final ship, *Impero*, was never completed. The Regia Marina was not alone in being unprepared for war: the suddenness of Mussolini's announcement led to about a quarter of Italian merchant ships being interned abroad, a serious loss that the country would regret later.

Many of the Regia Marina's officer corps were not committed fascists, their traditional allegiances leaning more towards the monarchy but, despite a lack of training in night-fighting, morale was high and when war was declared, they embraced their task with enthusiasm and confidence. This optimism was not shared by Supermarina, the navy's high command, which saw the navy's task as ensuring safe passage to Libya for convoys carrying reinforcements and supplies to the Italian army in North Africa. Supermarina took a cautious and pragmatic view of the navy's ability to carry out Mussolini's grandiose plans for immediate conquest and victory; understandable when four additional battleships were only weeks from joining the fleet.

Following the outbreak of war with Germany on 3rd September 1939, Britain's initial strategic objective in the Mediterranean was to maintain Italy's neutrality but in May 1940, it became clear to the British that war was not only unavoidable but imminent. British Intelligence had been intercepting and deciphering Italian diplomatic messages and many naval and military communications since 1937, giving them advanced warning of Mussolini's intentions. This intelligence capability enabled the British to make an accurate assessment of the likelihood and timing of Italy's entry into the war, allowing the Admiralty to reduce the Mediterranean Fleet to deploy ships in home waters to contain the Kriegsmarine, while detaching others to hunt German raiders in the Atlantic and Indian Oceans. The impact of having a significantly smaller British naval presence in the Mediterranean was reduced by the strong French fleet based on Toulon and in North African ports. But as France crumbled and Britain's reliable intelligence indicated that Mussolini would seek to exploit this, the Admiralty began to rebuild the Royal Navy's strength in the Mediterranean.

By June, the Mediterranean Fleet, commanded by the very able and aggressive Admiral Sir Andrew Cunningham, was based at Alexandria in Egypt, because its traditional base in Malta, only 60 miles from Sicily, was considered too vulnerable to Italian bombers. On paper, it was a powerful force of four battleships, an aircraft carrier and six cruisers but, in reality, it left much to be desired as a fighting force and was markedly inferior to the Italian fleet in some respects. The only capital ship approaching modern standards was Cunningham's flagship, HMS *Warspite*, already famous for her decisive role in the Second Battle of Narvik, barely eight weeks earlier during the Norwegian campaign. The *Warspite* had been completed during WW1 in time to fight at Jutland 24 years before but she had been completely reconstructed and modernised in the mid 1930s, somewhat along the lines of the Italian *Conti di Cavour* and *Giulio Cesare*, although she had not been lengthened and did not have their turn of speed, new machinery giving her a maximum of 24 knots; nor did she have their sleek appearance, looking more solid and purposeful than graceful. However, she did have one significant advantage over the Italian ships: her main armament of eight 15-inch (38cm) guns fired shells weighing over 1900lb each, compared with less than 1200lb for the Italian 32cm (12.6-inch) weapons. In addition, the maximum elevation of her guns had been increased to 30 degrees, allowing her to shoot to a range of 32,200 yards, more than matching the 31,280 yards range of the Italian ships.

The other battleships in the Mediterranean Fleet were less effective; the best of them being HMS *Malaya*, built as a sister-ship to the *Warspite* but not modernised to the same extent. She retained her original machinery and carried extra weight from additions and alterations in the early 1930s, making her significantly slower than the *Warspite*. In addition, the maximum elevation of her 15-inch main armament remained at the original 20 degrees, restricting her guns to a range of 23,400 yards. This considerable operational limitation applied to Cunningham's other two WW1-vintage battleships, the *Royal Sovereign* and *Ramillies*, sisters that also mounted eight 15-inch guns but had received even less modernisation than the *Malaya*. With a designed speed four knots slower than the original 25-knot *Queen Elizabeth* class, to which the *Warspite* and *Malaya* belonged, their maximum speed by 1940 was only 19-20 knots – less when they were long out of dock – and their old machinery was unreliable and prone to breakdown. The elderly aircraft carrier HMS *Eagle*, converted from an incomplete battleship hull at the end of WW1, gave Cunningham a certain advantage over the Italian fleet but she was limited by her slow speed, vulnerability to air and submarine attack and, most seriously, by the small size of her air group – only 17 Fairey Swordfish torpedo bomber/reconnaissance aircraft. However, she had taken aboard three obsolescent Gloster Sea Gladiator biplane fighters found in store at Alexandria and these, agile aircraft flown by her Commander (Flying) and volunteer Swordfish pilots, gave her some ability to defend the fleet from air attack.

The Battle of Calabria, 9th July 1940

The Royal Navy and the Regia Marina had similar primary tasks: to run convoys through the Mediterranean and to attack convoys run by their opponents. It was obvious to both sides that the intersection of Italian north-south convoys with British east-west and west-east convoys would bring the two fleets together sooner rather than later. A preliminary skirmish took place on 28th June, when British cruisers covering two convoys from Malta, intercepted and pursued three Italian destroyers taking troops and ammunition to Tobruk, sinking the *Espero* in the fading evening light but expending so much six-inch ammunition in the long chase that the engagement seriously depleted the Mediterranean Fleet's limited stocks.

Within a month of Mussolini's declaration of war, the anticipated clash of British and Italian fleets occurred in an action known to the British as the Battle of Calabria, after the region forming the 'toe' of Italy, and to the Italians as the Battle of Punta Stilo, after the nearest headland on that coast. Admiral Cunningham, flying his flag in the battleship HMS *Warspite*, was protecting two convoys evacuating surplus stores and non-essential personnel – including Cunningham's wife and two nieces – from Malta to Alexandria and had in company two other battleships, the *Malaya* and *Royal Sovereign*, together with the aircraft carrier *Eagle*, five cruisers and 16 escorting destroyers. Admiral Inigo Campioni was at sea in his flagship, the battleship *Giulio Cesare,* with her sister-ship, the *Conti di Cavour,* to protect a large convoy from Naples to Benghazi, carrying tanks, vehicles, troops, fuel and stores for Marshal Graziani's army in Libya. Apart from his two battleships, Campioni had 14 cruisers, including six heavy cruisers mounting eight-inch guns, and 20 destroyers.

The British and Italian commanders were well-informed of each other's movements: in addition to established British intelligence sources from broken Italian cyphers, the Royal Navy had captured two Italian submarines, the *Galileo Galilei* on 19th June and the *Uebi Scebeli* on 29th, both with their code and cypher books intact. This intelligence windfall gave Cunningham a significant tactical advantage for a few weeks, until the Italians changed their codes and cyphers, and it ensured that he was fully aware of Campioni's intentions and movements during the Battle of Calabria. Although the information available to Campioni was much less detailed, the highly effective German naval intelligence and monitoring service, *Beobachtungsdienst* or *B-Dienst*, in Berlin, passed the position and course of Cunningham's fleet to Supermarina. This did something to fill the void left by the Regia Aeronautica, which incurred Campioni's wrath for not providing him with tactical air reconnaissance comparable to that received by Cunningham from his carrier-borne Swordfish and RAF flying boats at Malta.

Both commanders were keen to engage but, before they did so, each tried to manoeuvre the other into a position of disadvantage. Cunningham sought to insert his ships between the Italian fleet and its base at Taranto; an ambitious plan, given the speed advantage enjoyed by the Italian battleships. Meanwhile, Supermarina instructed Campioni to draw Cunningham's fleet within range of the Regia Aeronautica's bombers and towards a screen of submarines positioned off the coast of Sicily, in the expectation that some of the major British ships would be sunk or disabled before the fleets met. When contact was made, Cunningham's determination to cut off the Italian fleet from its base, together with his innate impatience, led him to press on with the *Warspite* and her escorting destroyers as a 'fast division' to support the cruisers of his advanced scouting screen under Vice Admiral Tovey, while leaving the slower *Malaya* and *Royal Sovereign* to follow with their escorts at best speed. In doing this, he risked an engagement with superior forces but when the Italian battle squadron was sighted, he allowed the *Malaya* to make up some ground, although her unmodified guns had four miles less range than those of the *Warspite* and her few salvoes fell 3,000 yards short. The *Royal Sovereign* was left so far astern that she was never able to come into action, despite her elderly machinery being strained to the utmost and marking her progress with a dense pall of funnel smoke.

The action began with British and Italian cruisers exchanging accurate long-range salvoes at 22,000 yards, until the *Warspite,* coming up in support, opened fire on the Italian cruisers at 26,400 yards. The critical point of the battle came during the subsequent brief long-range artillery duel between the *Warspite* and the *Cesare* and *Cavour*. The Italian battleships, supporting their own cruisers, opened fire to starboard from a range of over 28,000 yards; the *Warspite*, shooting to port less than two minutes later, straddled the *Cesare* with her first salvo at a range of 26,000 yards. The Italians also soon found the range and shells began to bracket both flagships, one Italian salvo coming within 400 yards, other rounds overshooting and causing minor splinter damage to two British destroyers on the *Warspite*'s disengaged starboard side. The Italian heavy cruiser *Trento*, one of the squadron under Vice Admiral Paladini, also fired on the *Warspite* briefly from her maximum range of 28,000 yards before being ordered to join her five consorts in shooting at 22,000 yards on the British cruisers, all of which were becoming increasingly concerned that their six-inch ammunition was being rapidly consumed. When it became clear that both Italian battleships had accurately established the *Warspite*'s range and bearing, the British flagship increased speed and altered course to spoil the aim of the Italian gunners. Immediately before doing this, however, the *Warspite* fired a 15-inch salvo at 26,200 yards and one of these shells, weighing almost a ton, plunged down at a steep angle of descent, passed through the *Cesare*'s after funnel and struck her to port at its base.

The Italian flagship shook violently as the shell detonated; men in the aft conning tower being thrown into the air. Huge volumes of smoke immediately began pouring out of the ship from fires which broke out above and below decks, and from a 20 foot hole torn in her after funnel. Ventilator fans drew noxious fumes into four of the boiler rooms, overcoming the engineering personnel and reducing the *Cesare's* speed to 18 knots, as the affected boiler rooms were evacuated.

This loss of speed, together with the vast quantities of thick smoke obscuring his flagship aft of her funnels, convinced Admiral Campioni that the *Cesare* had been seriously damaged and he ordered the Italian fleet to turn away under cover of smoke. Their retirement was covered by a threat of torpedo attack by the numerous Italian destroyers on any British ships rash enough to penetrate the smoke screen and by Paladini's heavy cruisers dashing in and out of the smoke, shooting at the *Warspite* and Tovey's cruisers at every opportunity but without effect. This was not without cost to the Italians, as HMS *Neptune* hit the *Bolzano*, the leading heavy cruiser, with three six-inch shells from a salvo. One chopped the end from B turret's starboard eight-inch gun barrel, the second hit the torpedo room, killing two men and accidentally launching six torpedoes, while the third holed the hull aft, temporarily jamming her helm and causing the ship to take on 300 tons of water, although she stayed in action when the helm was restored.

With one of his two battleships damaged and reduced in speed, Admiral Campioni was not prepared to risk action with three British battleships carrying 15-inch guns and he set course for the Straits of Messina, as Cunningham still threatened to cut him off from his base at Taranto. Cunningham, meanwhile, had no intention of playing Campioni's game by exposing his heavy ships to torpedo attack from Italian destroyers darting through their smoke screen and he was also well aware, from accurate intelligence reports, that there was a submarine screen to the south, waiting in ambush if he pursued Campioni towards Sicily. The fleet action therefore petered out, to be replaced by heavy but ineffective high-level bombing attacks carried out by the Regia Aeronautica on the British and Italian fleets alike as they retired. The following day, Swordfish torpedo bombers from HMS *Eagle* attacked Augusta in Sicily in the hope of catching some of Campioni's ships but found only a destroyer, which they sank, and a tanker, which they damaged.

The shooting of both sides at the Battle of Calabria was impressively accurate, considering the extreme ranges at which the action was fought and that it took place before the advent of gunnery radar. The hit scored by HMS *Warspite* on the *Giulio Cesare* at 26,200 yards – over 13 nautical miles – stands as one of the longest-range hits on a moving target ever recorded. Italian shooting, though accurate, was marked by excessive shell spread within salvoes, something that adversely affected Regia

Marina gunnery throughout WWII. Italian authorities attributed the cause to their shells being of slightly different weights, due to inadequate quality-control during manufacturing, and also to the extremely high muzzle velocities of their heavy naval guns causing rapid barrel wear. In contrast, the Italians reported to the Germans that Royal Navy salvoes were notably well concentrated. British cruisers shot rapidly, consuming ammunition so quickly that the shell rooms of some ships became seriously depleted, a major concern in a theatre of war with limited ammunition reserves. As the war in the Mediterranean developed, British naval operations became limited as much by ammunition usage as by fuel consumption and this was to have grave consequences the following year, when ships were lost after running short of anti-aircraft ammunition during the evacuation of British and Dominion troops from Crete.

During the action off Calabria, both commanders handled their fleets aggressively, Campioni to the very limit of his restrictive orders from Supermarina, and the convoys that brought about the battle were delivered without loss. British morale was boosted by what they saw as a precipitate retreat by the Italian battle fleet after their flagship suffered only one shell hit, while the Italians felt that they had fought well against unfavourable odds and extricated their ships when fortune turned against them. The enthusiastic but inaccurate bombing of the Italian fleet by the Regia Aeronautica after the battle led to the painting of prominent red and white oblique stripes on the forecastles of Italian warships to facilitate recognition from the air. The Regia Marina realised that co-operation and co-ordination with the Regia Aeronautica was wholly unsatisfactory, although little subsequent improvement was obtained. Nevertheless, it was agreed that high-level bombing was ineffective against ships and this led to the deployment, within six months, of Ju87 Stuka dive bombers, a weapon that would severely test the Royal Navy in the Mediterranean and cause significant losses, particularly when wielded by Flieger Corps X of the Luftwaffe.

The action made clear to Admiral Cunningham the futility of deploying battleships that were up to seven knots slower than their opponents and whose guns were out-ranged by 8,000 yards. He also felt the lack of heavy cruisers armed with 8-inch guns, being conscious that Tovey's cruiser screen had been out-gunned as well as outnumbered. Cunningham was impressed with the performance of the *Eagle* but considered that more damage might have been done to the Italian ships and more protection given to his own fleet by a new aircraft carrier with modern fighters. The First Sea Lord, Admiral Sir Dudley Pound, was sympathetic and agreed to send Cunningham the newly rebuilt, radar-equipped battleship HMS *Valiant*, and the less modernised HMS *Barham*, both originally sister-ships of the *Warspite*, in exchange for the desperately slow and out-dated *Royal Sovereign* and *Ramillies*.

Pound also authorised despatch of the new armoured carrier HMS *Illustrious*, two heavy cruisers and two anti-aircraft cruisers to the Mediterranean. Although this large-scale reinforcement could not be effected immediately, it was a surprisingly complete answer to Cunningham's needs, particularly in the Summer of 1940, when the Admiralty was preoccupied with the threat of imminent invasion and felt compelled to retain sufficient ships in home waters to repel and destroy the German invasion fleet then being assembled across the Channel. This task was fundamental to the country's survival and, of necessity, would have to be undertaken by the Royal Navy, whatever the outcome of large-scale air battles then developing over southern England.

The Action off Cape Spada, 19th July 1940

Only ten days after the Battle of Calabria, the Mediterranean Fleet and the Regia Marina clashed again but on a smaller scale, off the northern coast of Crete. Captain J. A. Collins, Royal Australian Navy, in the cruiser HMAS *Sydney*, commanded a force of five destroyers, four of which had fought at Calabria, as had the *Sydney* herself. The Italian squadron comprised two cruisers under Rear Admiral Casardi, the *Giovanni della Bande Nere* and the *Bartolomeo Colleoni*, acclaimed as the fastest warships in the world when new in 1932; the *Bande Nere* reaching 41 knots on trials and the *Colleoni* making just under 40 knots, while another sister ship exceeded 42 knots. However, these much-vaunted speeds were misleading, as sea trials were run lightly loaded and the builders forced the machinery to give nearly 25% over designed power, to capitalise on the Italian navy's policy of paying a premium for each knot achieved over contract speed. The ships proved slower in service but the quest for high speed sacrificed armour protection and structural robustness, while their hull design conferred poor sea-keeping qualities in anything approaching rough weather. The Australian and Italian cruisers carried similar main armaments of eight six-inch guns but HMAS *Sydney* was better protected, although slower – her trial speed in 1935 had been 33 knots. Nevertheless, the *Sydney* had the considerable advantage that the surface action off Cape Spada would be her third against the Italian navy in as many weeks, having previously sunk the *Espero* on 28th June and been part of Admiral Cunningham's cruiser screen at Calabria.

The British ships were in two groups, both steering westerly courses between Greece and Crete. Four destroyers under Cdr H. St.L. Nicolson RN in HMS *Hyperion* were off northern Crete in line abreast, hunting for submarines, while Collins in HMAS *Sydney*, with a fifth destroyer, HMS *Havock*, sought Italian surface shipping 20 miles further north but ensured he kept within supporting distance of Nicolson. The Regia Aeronautica failed to provide Casardi with air reconnaissance and British cryptanalysts had yet to break the new Italian naval cypher introduced only two days earlier. Additionally, the *Sydney* was without aerial reconnaissance of her own, having received no replacement for her catapult-mounted Supermarine Walrus amphibian that had been lost earlier. Therefore, neither side knew the other's position, as the two Italian cruisers steamed eastwards through the Antikithera Channel off the north west tip of Crete, having had a rough passage from Tripoli. Casardi was on course for the island of Leros, from where he intended to attack British shipping in the Aegean; the Italian naval attaché in Istanbul having reported a convoy of British tankers leaving the Bosphorus carrying Romanian oil. The Italian ships had barely reached more sheltered waters off Cape Spada, when they sighted and were sighted by Nicolson's four destroyers. Casardi engaged but was wary of the out-ranged British ships being the escort for superior forces and of them attacking him with torpedoes, so he did not seek to close as Nicolson turned to the north-east, leading the Italians towards the *Sydney*, while the rear destroyer in the British line, HMS *Hasty*, signalled cheerfully to HMS *Hero*, the next ahead: "Don't look now but I think we are being followed.". Casardi's decision to engage from astern, keeping just within range of his main armament, lost him the opportunity to use his heavier guns decisively as he was soon frustrated by a combination of mist, British smoke and glare from the low sun.

HMAS *Sydney* received Nicolson's sighting reports and steered to intercept Casardi but kept radio silence to conceal her presence until she commenced shooting at 20,000 yards, lighting up a bank of low mist that shrouded her. Both Italian cruisers returned fire but after a six-inch shell struck the *Bande Nere* amidships and Nicolson's destroyers reversed course to engage, Casardi turned away and the action became a pursuit. Funnel smoke from the Italian ships interfered with the *Sydney*'s shooting and she frequently changed target between them, while the Italians replied with their after turrets but shot slowly, as they were rolling heavily. Nevertheless, they scored one hit that blew a small hole near the top of the *Sydney*'s fore funnel but, three minutes later, a shell from the Australian cruiser jammed the *Colleoni*'s rudder. Then the Italian ship was hit by several shells in quick succession, 4.7-inch from the British destroyers, now in range, as well as 6-inch from the *Sydney*. These caused severe casualties on the bridge and started serious fires before another hit in the boiler room stopped her dead in the water and disabled the main armament. The destroyers *Ilex* and *Hyperion* sank her with torpedoes, while the *Sydney* and two other destroyers sped off in pursuit of the *Bande Nere*, as she rounded the western extremity of Crete and set course southwards, after Casardi briefly turned back to confirm that the unfortunate *Colleoni* was beyond aid. The *Bande Nere* gradually drew away from the *Sydney*, returning fire with reasonable accuracy but she was hit again at 20,000 yards before disappearing into the haze at 22,000 yards, after which Collins broke off the chase, having only ten rounds left for the *Sydney*'s forward turrets. Dramatic photographs of the burning *Bartolomeo Colleoni*, her bows blown off by a torpedo from HMS *Ilex*, were widely published around the world as evidence that the Royal Navy had the upper hand in the Mediterranean, while the action reinforced the identity of the Royal Australian Navy, echoing a ship to ship action in 1914, when the previous HMAS *Sydney* sank the German cruiser *Emden*.

Other Mediterranean Surface Actions in 1940

On 12th October, British and Italian surface ships fought another action when Admiral Cunningham's battle fleet was at sea in heavy weather, covering supply convoy MB6 from Alexandria to Malta and the emptied freighters on their return voyage. At the extremity of Cunningham's scouting screen was the cruiser HMS *Ajax*, a veteran of the destruction of the German 'pocket battleship' *Graf Spee* at the Battle of the River Plate, ten months earlier. The Italians had their light craft at sea and, in improving weather off Sicily's Cape Passaro, the *Ajax* ran into two flotillas, one of four fleet destroyers and the other of three light destroyers. In a fast and confused moonlit night action, resolutely fought by both sides, the *Ajax* was hit several times, suffering 10 killed and 20 wounded, but she sank the light destroyers *Ariel* and *Airone* and crippled the fleet destroyer *Artigliere*, which was finished off the following morning by the heavy cruiser HMS *York*.

A month later, as part of a British plan to take the naval war into Italy's home waters, a force of three cruisers, HMS *Orion*, HMS *Ajax* and HMAS *Sydney* – seemingly always on the spot when a surface action was in prospect – entered the Adriatic with two Tribal class destroyers, and intercepted an Italian convoy in the Straits of Otranto, sinking all four merchant ships, damaging their escorting light destroyer and putting to flight the other escort, an armed merchant cruiser. On the same night, 11th November, 21 Fairey Swordfish torpedo bombers from the fleet carrier HMS *Illustrious* attacked the Italian naval base at Taranto and sank or crippled three of the Regia Marina's six battleships; one of which, the *Conti de Cavour*, never returned to service.

The Action off Cape Spartivento, 27th November 1940

The last surface action between British and Italian fleets in 1940 was fought off southern Sardinia on 27th November and is known to the Royal Navy as the Battle of Cape Spartivento but to the Regia Marina as the Battle of Cape Teulada. The Royal Navy had partly compensated for the French fleet no longer controlling the western Mediterranean, by basing at Gibraltar a small squadron, Force H, commanded by Vice Admiral Sir James Somerville in the battlecruiser HMS *Renown*, with the aircraft carrier HMS *Ark Royal* and the radar-equipped cruiser HMS *Sheffield*. This force was to earn lasting fame six months later when it was instrumental in the destruction of the German battleship *Bismarck* in the Atlantic. The *Renown* had seen service in WW1, but was comprehensively reconstructed and modernised between 1936 and 1939, with new machinery and dual-purpose secondary armament, improved protection and with the elevation of her main armament of six 15-inch guns increased to 30 degrees, giving the same 32,200 yard range as the guns of the *Warspite*. Although the *Renown* had pursued the German battlecruisers *Scharnhorst* and *Gneisenau* off Norway seven months earlier, making 29 knots in heavy weather to hit the *Gneisenau* three times at 18,000 yards, her armour protection was weak by battleship standards. This would be a considerable handicap in any fleet action against modern Italian capital ships of the *Littorio* class that were significantly better protected and carried nine 15-inch guns.

Admiral Somerville took Force H to sea in support of a double convoy operation from Gibraltar and Alexandria that also involved Admiral Cunningham transferring the unmodernised battleship HMS *Ramillies* and two cruisers with machinery defects from the Mediterranean Fleet to Gibraltar, en route to home waters; Somerville was due to rendezvous with the three west-bound ships south of Sardinia. The east-bound convoy from Gibraltar was particularly important and was routed straight through to Alexandria, carrying an armoured brigade, complete with tanks and heavy equipment. The convoy also included the cruisers *Manchester* and *Southampton*, each carrying 700 key military and RAF personnel from Gibraltar to Malta. The Italians were aware of the British ships leaving Gibraltar and Admiral Campioni sailed from Naples with the new battleship *Vittorio Veneto* and the *Giulio Cesare,* repaired after the Battle of Calabria four months earlier, and six heavy cruisers, hoping to intercept an inferior British squadron. Somerville had to rely on aerial reconnaissance to alert him to Campioni being at sea, as British cryptanalysts had yet to break the new Italian surface fleet cyphers introduced in mid-July, or the highest-level naval cyphers that had been changed on 1st October.

Somerville's actions were governed by the clear and unambiguous *Royal Navy Fighting Instructions* that required him to place the safe arrival of the convoy above all other considerations. In contrast, Supermarina had issued Campioni with imprecise and contradictory orders that told him not to refuse an encounter but to avoid action with a superior enemy and to show aggression but to minimise losses. When the British and Italian fleets met, Somerville was north of the convoy to rendezvous with the three west-bound ships. He just had time to combine these disparate forces into one squadron, forming an ill-matched battle line with the *Renown* and the *Ramillies*. He created a cruiser screen by including the returning *Newcastle* and *Berwick*, accepting that neither was able to achieve full speed because of machinery defects, and by withdrawing the *Manchester* and *Southampton* from the convoy, despite their handicap of being temporary fast troop transports. He completed the screen with his only fully effective cruiser, HMS *Sheffield*. Campioni had been pressing on, hoping to engage Force H before it could be reinforced but when he found that the British squadrons had joined forces, he judged that he faced a superior force and should return to port. The action then became a running fight, with the Italian heavy cruisers exchanging salvoes with the pursuing British cruiser screen. HMS *Berwick*, Somerville's only heavy cruiser, was twice hit aft, firstly by the *Pola* and then, 13 minutes later, by the *Trieste*, although the *Berwick* remained in action, bracketing the *Trieste* with 8-inch shells. The *Renown* developed a hot bearing on her starboard inner shaft and was restricted to 27.5 knots but began shooting at ranges up to 30,700 yards in support of the British cruisers, whenever she could see a target through the Italian smoke, her 15-inch shells raising towering splashes close astern of the *Bolzano*. Remarkably, the *Ramillies* worked up to nearly 21 knots and also began shooting but her two salvoes fell well short and the old ship gradually dropped astern of the action as it continued north-eastwards at high speed. Attacks on the fast moving, smoke-shrouded Italian ships by the *Ark Royal's* inexperienced Swordfish torpedo bombers and her small force of Skua dive bombers were unsuccessful, while 15-inch salvoes fired at the British cruisers by the *Vittorio Veneto* from about 30,000 yards caused only light splinter damage to HMS *Manchester*. The only Italian casualty was the fleet destroyer *Lanciere*, which was badly damaged by six-inch gunfire from HMS *Southampton* but made port under tow.

When the British ships were 30 miles from the Sardinian coast, it became clear to Somerville that the Italians were pulling away from the *Renown*. He confirmed with Vice Admiral Holland, commanding the scouting screen, that his cruisers also were unable to catch the Italian fleet and reluctantly abandoned the chase, in order to return to the convoy before dark. The British convoy operations were successful, with all ships reaching their destinations.

Admiral Somerville's decisions and actions were in accordance with the letter and spirit of the *Royal Navy Fighting Instructions* and properly reflected his command responsibility to balance engaging and seeking to destroy the enemy fleet with his primary task of ensuring the safety of the convoy under his protection. Nevertheless, a day after Force H returned to Gibraltar, the Admiralty informed him that a Board of Enquiry would be convened to consider his conduct of the action; its members left for Gibraltar in a destroyer, even before the Admiralty received Somerville's detailed account of the action that amplified his summary report signalled from sea. It was clear to Somerville that his handling of the action was being viewed as insufficiently aggressive, in that he called off his pursuit of Campioni's superior squadron.

The root of the Admiralty's attitude ran deeper than the Battle of Cape Spartivento and reflected the outspoken Somerville's unpopularity in London at that time. This stemmed from his undisguised distaste for the policy that led to his being ordered to fire on the Vichy French fleet at Mers-el-Kébir on 3rd July. He had also alienated Prime Minister Winston Churchill and the Admiralty by his subsequent robust support of Vice Admiral Sir Dudley North, who was removed as Flag Officer Commanding North Atlantic, at Gibraltar, for not preventing a Vichy French cruiser squadron reaching Dakar from Toulon. Also, in September, Somerville had fanned the flames of official hostility still further by expressing his view that a British-supported, Free French attack on Dakar would fail if Vichy forces resisted; in this he was proved absolutely right and perhaps that was his greatest sin. Therefore, when an opportunity arose that could possibly justify Somerville's removal from command of Force H, it seems that no time was lost in setting the wheels in motion. Within a week, the Board of Enquiry convened at Gibraltar but, after five days, it upheld Somerville's decisions and exonerated him in all respects.

During the following year, Somerville had responsibility for escorting several other convoys from Gibraltar to Malta and orders that he issued for the Operation Excess convoy in January 1941, only a month after the Board of Enquiry, make it clear that the experience had not altered his priorities:

> *"Should there be reasonable prospects of destroying one or more enemy capital ships, it is my intention to accept a certain degree of risk to the convoy: but unless I am satisfied that the destruction of enemy capital ships can probably be effected, the safety of the convoy will remain my primary object."*

Sir James Somerville was promoted to Admiral in 1942 and took up the poisoned chalice that was command of the hastily assembled and ill-assorted Eastern Fleet in the Indian Ocean, before going to Washington DC in 1944 as Head of the British Admiralty Delegation, where he built a surprisingly good working relationship with the irascible, opinionated and equally outspoken Admiral Ernest King, US Chief of Naval Operations.

In the action off Cape Spartivento, Admiral Campioni missed an opportunity for the Regia Marina to inflict a defeat on the Royal Navy in a surface action, when he failed to engage Somerville with a superior squadron that included the powerful new battleship *Vittorio Veneto*. His tactics were governed by understandable caution, however, following the loss of three Regia Marina battleships only two weeks previously in the Fleet Air Arm attack on Taranto. Although Campioni's actions were subsequently approved by Supermarina and by Mussolini, he was replaced as Fleet Commander by Admiral Iachino on 9th December 1940. Admiral Campioni later became Governor of the Dodecanese and supported the new pro-Allied regime in Italy after the overthrow of Mussolini but he was arrested by the Germans and shot for treason on 24th May 1944, together with several other Italian senior officers who refused to co-operate with the Nazis. He was posthumously awarded the Medaglia d'Oro al Valor Militaire, Italy's highest military decoration.

The surface actions fought by the Royal Navy and the Regia Marina in 1940 led to the most decisive engagement between them off Cape Matapan in March of the following year. This resulted in the loss of three Italian heavy cruisers and two destroyers, with serious torpedo damage inflicted by carrier-borne torpedo bombers on the Italian flagship, the battleship *Vittorio Veneto,* and is the subject of "*Dark Seas*", a previous volume of the Britannia Naval Histories of World War II.

The three Battle Summaries in this book were first issued in 1942/43 as instructional and training documents, classified as Confidential, one level down from Secret, and given limited distribution within the Royal Navy. They were derived only from official British sources and, for that reason, contained unavoidable inaccuracies in respect of the detailed movements of Italian ships involved in the actions. These became clear from Italian records after the end of WWII and all three Battle Summaries were rewritten by August 1954, being issued as a combined volume in March 1957. Prosaically titled *Selected Operations (Mediterranean), 1940,* with the lesser classification of Restricted, the volume also included a revision of Battle Summary 10, covering the Fleet Air Arm attack on Taranto on 11th November 1940, which will be the subject of a separate volume of the Britannia Naval Histories of World War II. The document was declassified in the early 1970s and retained in the archives of Britannia Royal Naval College, Dartmouth as an important naval history source. Also included in this volume are despatches submitted to the Admiralty by Admirals Cunningham and Somerville for the battles of Calabria and Cape Spartivento respectively and published as *Supplements to the London Gazette.*

Bibliography

Ando, E. & Bagnasco, E., (1999), *Navi E Marinai Italiani nella seconda guerra mondiali,* Ermanno Albertelli.

Bagnasco, E. and De Toro, A., (2011), *The Littorio Class,* Seaforth Publishing.

Bagnasco, E. and Grossman, M., (1986), *Regia Marina, Italian Battleships of World War Two,* Pictorial Histories Publishing.

Beevor, A., (2012), *The Second World War,* Weidenfeld & Nicholson.

Brescia, M., (2012), *Mussolini's Navy, A Reference Guide to the Regia Marina 1930- 1945,* Seaforth Publishing.

Brown, D. K., (1999), *The Grand Fleet, Warship Design and Development 1906-1922,* Chatham Publishing.

Brown, D. K., (2000), *Nelson to Vanguard, Warship Design and Development 1923-1945,* Chatham Publishing.

Burt, R. A., (2012), *British Battleships 1919-1945,* Seaforth Publishing.

Collins, Vice Admiral Sir John, (1971), *HMAS Sydney,* Naval Historical Society of Australia.

Cumming, A. J, (2010), *The Royal Navy and the Battle of Britain,* Naval Institute Press.

Cunningham of Hyndhope, Viscount, (1951), *A Sailor's Odyssey,* Hutchinson.

Danreuther, R., (1995), *Somerville's Force H,* Aurum Press.

Gay, Franco and Valerio, (1987), *The Cruiser Bartolomeo Colleoni,* Conway Maritime Press.

Giorgerini, G. and Nani, A., (1966), *Le Navi Di Linea Italiane 1861-1961,* Ufficio Storico Della Marina Militaire.

Giorgerini, G. and Nani, A., (1967), *Gli Incrociatori Italiani 1861-1967,* Ufficio Storico Della Marina Militaire.

Greene, J. and Massignani, A., (1998), *The Naval War in the Mediterranean 1940-1943,* Chatham Publishing.

Harrold, J. E. (Ed), (2012), *Dark Seas: The Battle of Matapan,* University of Plymouth Press.

Hinsley, F. H., et al., (1979), *British Intelligence in the Second World War, Vol 1,* HMSO.

Ireland, Bernard, (2004), *The War in the Mediterranean,* Leo Cooper.

Jones, B. (Ed), (2012), *The Fleet Air Arm in the Second World War, Vol 1, 1939-1941*, Ashgate Publishing for The Naval Records Society.

Macintyre, D., (1964), *The Battle for the Mediterranean*, Batsford.

McCart, N., (2012), *Town Class Cruisers*, Maritime Books.

O'Hara, V., (2009), *The Struggle for the Middle Sea*, Conway.

Pearce, M J (Ed), (2013), *Between Hostile Shores: Mediterranean Convoy Battles 1941- 42*, University of Plymouth Press.

Raven, A. and Roberts, J., (1980), *British Cruisers of World War Two*, Arms and Armour Press.

Simpson, M. (Ed), (1995), *The Somerville Papers*, Scolar Press for The Naval Records Society.

Simpson, M. (Ed), (1999), *The Cunningham Papers Vol 1*, Scolar Press for The Naval Records Society.

Smith, P. C., (1980), *Action Imminent*, William Kimber.

Stephen, M., (1991), *The Fighting Admirals*, Leo Cooper.

Stille, M., (2011), *Italian Battleships of World War II*, Osprey Publishing.

Warner, O., (1967), *Cunningham of Hyndhope, Admiral of the Fleet*, John Murray.

Whitley, M. J., (1999), *Cruisers of World War Two*, Brockhampton Press.

Winton, J., (1998), Cunningham: The Greatest Admiral Since Nelson, *John Murray.*

Wright, Malcolm, (2016), *British and Commonwealth Warship Camouflage of WWII Vol. 3*, Seaforth Publishing.

CONFRONTING ITALY

Exploding the myth of Mussolini's 'Mare Nostrum'

PART I

Illustrations

Major British Warships Engaged

Line drawings illustrating some of the ships involved in the Mediterranean surface actions of 1940 have been reproduced from an original, formerly classified United States Naval Intelligence recognition manual issued in 1943.

Queen Elizabeth Class – *Warspite*

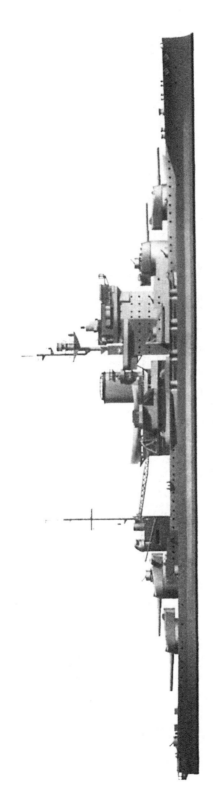

HEIGHT IN FEET:

	to Top of Stack – 79′	to Top of Foretop – 120′
from W. L.		
from Foc'sle Deck	to Top of Stack – 56′	to Top of Foretop – 97′

LENGTH: 634½′ (W. L.). BEAM: 104′

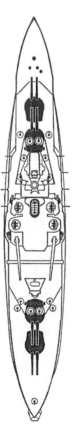

Queen Elizabeth Class – *Malaya*

HEIGHT IN FEET:

from W. L.	to Top of Stack – 81'	to Top of Foretop – 113'
from Foc'sle Deck	to Top of Stack – 55½'	to Top of Foretop – 87'

LENGTH: 634½' (W. L.).   BEAM: 104'

Royal Sovereign Class –Royal Sovereign, Ramillies

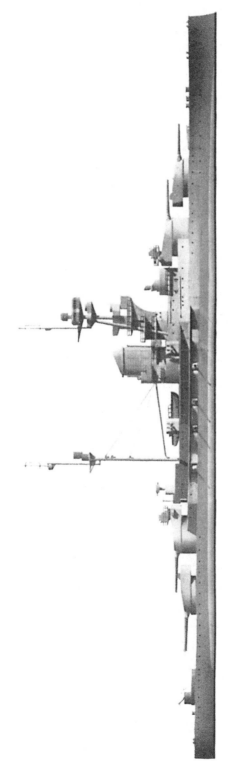

HEIGHT IN FEET:

	to Top of Stack–80'	to Top of Foretop–122'
from W. L.		
from Foc'sle Deck	to Top of Stack–56'	to Top of Foretop– 98'

LENGTH: 614½' (W.L.). BEAM: 102½'

Repulse Class – *Renown*

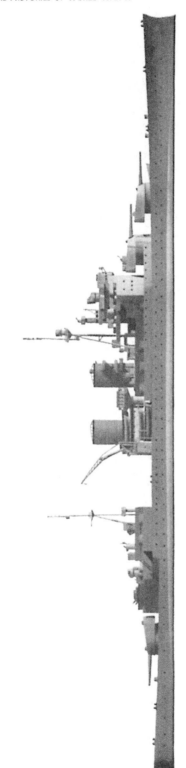

HEIGHT IN FEET:

from W. L.	to Top of Stack – $84\frac{1}{2}'$	to Top of Foretop – 123'
from Foc'sle Deck	to Top of Stack – $59\frac{1}{2}'$	to Top of Foretop – 98'

LENGTH: $787\frac{1}{2}'$ (W. L.). BEAM: 102'

Kent Class – *Berwick*

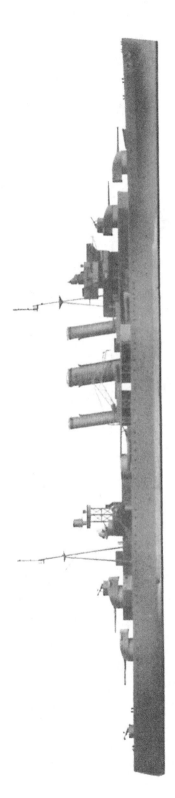

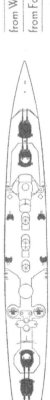

HEIGHT IN FEET:

from W. L.	to Top of Stack – 79'	to Top of Bridge – $73\frac{1}{2}'$
from Foc'sle Deck	to Top of Stack – $53\frac{1}{2}'$	to Top of Bridge – $45\frac{1}{2}'$

LENGTH: 624' (W. L.). BEAM: $68\frac{1}{2}'$

Leander Class – Ajax, Neptune, Orion

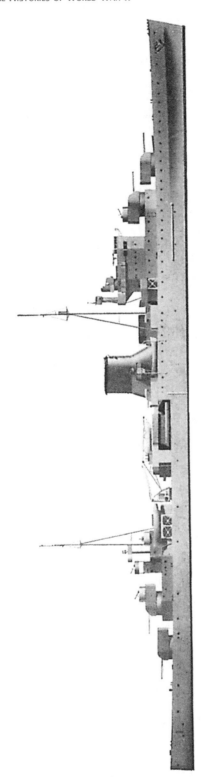

HEIGHT IN FEET:

		to Top of Stack – 63'	to Top F'w'd Director – 70'
from W. L.	to Top of Stack – 63'	to Top F'w'd Director – 70'
from Foc'sle Deck	to Top of Stack – 39'	to Top F'w'd Director – 46'

LENGTH: 554½' (O. A.).   BEAM: 55½'

Southampton Class – *Southampton, Sheffield, Newcastle, Manchester, Gloucester*

HEIGHT IN FEET:

from W. L.	to Top first Stack–76'	to Top f'w'd Director–90'
from Foc'sle Deck	to Top first Stack–44'	to Top f'w'd Director–58'

LENGTH: 584' (W. L.). BEAM: 62¼'

Cruiser HMAS *Sydney*

Major Italian Warships Engaged

Cruiser *Bartolomeo Colleoni* sinking off the coast of Crete, 19th July, 1940.

Cavour Class – Conte di Cavour, Giulio Cesare

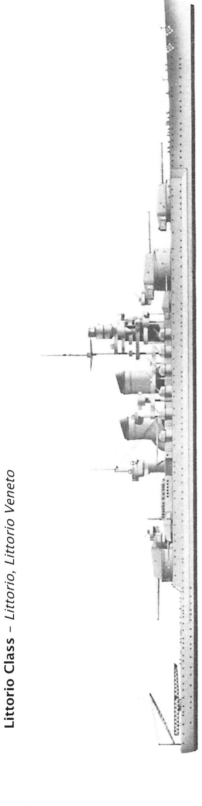

Littorio Class – *Littorio, Littorio Veneto*

Bolzano

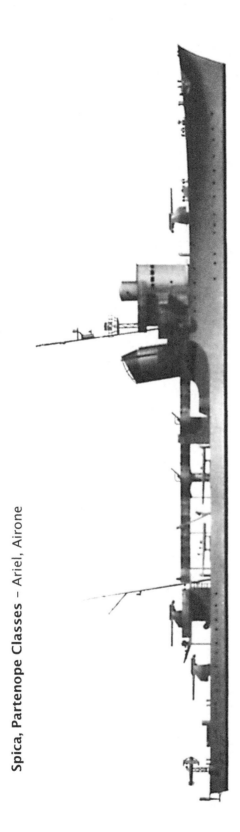

Spica, Partenope Classes – Ariel, Airone

PART II

C.B. 3081 (27)   BR 1736

NAVAL STAFF HISTORY
SECOND WORLD WAR

BATTLE SUMMARIES No 2, 8 & 9

Selected Operations (Mediterranean) 1940

T.S.D. 21/46
Training and Staff Duties Division (Historical Section), Naval
Staff, Admiralty, S.W.1

The Battle Summaries superseded by this volume were originally issued in 1942 and were contained in three separate books. In the present volume, they have been largely re-written to include information from the opposing side and other sources not available at the time they were produced, and have been rearranged as a separate chapter. They have also been amended in matters of detail, where such have proved in error.

The most interesting additions which have been made are an account of the plan and movements of the Italian fleet prior to and during the indecisive action off Calabria (Chapter I), and information derived from Italian sources on Sir James Somerville's action off Cape Spartivento, Sicily (Chapter III).

It must be remembered that all these events took place in the early days of radar. Few ships were fitted with sets other than for detection of high-flying aircraft. No ships as yet had fighter direction equipment.

Plans illustrating the events described have been completely re-drawn to include up to date information. As might be expected, the composition and movements of the Italian Forces in the actions off Calabria and Cape Spartivento differ somewhat from the contemporary estimates of the British. They will be found at the end of the volume, together with a reference chart of the Mediterranean Sea.

August, 1954

Abbreviations

A.A.	Anti-Aircraft	H.Q.	Headquarters
A.B.V.	Armed boarding vessel	M.A.S	Motor anti-submarine
A/C	Aircraft	ME.	Malta – East (convoy)
ac	Aircraft carrier	MF.	Malta – Fast (convoy)
A.N.	Aegean – North (convoy)	MS.	Malta – Slow (convoy)
A.S.	Aegean – South (convoy)	M/S	Minesweeper
A/S	Anti-Submarine	M.T.	Mechanical transport
bc	Battlecruiser	M.V.	Merchant vessel
bs	Battleship	MW.	Malta – West (convoy)
C.-in-C.	Commander-in-Chief	N.A.	Naval Attaché
C.P.B.C.	Common pointed ballistic	R.A.(A.)	Rear-Admiral. Aircraft Carriers
	capped shell	R.A.1	Rear-Admiral 1st Battle Squadron
C.S.	Cruiser Squadron	R.A.F.	Royal Air Force
D.C	Depth Charge	R/C	Reconnaissance
D.C.T.	Director Control Tower	R.D/F	Radio direction finder (Radar)
D.F.	Destroyer Flotilla	S.A.P.	Semi armour piercing
dr.	Destroyer	S/M	Submarine
F.A.A.	Fleet Air Arm	S.O.	Senior Officer
F.B.	Flying Boat	T.O.O.	Time of origin
F.O.	Flag officer	T.S.R.	Torpedo Spotter Reconnaissance
F.O.(H)	Flag officer Commanding Force	T/B	Torpedo Bomber
G.R.T.	Gross registered tons	Tr.	Trawler
H.A.	High angle	V.A.(D)	Vice-Admiral, Destroyer Flotillas
H.E.	High explosive	V.A.L.F.	Vice-Admiral, Light Forces
H.L.B.	High level bombing	W/T	Wireless Telegraphy
		Asdic	Early form of sonar used to detect submarines.

Operation M.A.5 and Action off Calabria July 1940

Strategical Situation, June–July 1940

With the declaration of war by Italy on 11th June 1940 and the collapse of France on the 22nd, the strategic balance in the Mediterranean underwent a radical change, much in favour of the Axis Powers. Prompt decisions by H.M. Government restored the situation remarkably quickly. Stern measures to ensure that no important units of the French Fleet should fall intact into the hands of the enemy, as well as the formation of a powerful force at Gibraltar, had largely neutralised the effect of the French defection in the Western Mediterranean within a fortnight. While in the Eastern basin, Admiral Sir Andrew Cunningham had speedily induced the French Admiral Godfroy to demobilise his ships at Alexandria, and as early as 25th June had decided to resume the running of convoys to and from the Aegean and Egypt, and also between Malta and Alexandria.[1]

Having settled the distressing question of the French Fleet, the British Naval Forces in the Mediterranean could turn their undivided attention to the Italians, and put Mussolini's much vaunted pre-war claim to the control of the Mediterranean to the test.

Possessing numerically superior forces and well-situated bases, they had the advantage of being able to concentrate quickly, but as the lines of communication to their African colonies intersected the important British route from Gibraltar to the Suez Canal, neither side could control their communications without anticipating constant attack. The initiative that the enemy would display in attempting to interfere with the British communications was an open question. He could employ his forces – air, surface or submarine – singly or in combination. The first and third could yield only limited results, but the second or a combination of all three might prove a very difficult problem to tackle.

Early in July, Sir Andrew Cunningham drew up plans for an operation termed M.A.5. In this operation he proposed to employ practically the whole strength of his Fleet in making an extensive sweep into the Central Mediterranean almost as far as the Italian coast, while two convoys were passing from Malta to Alexandria.

It so chanced that Operation M.A.5 synchronised with the passage of an important Italian military convoy from Naples and Catania to Benghazi, covered by the bulk of the Italian Fleet. This led to the first surface action between the British and Italian Fleets, an encounter which took place off the Calabrian coast on 9th July 1940.

Operation M.A.5: Object and Organisation (Fig. 1)

The primary object of Operation M.A.5 was to ensure the safe passage of two convoys from Malta to Alexandria. These consisted of a fast convoy (M.F.1) of three 13-knot ships[2] carrying evacuees, and a slow convoy (M.S.1) of four 9-knot ships[3] with stores. They were to sail from Malta at 1600,[4] D3,[5] and steer to pass through 34° 40' N., 21° 50' E. (Position "Q").

Governing the convoy movement was the determination to seize any opportunity of bringing the enemy to action, whenever or wherever he might be encountered; and it was also intended to attack ships in Augusta with aircraft from the *Eagle*, while the Fleet was in Central Mediterranean waters.

For the Operation, the Fleet was organised in three forces, viz.: Force "A", under Vice-Admiral (D) J. C. Tovey, consisting of five 6-inch cruisers of the 7th Cruiser Squadron and the destroyer *Stuart*; Force "B", the fast battleship *Warspite*,[6] flying the flag of the C.-in-C., and five destroyers; Force "C", under Rear-Admiral H. D. Pridham-Wippell, the battleships *Royal Sovereign* and *Malaya*, the carrier *Eagle*, and 11 destroyers.

An escort force of four or five destroyers, known as Force "D", was to be detached to Malta after the Fleet reached a position east of Cape Passero (Sicily). This force, augmented by the *Jervis* (Lieutenant-Commander A. M. McKillop) and *Diamond* (Lieutenant-Commander P. A. Cartwright) which were already at Malta, would form the convoy escorts.

The three forces were routed to arrive independently at about 1600, D3 (9th July), at which time the slow convoy was to sail from Malta, in the following positions: –

Force "A" 36° 30' N., 16° 20' E. (60 miles 100° from Cape Passero),
Force "B" 36° 00' N., 17° 00' E. (100 miles 115° from Cape Passero),
Force "C" 35° 50' N., 180 40' E. (180 miles 105° from Cape Passero).

From these positions they were to work to the eastward under their respective senior officers, keeping pace with the convoys to the northward of their route till D6, when Forces "B" and "C" were to return to Alexandria, followed by Force "A",

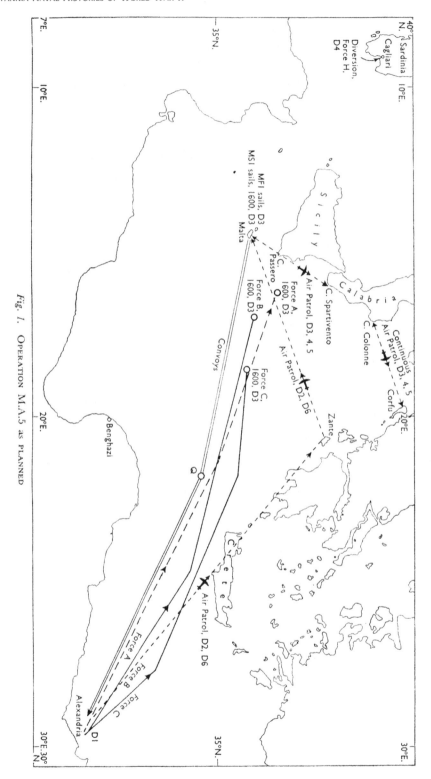

Fig. 1. OPERATION M.A.5 as PLANNED

which was to keep to the north-westward, of Convoy M.S.1 till nightfall that day.[7]

Arrangements were made for F/B patrols of 201 Group to operate in conjunction with the Fleet on each day from 8th to 13th July. These patrols were to operate as follows: –

D2 and D6 (8th and 12th July): F/Bs on passage Alexandria-Zante-Malta.

D3, 4, 5 (9th–11th July): continuous patrol on lines Malta-Cape Spartivento (Calabria) and Cape Colonne-Corfu.

D7 (12th July): to a depth 60 miles to westward of Convoy M.S.1.

During the operation a diversion by Force "H",[8] under Vice-Admiral Sir James Somerville, which had arrived at Gibraltar on 6th July after operations off Oran, was staged in the Western Mediterranean. The diversion was to take the form of an air attack by the F.A.A. of the *Ark Royal* on Cagliari (Sardinia), at dawn, 10th July (D4) – the day following the convoys' first night out from Malta.

Italian Plan of Operations (Plan 1)[9]

While Admiral Cunningham was making the arrangements just described, the enemy were planning to run an important troop and military stores convoy from Naples to Benghazi at about the same time. Leaving Naples on 6th July, the convoy was to pass through the Strait of Messina in the forenoon of the 7th (M.A.5, D1) and follow the Sicilian coast till off Syracuse, when it was to steer a diversionary course for Tobruk, altering direct for Benghazi after dark. At 0500, 8th (M.A.5, D2) when it was expected to be in 34° 54' N., 17° 58' E., the convoy was to split into a fast (18-knot) and a slow (14-knot) section, due to arrive at Benghazi 1600 and 1900 that evening respectively.

The convoy was to be escorted by two 6-inch cruisers,[10] four fleet destroyers and six torpedo boats, while distant cover was to be provided to the eastward of the route by six 8-inch cruisers[11] and 12 destroyers, and to the westward by four 6-inch cruisers[12] and four destroyers. Two battleships, the *Cesare* flying the flag of the C.-in-C. – Admiral I. Campioni, and *Conti di Cavour*, with six 6-inch cruisers[13] and 16 destroyers, were to cruise in support.

The surface forces were to remain in their covering positions till the afternoon of 8th July, when they were to return to their bases.

Special submarine dispositions between 6th and 11th July, were ordered west of a line joining Cape Passero-Malta-Zuara (32° 50' N., 12° 32' E.) to cover the approaches from the Western Mediterranean, and in the Eastern basin east of a line joining Cape Matapan – Ras el Hilal (33° N., 22° 10' E.), as shown in Plan 1.

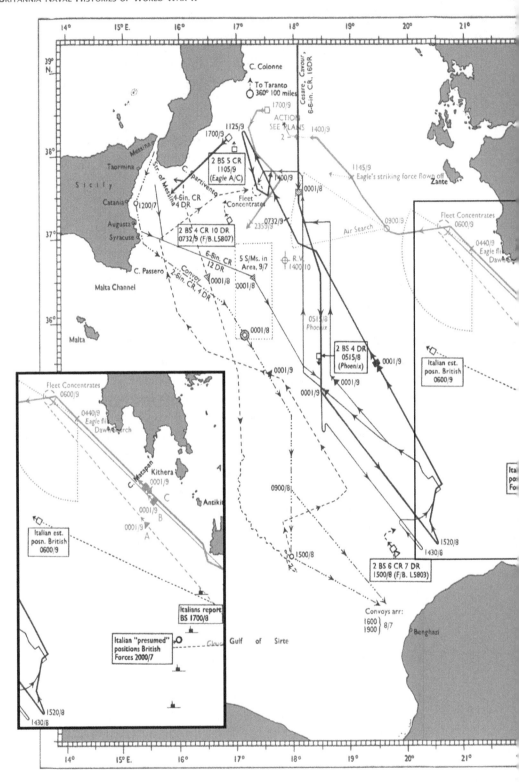

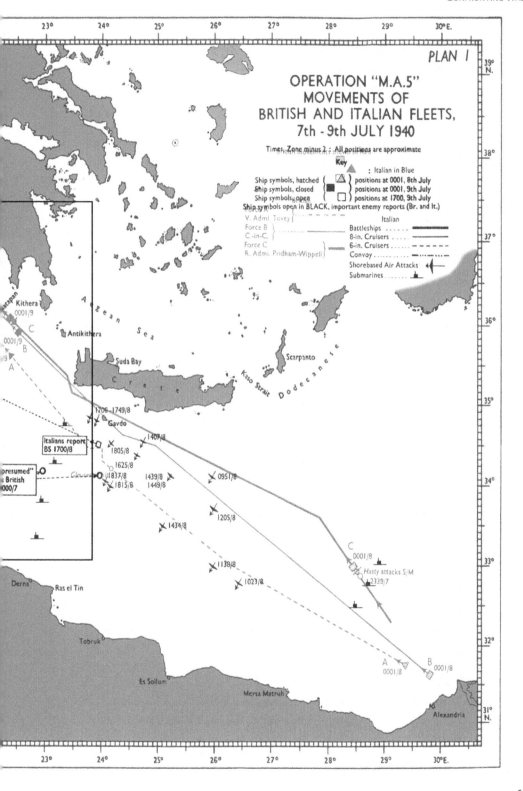

PLAN I

OPERATION "M.A.5"
MOVEMENTS OF
BRITISH AND ITALIAN FLEETS,
7th - 9th JULY 1940

Times, Zone minus 2 : All positions are approximate

Initial Moves, Operation M.A.5, 7th–8th July (Plan 1)

Operation M.A.5 started in the afternoon of 7th July, when Rear-Admiral Pridham-Wippell sailed from Alexandria with Force "C"[14]. That same afternoon, some 900 miles to the north-westward, the Italian squadrons were putting to sea from Palermo, Augusta, Taranto and Messina.

After clearing the swept channel, the *Eagle* embarked No. 813 Squadron from Dekheila,[15] and course was then set for the Kaso Strait. Forces "A"[14] and "B"[14] sailed that evening, and by midnight 7th/8th July all ships[16] were clear of the harbour, and steering to pass through the following positions: –

Force "A" – 35° 00' N., 21° 30' E.;
Force "B" – 34° 15' N., 24° 50' E.;
Force "C" – 33° 20' N., 27° 50' E.

Evidence was soon forthcoming that the enemy was keeping watch on the approaches to Alexandria, when at 2339, 7th, the *Hasty* sighted and attacked a submarine on the surface at 1,000 yards range in 32° 35' N., 28° 30' E. A full pattern of depth charges was dropped and it was considered that the submarine was probably sunk. When proceeding to rejoin Force "C", the *Hasty*, at 0100, 8th, attacked a confirmed contact and possibly damaged second submarine.[17]

A few hours later the *Imperial* burst a feed tank, and was ordered to return to Alexandria. Enemy submarines were reported by the *Eagle's* aircraft on A/S patrol at 0658 and 0908; the latter was attacked with bombs.

During the night, the C.-in-C. with Force "B" set a mean line of advance 305°, 20 knots. The original plan was modified, and a rendezvous appointed for all forces at 1400, 10th July, in 36° 30' N., 17° 40' E.

Meanwhile, unknown to the C.-in-C., Admiral Campioni's forces were at sea, steering southerly courses in pursuance of their plan for covering their convoy to Benghazi.

The first intelligence of the enemy Fleet being at sea was received in the *Warspite* at 0807, 8th, from the submarine *Phoenix* (Lieutenant-Commander G. H. Nowell), who reported that at 0515 she had made an unsuccessful attack at extreme range on two battleships and four destroyers steering 180° in 35° 36' N., 18° 28' E. (about 185 miles to the eastward of Malta). This enemy activity might well be due to movements covering an important convoy and the C.-in-C. ordered the Vice-Admiral, Malta[18], to arrange for a F/B to search for and shadow the enemy force. Pending further information, the Fleet maintained its course and speed.

During the day of 8th July, all three forces experienced heavy bombing attacks by formations of aircraft coming apparently from the Dodecanese bases. Between 1023 and 1837, five attacks were made on Force "A", in the last of which the *Gloucester*, seemingly singled out as a special target, was hit by a bomb on the compass platform. This unhappily caused the following casualties: officers, 7 killed (including Captain F. R. Garside), 3 wounded; ratings, 11 killed, 6 wounded. The damage to the *Gloucester's* bridge and D.C.T. obliged her to steer from aft and use her after gun control.

Force "B" was attacked seven times between 1205 and 1812, some 120 bombs being dropped without result. Six attacks were made on Force "C" between 0951 and 1749. No hits were made, though about 80 bombs were dropped, the *Eagle* being the chief target. In these attacks, which were all delivered from levels between 10,000 and 14,000 ft., there were a number of near misses.

Further information of the Italian fleet was received at 1557, 8th – a signal from F/B L.5803, reporting two battleships, six cruisers and seven destroyers in 33° 08' N., 19° 45' E.[19] (60 miles north of Benghazi) steering 340° at 1500. Later, the F/B reported that the enemy had altered course to starboard, and gave their course at 1630 as 070° 20 knots: it was obliged to return to Malta at 1715 and no relief was then available to continue shadowing the enemy fleet.

Suspecting that the "battleships" reported by the F/B were probably 8-inch cruisers, the C.-in-C. was of opinion that the enemy had some special reason for wishing to keep the British Fleet away from the Central Mediterranean. The intensive bombing already experienced strengthened his impression that the Italians might be covering the movement of an important convoy – probably one to Benghazi. Acting on this conclusion, he decided to abandon temporarily the operation in progress and to proceed at best possible speed in the direction of Taranto, in order to get between the enemy and that base. He accordingly took the following steps. Forces "A", "B" and "C" were ordered to concentrate to the southward of Zante (36° 55' N., 20° 30' E.) at 0600, 9th July.[20] Two F/B searches were ordered to commence at dawn, one between 070° and 130° from Malta, the other westward of a line 180° from Cape Matapan between 35° N. and the African coast. At the same time, the *Eagle* was to fly off a search to a depth of 60 miles between 1800 and 300°. The submarines *Rorqual* and *Phoenix* were ordered to positions on a line 160° from Taranto – the *Rorqual* as far north as possible, the *Phoenix* south of 37° 30' N.

During the night 8th/9th July the C.-in-C. maintained a mean line of advance of 310°, 20 knots, Forces "A" and "C" adjusting courses and speeds as necessary to make the rendezvous.

Movements of Italian Fleet, 8th–9th July (Plan 1)

Meanwhile, the Italians had carried out their convoy movements almost exactly as planned. At 0150, 8th July, Admiral Campioni received a signal from the Italian Admiralty reporting that British forces from Alexandria were estimated to be in positions 34° 10' N., 23° 00' E. and 34° 5' N., 24° 00' E. at 2000, 7th July.[21]

Steps were taken to concentrate the covering forces, and just before 0500 the convoy's course was altered to 180° till the situation should be clarified. Air search at dawn to the eastward and south-eastward of the *Cesare* to a depth of 100 miles having proved negative, the convoy resumed its course for Benghazi during the forenoon and arrived there without incident that evening.

Between 1430 and 1520, 8th, the covering forces turned to the N.N.W to return to Italy, the battleships then being about 75 miles to the north-east of Benghazi and the 8-inch cruisers some 30 miles north-west of the battleships. It was shortly after the 8-inch cruisers had made this turn that they were sighted and reported by F/B L.5803.[22] Soon after this, on the strength of an air report of three enemy battleships and eight destroyers to the south of Crete, Admiral Campioni decided to steer to intercept them, and altered to a N.N.E.'ly course, the cruiser forces altering to close him; but at 1820 the Italian Admiralty intervened and cancelled this movement, pending further orders. Course 330° was therefore resumed.

The Italian Admiralty had intercepted and decyphered enemy signals, which indicated that early next afternoon (9th) the British Fleet would be some 80 miles east of Sicily. This information seemed to offer a golden opportunity of engaging the main British naval force in their own waters with shore-based aircraft, submarines and surface forces. They accordingly directed Admiral Campioni to steer for this area (later amended to one further north, off Calabria), at the same time ordering five submarines to take up positions between 35° 50' N. and 37° N. and 17° and 17° 40' E.

The plan was a good one, but it did not quite take into account Admiral Cunningham's offensive spirit, which led him to change his aim as soon as he saw a chance of getting between the enemy fleet and its base, and to thrust boldly towards Taranto, thereby, as things turned out, leaving the submarine trap some 60 miles to the southward of him.

These intentions and the information on which they were based were communicated to Admiral Campioni during the night, who continued to steer 330°. At midnight 8th/9th July the *Cesare* was approximately 200 miles west of the *Warspite*, both the opposing forces making to the north-westward on slightly converging courses. Soon after this, Admiral Paladini – as the result of a signal from the Italian Admiralty giving warning of the presence of two British submarines –

altered the course of his 8-inch cruisers to 000°, 20 knots, without informing the C.-in-C., thereby getting to the eastward of the battleships next morning. The four light cruisers of the 7th Division, which after covering the convoy to the westward were proceeding to Palermo, continued steering towards the Strait of Messina till soon after 0600, 9th, when they were ordered to join the C.-in-C. to the east of Cape Spartivento.

Action off Calabria: The Approach (Plans 1, 2)

To return to the British Mediterranean Fleet.

The concentration of the fleet was effected south of Zante at 0600, 9th July, in 36° 55' N., 20° 30' E., and the fleet took up the following formation: Force "A" in the van eight miles ahead of Force "B", with Force "C" eight miles astern of the *Warspite*, the mean line of advance being 260° at 15 knots.

The air searches ordered the evening before had commenced at dawn, the *Eagle* having flown off her aircraft at 0440, and reports of the enemy began to come in. The first came from F/B L.5807 at 0732 – two battleships, four cruisers and ten destroyers steering 350°, 15 knots in 37° 14' N., 16° 51' E. Further air reports quickly followed of a group of six cruisers and eight destroyers bearing 080°, 20 miles from the main fleet at 0739, and then at 0805 that the main fleet had altered course to 360°. According to this information, the main enemy fleet now bore about 280°, 145 miles from the *Warspite*. The C.-in-C. altered course to a mean line of advance of 305° and an hour later to 320° at 18 knots in the endeavour to work to the northward of the enemy and so reach a position between him and Taranto.

At 0858, 9th, the *Eagle* flew off three aircraft to search the sector between 260° and 300° to a maximum depth. Several reports from these reconnaissance aircraft and from F/Bs 5807 and 9020 were received between 1026 and 1135. These, though they differed considerably, seemed to afford fairly reliable information of the enemy's movements. Thus, at 1105, one of the *Eagle*'s aircraft reported two battleships and a cruiser with four other cruisers near by in 38° 07' N., 16° 57' E., while at 1105, F/B L.5807 reported the enemy battlefleet in 38° 06' N., 17° 48' E., steering North. It seemed probable that the ships in the latter report were, if correctly identified, actually considerably further to the westward.

These reports indicated that the enemy fleet consisted of at least two battleships, 12 cruisers and 20 destroyers, dispersed in groups over a wide area. It looked, too, as if the group of cruisers and destroyers reported at 0739, had made a wide sweep to the north-eastward and had been joined by another group of cruisers and destroyers, possibly those reported as being in company with the battlefleet.

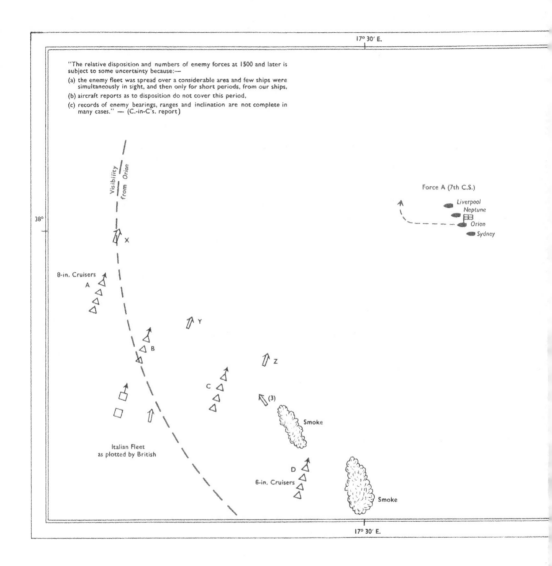

"The relative disposition and numbers of enemy forces at 1500 and later is subject to some uncertainty because:—

(a) the enemy fleet was spread over a considerable area and few ships were simultaneously in sight, and then only for short periods, from our ships,

(b) aircraft reports as to disposition do not cover this period,

(c) records of enemy bearings, ranges and inclination are not complete in many cases." — (C.-in-C's. report)

17° 30′ E.

Visibility from Orion

Force A (7th C.S.)

Liverpool
Neptune
Orion
Sydney

38°

X

8-in. Cruisers
A

Y

B

Z

C

(3)

Smoke

Italian Fleet
as plotted by British

D

6-in. Cruisers

Smoke

17° 30′ E.

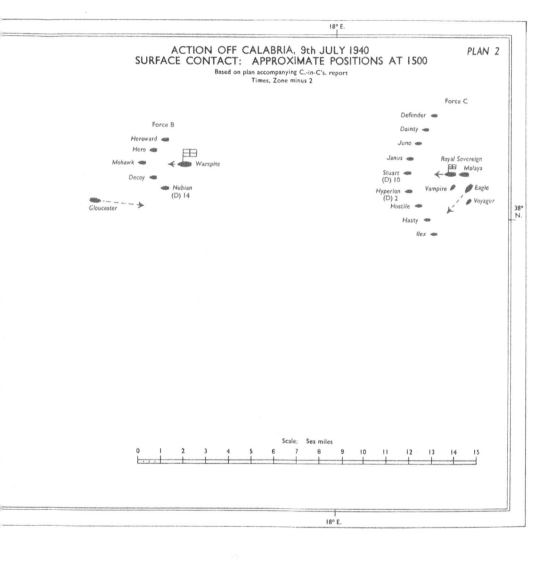

ACTION OFF CALABRIA, 9th JULY 1940
SURFACE CONTACT: APPROXIMATE POSITIONS AT 1500
Based on plan accompanying C.-in-C's. report
Times, Zone minus 2

PLAN 2

Scale: Sea miles

At 1145, 9th, acting on the assumption based on the air reports that the enemy fleet was then steaming north in a position 295°, 90 miles from the *Warspite*, a striking force of nine Swordfish aircraft were flown off from the *Eagle* to attack with torpedoes. But owing to a lack of reconnaissance aircraft and to unavoidable delay in flying off relief shadowers, air touch had been lost ten minutes earlier (1135), and it so happened that just before Admiral Campioni, deeming that he was getting too far to the northward, had altered the course of the battlefleet to 165° in order to concentrate his fleet in about 37° 40' N., 17° 25' E.

Air touch was regained at 1215, when F/B L.5803 reported six cruisers and ten destroyers in 37° 56' N., 17° 48' E. steering 220°, and five minutes later a group of three 8-inch cruisers in 37° 55' N., 17° 55 ' E. steering 225°; but owing to the battlefleet's turn to the southward, the striking force failed to find it, though at 1252 it sighted a large number of enemy ships and working round to the westward of this group, at 1330, attacked the rear ship. The ship was thought at the time to be a battleship, but actually it was one of Admiral Paladini's 8-inch cruisers which were then steering for the rendezvous; no hits were made in this attack, which had to face heavy A.A. fire, though the aircraft suffered little damage.

Meanwhile the *Warspite* had maintained her course 320°, and at noon estimated her position as 37° 30' N., 18° 40' E. An air report at 1330 that there were no enemy ships between 334° and 291° to a depth of 60 miles from 38° N., 18° E., made it clear that the enemy battlefleet had turned to the southward, and that the cruiser groups which were thought to have been sweeping to the north-eastward had altered to the south-westward. The indications were that the enemy fleet was concentrating south-east of Calabria in the approximate position 37° 45' N., 17° 20' E.

Further air reports helped to establish its position and movements: thus, at 1340, F/B 9020 reported three battleships and a large number of cruisers and destroyers in 37° 58' N., 17° 55' E., steering 220°, and at 1414 gave their course and speed as 020°, 18 knots.

Apparently the enemy had by that time completed his concentration, and turning to the northward, was maintaining a central position with three directions open for retreat. Whether he intended to stand and fight in an area of his own choosing was still a matter of conjecture. The British Fleet on its north-west course was rapidly closing and at 1400, having achieved his immediate object of cutting him off from Taranto, the C.-in-C. altered course to 270° to increase the rate of closing. Though the cruisers were well ahead, the *Royal Sovereign*'s speed limited the rate of approach, and at 1430, in 38° 02' N., 18° 25' E., the *Warspite* increased speed to 22 knots, acting as a battle-cruiser to support the 7th C.S., which in comparison with the enemy cruiser force was very weak, being fewer in numbers and lacking 8-inch gun ships.

At 1434, the *Eagle's* striking force had landed on and an air reconnaissance report received at 1435 gave the enemy's course and speed as 360°, 15 knots. This was amplified four minutes later when the enemy's bearing and distance from the *Warspite* was signalled as 260°, 30 miles. Force "A", less the *Stuart*, which had just been ordered to join the *Royal Sovereign's* screen, was then eight miles ahead of the *Warspite* while Force "C" was about ten miles astern of her.

At this stage, when the period of approach may be considered to end, there was a general impression that the enemy proposed to vindicate Mussolini's claim of Mare Nostrum concerning the Mediterranean. The moment for which the Italian Fleet had been built up was at hand, if the Italian C.-in-C. was prepared to accept the gauge of battle.

This impression was not far wrong. The first enemy report received by Admiral Campioni that day had come from an aircraft at 1330. The signal, which arrived at rather an awkward moment, just as he was concentrating his fleet – a manoeuvre complicated by the F.A.A. attack on the heavy cruisers – made it clear that the British had been steering for an objective further north than had been conjectured the night before. He determined, therefore, to interpose his fleet between the Italian coast and the enemy, and if possible to get between him and Taranto, accepting battle and relying on his superiority of speed to enable him to break off the action if the superior weight of gunfire of the British capital ships should prove too much for him.

He then had in company the two battleships, six 8-inch cruisers, eight 6-inch cruisers and 24 destroyers[23]. The four light cruisers of the 7th Division were still some distance to the south-westward, but in view of the urgency to keep open the route to Taranto and the marked numerical superiority in cruisers and destroyers he already possessed, he decided to steer to the northward without waiting for them.

Action off Calabria: Surface Contact (Plan 2)

At 1447, 9th July, the *Orion* sighted white smoke bearing 230° and two minutes later black smoke, bearing 245°, being laid by a destroyer. Apparently the enemy was completing his concentration behind this cover of smoke. At 1452 the *Neptune* reported two enemy ships in sight bearing 236°. These reports were amplified by further details at 1455 and 1500 from the *Orion*.

On first sighting the enemy the damaged *Gloucester* was ordered to join the *Eagle*, which – screened by the *Voyager* and *Vampire* – was taking station ten miles

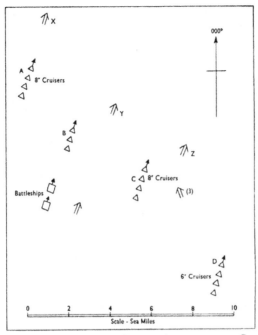

Fig. 2. ITALIAN DISPOSITION, 1500, AS IT APPEARED TO THE BRITISH

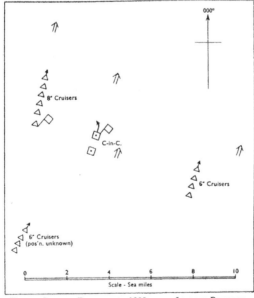

Fig. 3. ITALIAN DISPOSITION, 1500, FROM ITALIAN RECORDS
(*Positions of destroyers are unknown*)

to the eastward of the *Warspite*, while the air striking force was re-arming and re-fuelling in readiness to renew its attack. The remaining four cruisers, in order from north to south *Neptune, Liverpool, Orion, Sydney* (henceforth referred to as the 7th Cruiser Squadron) were formed on a line of bearing 320°, steering 270° at 22 knots, distant ten miles 260° from the *Warspite*.

At 1500 the enemy fleet appeared to be disposed in four columns or groups spread over a wide area, with intervals of about five miles between the columns, which were on a line of bearing 130°-310°. The direction of their advance was reported as 020°, speed 19 knots. Only a few of their ships were visible simultaneously to the British ships and then only for short periods (see Fig. 2). The difficulty of gauging their formation and what ships were present, can be seen by a comparison with Fig. 3, which shows it from Italian records.

Taking the enemy columns in order, as they appeared to the British: the port wing column (marked A in Fig. 2) consisted of five or six cruisers, including some of the *Bolzano* class, the next column (B) was thought to consist of two or three cruisers, ahead of two *Cavour* class battleships. In the third column (C) four cruisers, probably 8-inch, and in the starboard wing column (D) four 6-inch cruisers. In the van were a number of destroyers, probably three flotillas (X, Y and Z) while some others formed the battleship A/S screen.

Actually, this was an overestimate of the number of cruisers present in this opening stage, according to the Italian records. Admiral Campioni had been proceeding on a mean course 010°, the six 8-inch cruisers under Admiral Paladini in the *Pola* (in the rear), disposed three miles on his port beam, and four 6-inch cruisers (two from the 8th Division and two from the 4th) five miles on his starboard beam. At 1500 the 8-inch cruisers were going ahead to take station in the van, a movement facilitated by a turn to port by the battleships. The four cruisers of the 7th Division (which it will be remembered had been on their way home) were some distance off, coming up from the south-westward.

It was a fine day, with the wind north, force 4, sea slight, 1/10 cloud and visibility ranging from 13 to 18 miles.

Vice-Admiral Tovey was getting a long way ahead of the *Warspite*, and at 1508, in order to avoid becoming heavily engaged before she was in a position to support, he altered course together to 000°24. As he turned, the *Neptune* reported two battleships bearing 250°, 15 miles off. The 7th Cruiser Squadron was still closing the enemy and soon groups of enemy cruisers and destroyers were seen showing up between the bearings of 235° and 270° at distances of 12 to 18 miles. Course was again altered to 045° and at 1514 the squadron was formed on a line of bearing 350°.

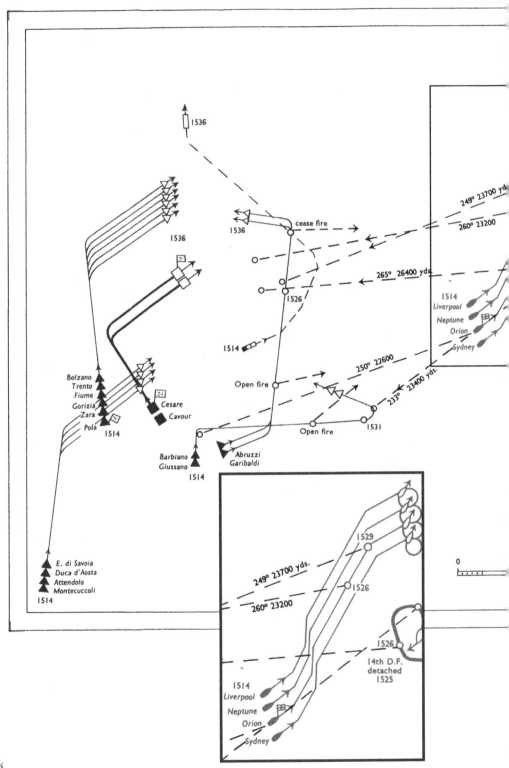

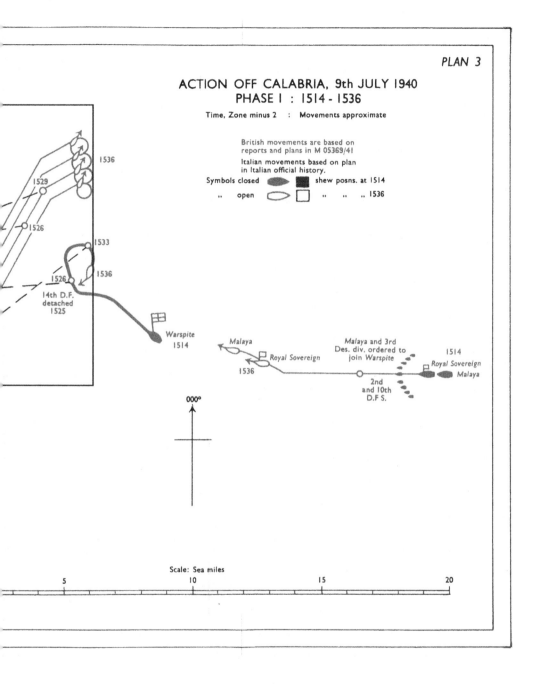

The surface action which ensued falls into three phases: –

(1) 1514 to 1536. Cruiser action, in which the *Warspite* intervened.
(2) 1548 to 1615. Battleships and cruisers in action, and F.A.A. attack by the *Eagle's* aircraft.
(3) 1615 to 1649. The Italian Fleet in full retreat; British cruisers and destroyers engaging enemy destroyers as opportunity offered.

From 1640 to 1925 the enemy shore-based aircraft carried out heavy but ineffective attacks on both fleets with complete impartiality.

Action off Calabria: Phase 1 (Plan 3)

At 1514 the enemy cruisers (C)[25] bearing 250° opened fire at a range 23,600 yards on the 7th Cruiser Squadron. Vice-Admiral Tovey increased speed to 25 knots at 1515 and a minute later altered course to 025° to open the "A" arcs. With the advantage of the sun behind him, the enemy's fire was good for range, but it fell off later. After a couple more alterations of course together to 355° and 030°, the 7th Cruiser Squadron was ordered at 1522 to engage an equal number of enemy ships.

The *Neptune* and *Liverpool* immediately opened fire, range 22,100 yards, followed by the *Sydney* at 1523 engaging the fourth cruiser from the right. The speed of the Squadron was increased to 28-knots and the *Orion*, at 1526, fired at a destroyer (Z) for three minutes, range 23,200 yards. When this destroyer altered course away, the *Orion* shifted target to the right-hand cruiser, then bearing 249°, range 23,700 yards. By this time the *Warspite* was intervening. It appeared urgently necessary to support the outnumbered cruisers, and at 1525 the C.-in-C. detached his destroyer screen, which formed single line ahead on the *Nubian*, and altered course to starboard to pass on the *Warspite's* disengaged side. A minute later (1526) the flagship opened fire on what was believed to be an 8-inch cruiser (C)[26] bearing 265°, range 26,400 yards. Blast from the first salvo damaged the *Warspite's* aircraft, which was subsequently jettisoned. Ten salvoes were fired, and it was thought a hit was scored by the last.[27] The enemy cruisers turned away under smoke; this took them out of range of the 7th Cruiser Squadron which checked fire at 1531.

During this opening stage of the action no hits had been observed on the enemy ships, whose fire had been equally ineffective. The British cruisers were straddled several times, but the only damage done was by splinters from a near miss to the *Neptune's* aircraft, which was jettisoned shortly afterwards as it was leaking petrol.

Sir Andrew Cunningham was finding the slow speed of his battlefleet a sore trial. Having ordered the *Malaya* to press on at utmost speed, he turned in the

Warspite through 360° and made an "S" bend to enable her to catch up. The 7ᵗʰ Cruiser Squadron, whose orders were not to get too far ahead of the C.-in-C., made a complete turn to conform with this movement. While under helm the *Warspite* fired four salvoes between 1533 and 1536 at each of two 6-inch cruisers, forcing them to turn away.[28] It was thought that these ships were attempting to work round towards the *Eagle*, as they were on an easterly course when sighted.

Apart from this burst of fire, there was a lull in the action till 1548. The C.-in-C. could do nothing but wait for his battleships to come up. There is a smack of old world courtesy – almost of apology – in the signal he flashed to Vice-Admiral Tovey at this time: – "I am sorry for this delay, but we must call upon reinforcements."

The situation of the British Fleet was then as follows: the 7ᵗʰ Cruiser Squadron, steering 310°, 28 knots, to close the enemy was 3½ miles to the northward of the *Warspite*, which was turning to 345°. The *Malaya* and *Royal Sovereign* – particularly the former – had gained considerably. The destroyers, all of which had been released from screening duties, were concentrating in their flotillas on the disengaged bow of the battlefleet. A squadron of six enemy cruisers (presumably column A) was in sight ahead of their battlefleet.

Action off Calabria: Phase 2 (Plan 4)

Just at this moment (1548) the second phase or battleship action began, when the enemy battleships opened fire on the *Warspite* at extreme range. Reserving her fire till 1553, the *Warspite* then fired at the right-hand enemy battleship (*Cesare*), bearing 287°, range 26,000 yards. Just previously, the *Eagle's* striking force of nine Swordfish of No. 824 Squadron, which had flown off at 1545, passed over her on their way to the attack.

The enemy's shooting was moderately good, most of his salvoes falling within 1,000 yards, some straddling, but nearly all having a wide spread. One closely bunched salvo fell about 400 yards off the *Warspite's* port bow. The destroyers, then passing to the eastward of her, under orders to join Admiral Tovey, were narrowly missed by salvoes of heavy shells, falling one to two miles over the Fleet flagship.

At 1600 a salvo from the *Warspite* straddled the *Cesare* at a range of 26,200 yards and a hit was observed at the base of her foremost funnel; The effect was immediate; the enemy ships altered course away and began to make smoke. The shell had exploded on the upper deck casing, starting several fires and killing or wounding 98 men. Four boilers were put out of action and her speed dropped to 18 knots, causing the ship to drop back on the *Cavour*. This meant that Admiral Campioni had lost the margin of speed on which he was relying to counter-balance the superiority of the British gunfire; he decided to break off the action without

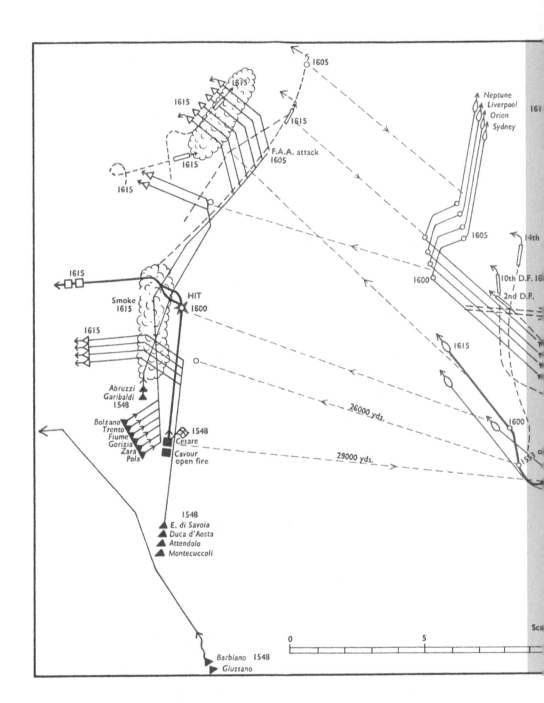

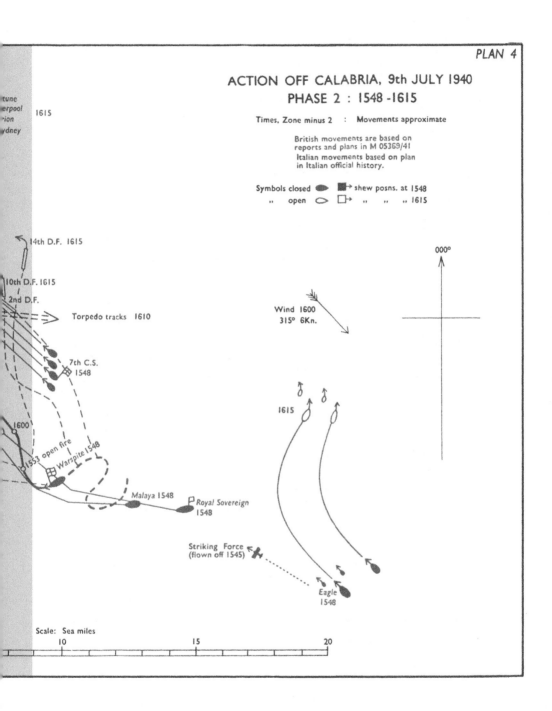

PLAN 4

ACTION OFF CALABRIA, 9th JULY 1940
PHASE 2 : 1548 -1615

Times, Zone minus 2 : Movements approximate

British movements are based on
reports and plans in M 05369/41
Italian movements based on plan
in Italian official history.

Symbols closed ⬤ ▮→ shew posns. at 1548
   „   open ◖ ▯→ „   „   „ 1615

000°

tune
erpool
-ion   1615
ydney

14th D.F. 1615

10th D.F. 1615

2nd D.F.

Torpedo tracks 1610

Wind 1600
315° 6Kn.

7th C.S.
1548

1615

1600

1553 open fire

Warspite 1548

Malaya 1548

Royal Sovereign
1548

Striking Force
(flown off 1545)

Eagle
1548

Scale: Sea miles
        10   15   20

69

more ado. Accordingly, he altered course to west and later to 230°, and ordered those destroyers suitably placed to lay smoke and attack the enemy fleet, though he recognised that in broad daylight against practically untouched ships they were unlikely to achieve material success. All he hoped was that they might delay the enemy from closing during the critical stage of disengaging.

The *Warspite* at 1602 tried to close the range by altering course to 310°. The *Malaya*, by then in station bearing 180° from her, fired four salvoes at extreme range, but all fell short. Three more salvoes, fired by her at 1608, had an equally disappointing result. The *Royal Sovereign*, unable to close the *Warspite* nearer than three miles, took no part in the action. At 1604 the enemy battleships became obscured by smoke, and the *Warspite* ceased fire, having got off 17 salvoes.

Just as this engagement between the battleships was ending, the *Eagle's* striking force attacked Admiral Paladini's 8-inch cruisers. After passing over the *Warspite*, the Swordfish had a bird's-eye view of both fleets opening fire and noticed several salvoes straddling the *Warspite*. When two-thirds of the way towards the enemy they came under A.A. fire at 6,000 feet. The enemy fleet, partially obscured by smoke, seemed to be in some confusion with 15-inch shell straddling their ships. Observing two large ships[29] at the head of a line of cruisers, the squadron leader, Lieutenant-Commander A. J. Debenham, decided to attack the leading ship, which at the moment was turning in a circle. After the attack by sub-flights had commenced, this ship became more distinct; though it then seemed probable she was a *Bolzano* class cruiser and not a battleship, he decided not to call off the attack. A.A. fire became general during the final approach, which was made at 1605 in three sub-flights from ahead. All the aircraft dropped their torpedoes successfully on the enemy ship's starboard side between her bow and beam bearings. Observers in the *Neptune* testified to the determined manner in which the attack was made. On account of smoke from the ships' guns, the aircraft crews were unable to establish definite claims to results, but five members reported individually having seen columns of water, smoke, or an explosion. On the strength of this evidence it was assumed that at least one torpedo got home, but it is now known that this was not the case.[30]

Meanwhile, the cruisers had renewed their action. The 7th Cruiser Squadron, steering 310°, endeavoured to close the enemy, who at 1556 reopened an accurate fire. The *Orion* replied at 1559, her target being a *Bolzano* class cruiser (A) bearing 287°, range 23,000 yards. At 1600, the *Neptune* and *Sydney* opened fire respectively at the second and fourth enemy cruisers from the right, and the *Liverpool* followed suit two minutes later. The course of the Squadron was altered to 010° and then 070°, but as the enemy was seen to be turning away at 1606, course 010° was resumed.

About this time, too, the D.F.s were coming into action. They had been ordered at 1545 to join the 7th Cruiser Squadron, and after their unpleasant experience among the "overs" while passing the *Warspite*, were reformed at 1555 by Captain P. J. Mack, the Senior Captain (D), on course 350° in the following order: –

14th D.F. *Nubian, Mohawk, Juno, Janus.*

2nd D.F. *Hyperion, Hero, Hereward, Hostile, Hasty, Ilex* (in single line ahead 25 knots on bearing 140° from *Nubian*).

10th D.F. *Stuart, Dainty, Defender, Decoy* (in single line ahead 27 knots on bearing 220° from *Nubian*).

From 1602 and 1605 the two leading flotillas (14th and 10th) came under heavy fire from the enemy cruisers but were not hit. The enemy destroyers were observed at this time by the *Warspite* moving across to starboard from the enemy's van, and at 1607 two destroyer salvoes could be seen landing close to the *Stuart*.

At 1609 the *Warspite* fired six salvoes at a cruiser bearing 313°, range 24,600 yards, which had drawn ahead of the enemy battleships. A minute later the tracks of three or more torpedoes were seen passing through the 14th Flotilla.

At 1611, the *Orion* shifted target to the right-hand cruiser bearing 308° range 20,300 yards,[31] which was then the only ship within range. The *Sydney* too fired a few salvoes at this ship, her previous target having become very indistinct. The *Neptune* straddled her target which she claimed to have hit, and the *Liverpool* straddled with her fifth salvo, after which the enemy ships altered course away, throwing her salvoes out for line. During this period of the action, a hot fire from the enemy destroyers, which were moving up to gain a position for attack, was a constant source of annoyance to the British cruisers. Their guns outranged the cruisers' 4-inch armament, but as soon as the enemy cruisers had disappeared in the smoke, the cruisers turned their 6-inch guns on to these hornets, which were quickly silenced and driven off. This ended the second phase of the action.

Action off Calabria: Phase 3

At the beginning of the third phase of the action (about 1615) the position was thus roughly as follows: –

The Italian Fleet was withdrawing to the westward, the damaged *Cesare* and *Cavour* sorting themselves out behind a smoke screen on a westerly course and the cruisers gradually conforming on north-westerly courses.[32] Their destroyers were either laying smoke, or proceeding to positions suitable for attack on the

British; one flotilla was already firing on Admiral Tovey's cruisers.

Turning to the British, the battleships on a north-westerly course were endeavouring to close the enemy battlefleet, with the D.F.s – bearing about 030° from the *Warspite* – steering to join Admiral Tovey, then some nine miles north of the *Warspite*; the 7th Cruiser Squadron had turned back to 010° to conform with the enemy's turn away, and was engaging the 8-inch cruisers.

At 1614 the signal for our destroyers to counter-attack the enemy destroyers was made. The flotillas were then about four miles N.N.E. of the *Warspite*; speed was increased to 29 knots and course altered to 270° to close the enemy, each flotilla manoeuvring as necessary to clear the others and keep their lines of fire open. Speed was increased to 30 knots at 1617 and at the same time, the 7th Cruiser Squadron altered course to 340° in support[33], but four minutes later altered away to 040° to avoid fouling our destroyers.

The 10th D.F. opened fire at 1619 on an enemy destroyer ahead, range 12,600 yards, and the *Stuart*'s first salvo appeared to hit.[34] The 2nd D.F. opened fire at 1626 on a destroyer bearing 290°, range 14,000 yards, and the 14th D.F. at 1629 on one of two destroyers bearing 278°, range 12,400 yards.

Apparently at this time a number of enemy destroyers, after working across to starboard of their main fleet, were attempting in a half-hearted manner to make a torpedo attack. After firing their torpedoes at long range, they turned away to the westward making smoke, the second flotilla retiring through the smoke made by the leading flotilla. On account of these cautious tactics, our flotillas were only able spasmodically to engage targets when they presented themselves within range, unobscured by smoke. No hits on either side were seen by the *Warspite*'s aircraft on observation duty.

To return to the 7th Cruiser Squadron, after turning to the north-eastward to clear the flotillas, the enemy quickly disappeared and fire was checked at 1622; at the same time a submarine was reported, which however, proved to be the wreckage of an aircraft. In order to place the cruisers in a better position to support the destroyers, Admiral Tovey then altered course round through south to 280°. The *Orion* then opened fire again on her former target, and the *Neptune* managed to get off a couple of salvoes at a cruiser, which showed up momentarily out of the smoke. The *Sydney*'s target, a smoke-laying destroyer, was engaged till she became obscured; and the *Liverpool* at 1625 fired four salvoes at a cruiser, range 19,000 yards, before she also disappeared into the smoke screen. At 1628, course was altered to 180°; the *Orion*, *Neptune* and *Sydney* fired occasional salvoes whenever they caught fleeting glimpses of enemy destroyers, and four minutes later Admiral

Tovey hauled round to 210° in pursuit of the enemy. At 1634, with all their targets rapidly disappearing in the smoke, the 7th Cruiser Squadron ceased fire. This marked the end of the cruiser action, apart from a few salvoes fired by a ship invisible to our cruisers at 1641. The principal feature of its desultory character, was the unanimous determination of the enemy cruisers to avoid close action. This they achieved with conspicuous success.

Meanwhile, the C.-in-C.in the *Warspite*, with the *Malaya* in company and the *Royal Sovereign* about three miles astern, had been steering a mean course 313° at 20 knots, and by 1630 was nearing the enemy's smoke screen. Several enemy signals had been intercepted, saying that he was "constrained to retire" at 20 knots and ordering his flotillas to make smoke, and to attack with torpedoes; there was also a warning that they were approaching the submarine line. "These signals," – wrote Admiral Cunningham afterwards – "together with my own appreciation of the existing situation, made it appear unwise and playing the enemy's own game to plunge straight into the smoke screen."[35] He therefore altered course to starboard to 340° at 1635, to work round to the northward and to windward of the smoke. A few minutes later, enemy destroyers came into view and between 1639 and 1641 the *Warspite* fired five salvoes of 6-inch and the *Malaya* one salvo at them and they disappeared into the smoke. The proceedings were enlivened by the first appearance that day of the Italian Air Force, which carried out an ineffective bombing attack on the *Warspite* at 1641.

The fitful engagement continued until 1649, our destroyers seizing every opportunity involuntarily offered by the enemy as he bolted in and out of the smoke cover. At 1640, two torpedoes were seen passing astern of the *Nubian*, and at 1647 she observed one of two enemy destroyers apparently hit and dropping astern. The 2nd D.F. passed through the smoke, while the 14th tried to work round it to the northward. All endeavours to get to close quarters were unsuccessful, and at 1654 orders were received from the C.-in-C., who three minutes earlier had altered course to 270° to rejoin the 7th Cruiser Squadron. When the destroyers finally cleared the smoke screen at 1700, the enemy was out of sight, having retired to the south-westward in the direction of his bases.

The flotillas then proceeded as necessary to join Vice-Admiral Tovey, who was to the north of the *Warspite* steering 280° at 27 knots, taking stations in accordance with Destroyer Cruising Order No. 3.[36]

To the east, the striking force was just getting back to the *Eagle*: all the Swordfish landed on safely at 1705. Another striking force was being got ready, but it could not be despatched before the general recall of aircraft was made at 1750. During the engagement the *Eagle* had also maintained aircraft, as available, on reconnaissance, as well as one acting as spotter for the *Royal Sovereign*.

The surface action was over; its indecisive character at all stages was due to the "safety first" tactics of the Italians. Throughout its course, their cruisers had kept at extreme ranges, the battleships called for smoke protection as soon as one was hit, and the destroyers – dodging in and out of the smoke screen – fired a few torpedoes at long range and then withdrew at their best speed. With the British Fleet between them and their main base (Taranto), they were hurriedly seeking shelter in other bases to the south and west. It was now the turn of the Italian Air Force to see if it could do better against Admiral Cunningham's fleet.

Action off Calabria: Italian Air Attacks, 9th July

The first appearance of enemy aircraft on the scene, as already mentioned, was at 1640 – just as the surface action was petering out – when the *Warspite* was attacked. From then till about 1930, the Fleet was subjected to a series of heavy bombing attacks by shore-based aircraft.

The *Warspite* and the *Eagle* were particularly singled out as targets, each being attacked five times;[37] but the 7th Cruiser Squadron received numerous attacks and many bombs fell near the destroyers. At 1654, the *Orion* fired on a formation of nine aircraft which attempted to bomb the flotillas. Vice-Admiral Tovey effectively disposed his cruisers in a diamond formation to resist these attacks, which were frequent till 1920.

Most of the bombing was extremely wild, from heights of between 10,000 and 15,000 feet, carried out by formations of aircraft varying in numbers from nine to a single aircraft, but generally in formations of three. No ships were hit during any of the attacks, but there were numerous near misses and a few minor casualties from splinters. The *Malaya* claimed to have damaged two aircraft by A.A. fire, but none were seen to fall.

During this period of the action, the coast of Italy was in sight, the high land of Calabria showing up prominently as the sun got lower in the West.

About 600 miles to the westward, Vice-Admiral Somerville with Force "H", who was then south of Minorca on his way to carry out the diversionary attack on Cagliari, which had been arranged for the next morning, was undergoing a similar experience at much the same time. Admiral Somerville, deeming that the risk of damage to the *Ark Royal* outweighed the importance of a secondary operation, cancelled the proposed attack and returned to Gibraltar.[38] No damage was suffered from the air attacks, but the destroyer *Escort* was torpedoed and sunk by a submarine on the return passage two days later.

Fleet Movements after Action (Plan 1)

To return to the Italians.

The sudden retirement behind the smoke screens had naturally thrown the fleet into considerable disorder and the manoeuvre had not been helped by the F.A.A. attack on the *Bolzano*, which had developed a few minutes later. The battleships steered a westerly course till about 1615 and then steadied on 230°, the other squadrons steering to the north-westward and gradually conforming.

By 1645 the *Cesare's* boilers had again been connected up, and Admiral Campioni considered the possibility of pushing towards Taranto and regaining contact with the British Fleet. Nothing could be seen of the enemy, owing to the smoke screens, and he had received no report of his movements since 1615; but he knew that their battleships were by that time concentrated and there would be danger of his being forced on to the Calabrian coast by their gunfire. He therefore decided to steer for the Sicilian ports. Shortage of fuel in his available destroyers prevented him from sending them to locate the enemy and subsequently attempt a night attack.

From this time onwards, the various units of the fleet were repeatedly bombed by their own shore-based aircraft.[39] "Signals were made with searchlights, wireless messages were sent, national flags were spread on the turrets and decks – but without results. Ships frequently replied with gunfire to the dropping of the bombs."[40] The marksmanship of the Italian pilots seems to have been no better on their own ships than on the British for none were hit "due to the quickness of the ships' manoeuvring"; but the attacks kept the fleet in disorder, and it was not till 1800 that it was reformed, the light cruiser squadrons and destroyers then taking station to the east and south-eastward, and the heavy cruisers disposed to the north-westward of the battleships.

At 1930, the destroyers which had been fuelling rejoined his flag, and the various units of the fleet arrived at Augusta, Messina and Palermo in the course of the evening – the majority, by order of the Ministry of Marine, sailing for Naples early on 10th July.

The British Fleet, meanwhile, had continued steering 270° from 1700 to 1735, 9th July. As it was plainly evident that the enemy had no intention of renewing the action and that it was impossible to intercept him, the C.-in-C., being then about 25 miles from the Calabrian coast, altered the course of the fleet to 200°. At 1830 the destroyers were ordered to resume their screening formations on the battleships and at 1910 the *Gloucester* was ordered to rejoin Vice-Admiral Tovey. A couple of alterations of course were made to open the land.

An enemy destroyer was believed to have been severely damaged, but on account of shortage of fuel in his own destroyers, Sir Andrew Cunningham reluctantly decided not to detach a force to deal with her. The last information of the enemy fleet received from the *Warspite's* aircraft reported it in 37° 54' N., 16° 21' E. (about 10 miles from Cape Spartivento) at 1905, steering 230° at 18 knots.

At 2115, 9th, Admiral Cunnigham altered course to 220° for a position south of Malta. During the night, which passed without incident, eight destroyers (*Stuart, Dainty, Defender, Hyperion, Hostile, Hasty, Ilex, Juno*) were detached to arrive at Malta at 0500, 10th, to complete with fuel.[41]

The Vice-Admiral, Malta, had been told to delay the sailing of the convoys for Alexandria. However, "on hearing that the fleets were engaged, he wisely decided that the Italians would be too busy to attend to convoys, so sailed the fast convoy [42] – M.F.1 – escorted by the *Diamond, Jervis* and *Vendetta* (Lieutenant R. Rhoades, R.A.N.) at 2300, 9th July.

Movements and F.A.A. Attack on Port Augusta, 10th July

At 0800, 10th July, the fleet was in 35° 24' N., 15° 27' E. (about 50 miles E.S.E. of Malta), steering west, and throughout the day cruised to the south of Malta, while the destroyers were fuelling. An air raid took place on Malta at 0855, but no destroyer was hit. Three or four enemy aircraft were shot down. The second group (*Hero, Hereward, Decoy, Vampire, Voyager*) proceeded to Malta at 1525, the last three being ordered to sail with Convoy M.S.1. Shortly after noon, the *Gloucester* and later the *Stuart* were detached to join Convoy M.F.1.

A flying-boat reconnaissance of Port Augusta having reported three cruisers and eight destroyers in harbour there, the *Eagle's* striking force of nine Swordfish aircraft were flown off at 1850, 10th, to make a dusk attack. Unfortunately, the enemy force had left before it arrived, and the only ships found were a destroyer of the *Navigatori* class and an oil tanker of 6,000 tons in a small bay to the northward. The destroyer – the *Leone Pancaldo* – was hit by two torpedoes' and sank after breaking in two; the tanker also was hit. All the aircraft returned safely, landing at Malta.

At 2000, 10th, the 7th Cruiser Squadron was ordered to search to the eastward in the wake of Convoy M.F.1; and half an hour later the *Royal Sovereign, Nubian, Mohawk* and *Janus* were sent in to Malta to refuel. As they neared the island, an air raid on the neighbourhood of Calafrana was seen to be in progress. The ships entered harbour at midnight and left at 0430, 11th to rejoin the C.-in-C.. The remainder of the fleet, at 2100, steered 180° from position 35° 28' N., 14° 30' E., till 0130, 11th July, when course was altered to the north for a rendezvous at 0800.

In view of the bombing attacks experienced on the 8th and 9th July, the Air

Officer, C.-in-C., Middle East, was requested to do everything possible to occupy the Italian air forces while the fleet and convoys were on passage to Alexandria.

Passage to Alexandria, 11th–15th July (Plan 5)

At 0800, 11th July, the ships which had been fuelling rejoined the flag in 35° 10' N., 15° 00' E., and the *Eagle* landed on her air striking force from Malta.

The slow convoy, M.S.1, escorted by the *Decoy, Vampire* and *Voyager* had left Malta at 2100, 10th, and at 0900,11th, the C.-in-C. in the *Warspite*, screened by the *Nubian, Mohawk, Juno* and *Janus* (Force "B")[43] went on ahead at 19 knots for Alexandria, while Rear-Admiral Pridham-Wippell in the *Royal Sovereign*, with the *Malaya, Eagle* and remaining destroyers (Force "C")[44] proceeded on a mean line of advance 080°, 12 knots, to cover the passage of the convoys. Vice-Admiral Tovey, who after being detached had kept to the southward of the track of convoy M.S.1, closing to about 20 miles from it at daylight, was then about 80 miles to the eastward of the *Warspite*, and had just opened fire on a shadowing aircraft which had appeared a few minutes previously. Considering that the protection against air attack – which cruisers of the *Orion* class could give to the slow convoy – was not of sufficient value to justify closing it, the Vice-Admiral decided to continue on a southeasterly course until he was 150 miles from Sicily, when he altered course to 0450 and took up a covering position.

As expected, it was not long before air attacks commenced. Between 1248 and 1815, 11th, 66 bombs were aimed at the *Warspite* and her destroyers in five attacks.[45] Force "C" – which had already experienced a submarine alarm when the *Defender* attacked a contact at 0955 without result – suffered 13 bombing attacks, mostly directed against the *Eagle*, between 1111 and 1804, about 120 bombs being dropped. The *Malaya* and the *Royal Sovereign* each claimed to have damaged an aircraft and one was shot down by a Gladiator in the course of these attacks. It was remarked that the attacks at lowest levels were made on destroyers, and that the seaplanes came in lower than other types of aircraft.

Convoy M.S.1 was attacked four times. None of the ships were damaged and there was only one casualty – Mr. J. H. Endicott, Commissioned Gunner of the *Vampire*, who died after transference to the *Mohawk*. Convoy M.S.1 was overhauled by the *Warspite* at 1500, and the *Janus* was then ordered to exchange stations with the *Vampire* in the convoy escort.

Further east, Admiral Tovey's cruisers also were bombed. Between 1445 and 1500, they were attacked by 15 aircraft in waves of three. No damage was done to either side, though one stick of bombs fell close to the *Neptune*. After the attack, an attempt to evade further attacks was made by altering course to 225° for 75

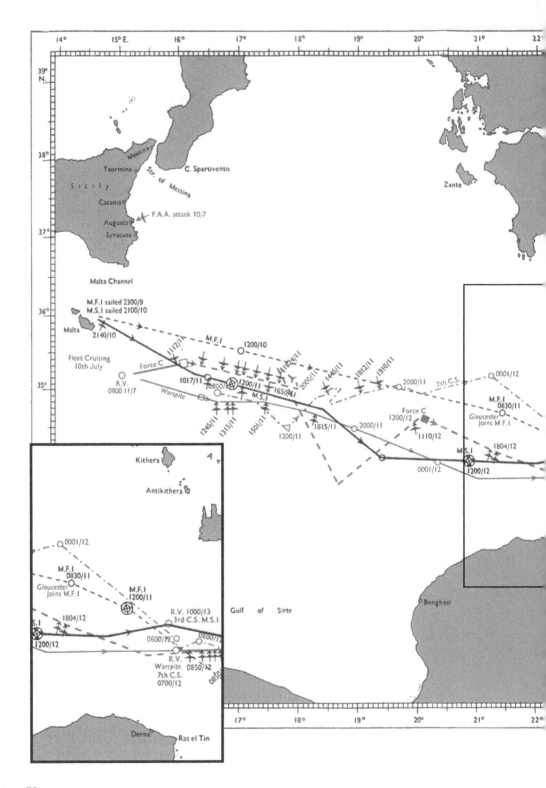

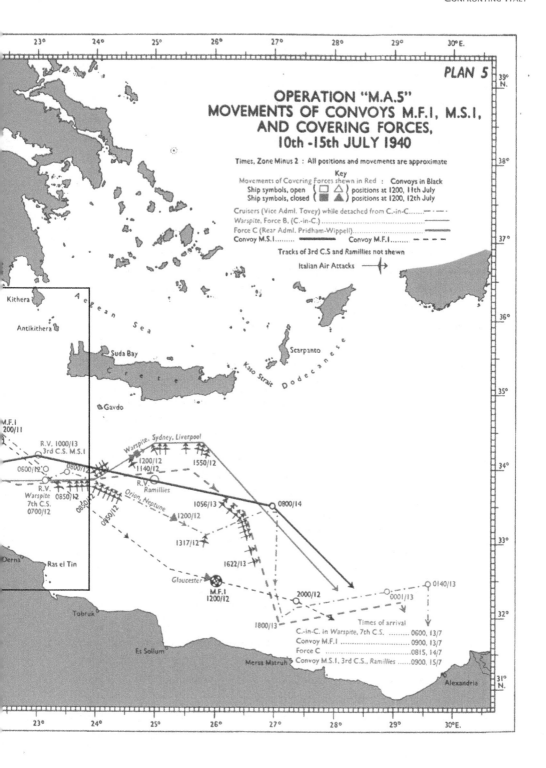

PLAN 5

OPERATION "M.A.5"
MOVEMENTS OF CONVOYS M.F.I, M.S.I,
AND COVERING FORCES,
10th -15th JULY 1940

Times, Zone Minus 2 : All positions and movements are approximate

Key
Movements of Covering Forces shewn in Red : Convoys in Black
Ship symbols, open positions at 1200, 11th July
Ship symbols, closed positions at 1200, 12th July
Cruisers (Vice Adml. Tovey) while detached from C.-in-C.
Warspite, Force B, (C.-in-C.)
Force C (Rear Adml. Pridham-Wippell)
Convoy M.S.I Convoy M.F.I

Tracks of 3rd C.S and Ramillies not shewn

Italian Air Attacks

Kithera
Antikithera
Aegean Sea
Suda Bay
Crete
Scarpanto
Kaso Strait   Dodecanese
Gavdo

M.F.I
200/11
R.V. 1000/13
3rd C.S. M.S.I
0600/12   0800/12
Warspite, Sydney, Liverpool
1200/12   1550/12
1140/12
R.V.
Warspite 0850/12   R.V.
7th C.S.   Ramillies
0700/12   Orion, Neptune
0850/12   1056/13   0800/14
1200/12
1317/12
1622/13

Derna   Ras el Tin
Gloucester
M.F.I
1200/12   2000/12   0001/13   0140/13

Tobruk
1800/13   Times of arrival
C.-in-C. in Warspite, 7th C.S. 0600, 13/7
Convoy M.F.I 0900, 13/7
Es Sollum   Force C 0815, 14/7
Mersa Matruh   Convoy M.S.I, 3rd C.S., Ramillies 0900, 15/7
Alexandria

79

minutes, after which course 070° was resumed but this proved unsuccessful, for another attack developed at 1812, when eight bombs – "all very bad shots" – fell ahead of the *Orion*. These aircraft, flying very high, were not engaged before they dropped their bombs. Another attack occurred at 1930, the bombs again falling wide. One aircraft hit in this attack made off to the north-west, then turned eastward losing height and with smoke coming from one of its engines. It was thought unlikely that it reached its base 180 miles away.

The night of 11th/12th July passed quietly. The C.-in-C., who was in 34° 22' N., 19° 17' E. at 2100, 11th, continued to the eastward, steering 110°. Force "C", after operating aircraft, at 2000, 11th, feinted to the north-west for an hour and a half, before turning to 150° at 2130 in order to keep to the westward of convoy M.S.1. At 0254, 12th July, the *Hasty* attacked a submarine contact. The 7th Cruiser Squadron, which had been ordered to join the C.-in-C. at 0800, 12th July, steered so as to approach the rendezvous from the northward. It sighted the *Warspite* at 0638,12th; the *Orion* and *Neptune* were then detached to join Convoy M.F.1, the *Liverpool* and *Sydney* remaining in company with the C.-in-C..

During this day, 12th July, the bombing attacks on the Warspite were intensified. Between 0850 and 1550, in seventeen attacks about 160 bombs[46] were dropped. The *Warspite* was straddled three times[47] and there were several near misses, splinters from one killing three ratings in the *Liverpool*, and wounding her executive officer and five ratings. As a result of these attacks, course was altered to close the Egyptian coast and No. 252 Wing was asked to send out fighter aircraft, but when these arrived late in the afternoon the attacks had ceased. Force "C", after flying off A/S patrols at dawn, had sighted Convoy M.S.1 at 0621, 12th. At 0925 the *Defender* was detached to find and escort the oiler *British Union* to Alexandria. As regards bombing, Force "C" got off lightly on this day, only three attacks being made between 1110 and 1804; 25 bombs were dropped, all of which fell wide. Haze overhead made sighting of aircraft difficult. The *Dainty* reported passing the body of an Italian airman at 1848.

Vice-Admiral Tovey with the *Orion* and *Neptune*, on parting company with the C.-in-C. at 0730, 12th, had set course 115°, 25 knots, in search of the fast convoy. Between 0850 and 0950 the two cruisers were attacked by 30 aircraft without result, and again at 1312 by a solitary aircraft, which dropped four bombs near the *Neptune*. The effect of these attacks was to deflect the ships to the northward, so that they did not gain touch with Convoy M.F.1 – then about 150 miles from Alexandria – till 1825. After passing the morning rendezvous to the *Gloucester*, the *Orion* and *Neptune* proceeded on course 080° to keep clear during the night and arrived at Alexandria at 0645 next morning (13th July). The C.-in-C., in the

Warspite, with the *Liverpool, Sydney* and destroyers had arrived three-quarters of an hour earlier, and Convoy M.F.1, with escort, arrived at 0900. The *Ramillies* (Captain H. T. Baillie-Grohman), screened by the *Havock* (Commander R. E. Courage), *Imperial, Diamond* and *Vendetta*, was then sailed to meet and cover Convoy M.S.1.

Meanwhile Rear-Admiral Pridham-Wippell with Force "C", had been slowly working to the eastward, adjusting his advance to keep to the westward of Convoy M.S.1. At nightfall 12th July, course was set to pass rather closer to Ras el Tin than to Gavdos, but as a result of instructions from the C.-in-C., an alteration to 085°, in order to increase the distance from the Libyan coast, was made at 0215, 13th. Some three hours later (0524) the *Capetown* (Captain T. H. Back) flying the flag of the Rear-Admiral, 3rd Cruiser Squadron (Rear-Admiral E. de F. Renouf) and the *Caledon* (Captain C. P. Clarke), which had sailed from Alexandria the previous day to meet Convoy M.S.1 about 60 miles south west. of Gavdos, hove in sight. These two cruisers then took over M.S.1 and Force "C" went on for Alexandria.

The first warning of trouble from the air came at 0802, when one of the *Eagle's* Gladiators reported a shadower, which it shot down a little later. Air attacks on Force "C" began at 1056 and continued till 1622. From 1110 to 1300 the attacks were too numerous to record precisely, the *Eagle* being the favourite target. The attackers found she could hit back, however, two of them being shot down by the Gladiators and a third so seriously damaged as to prevent its return home. A destroyer was sent to pick up the only airman seen to come down, but no body was found. The average height of the attacking aircraft was about 12,000 feet; although there were several near misses and straddles, no damage was done to any of the ships.

At 1210, 13th, Force "C" steered to close the coast off Mersa Matruh, in compliance with orders from the C.-in-C. and at 1800 course was altered to the E.N.E. to adjust the time of arrival at Alexandria next morning. Force "C" entered harbour at 0815, 14th July, and the 3rd Cruiser Squadron, *Ramillies* and Convoy M.S.1 on the morning of the 15th, thus bringing operation M.A.5 to a successful conclusion.

Remarks on Action off Calabria

Commenting on the action of 9th July, the C.-in-C., Mediterranean, remarked: –

> " ...It is still not clear what brought the enemy fleet to sea on this occasion, but it seems probable that it was engaged on an operation designed to cover the movement of a convoy to Libya. When our fleet was reported south of

Crete it seems that the enemy retired close to his bases, fuelled his destroyers by relays, and then waited hoping to draw us into an engagement in his own waters (under cover of his Air Force and possibly with a submarine concentration to the southward of him) whence he could use his superior speed to withdraw at his own time.

"If these were, in fact, the enemy's intentions, he was not altogether disappointed, but the submarines, if there were any in the vicinity of the action, did not materialise and fortunately for us, his air attacks failed to synchronise with the gun action.

"It will be noted that the whole action took place at very long range and that the *Warspite* was the only capital ship which got within range of the enemy battleships. *Malaya* fired a few salvoes which fell some 3,000 yards short. *Royal Sovereign*, owing to her lack of speed, never got into action at all.

"*Warspite's* hit on one of the enemy battleships at 26,000 yards range might perhaps be described as a lucky one. Its tactical effect was to induce the enemy to turn away and break off the action, which was unfortunate, but strategically it probably has had an important effect on Italian mentality.

"The torpedo attacks by the F.A.A. were disappointing, one hit on a cruiser being all that can be claimed,[48] but in fairness it must be recorded that the pilots had had very little practice, and none at high speed targets, *Eagle* having only recently joined the Fleet after having been employed on the Indian Ocean trade routes.

The enemy's gunnery seemed good at first and he straddled quickly, but accuracy soon fell off as his ships came under our fire.

"Our cruisers – there were only four in action – were badly outnumbered and at times came under a very heavy fire. They were superbly handled by Vice-Admiral J. C. Tovey, G.B., D.S.O., who by his skilful manoeuvring managed to maintain a position in the van and to hold the enemy cruiser squadrons, and at the same time avoid damage to his own force. *Warspite* was able to assist him with her fire in the early stages of the action.

"The enemy's smoke tactics were impressive and the smoke screens laid by his destroyers were very effective in completely covering his high speed retirement. With his excess speed of at least five knots there was little hope of catching him once he had decided to break off the action. An aircraft torpedo hit on one of his battleships was the only chance and this unfortunately did not occur...

"A feature of the action was the value, and in some cases the amusement, derived from intercepted enemy signals. We were fortunate in having the Italian Fleet Code, and some of his signals were made in plain language...

"My remarks on the bombing attacks experienced by the Fleet during the course of these operations are contained in my signal timed 1619 of 14th July 1940.[49]

"I cannot conclude these remarks without a reference to H.M.S. *Eagle*. This obsolescent aircraft carrier, with only 17 Swordfish embarked, found and kept touch with the enemy fleet, flew off two striking forces of nine torpedo bombers within the space of four hours, both of which attacked, and all aircraft returned. 24 hours later a torpedo striking force was launched on shipping in Port Augusta and throughout the five days' operations, *Eagle* maintained constant A/S patrols in daylight and carried out several searches. Much of the *Eagle's* aircraft operating work was done in the fleeting intervals between, and even during, bombing attacks and I consider her performance reflects great credit on Captain A. M. Bridge, Royal Navy, her Commanding Officer.

"The meagre material results derived from this brief meeting with the Italian fleet, were naturally very disappointing to one and all under my command, but the action was not without value. It must have shown the Italians that their Air Force and submarines cannot stop our fleet penetrating into the Central Mediterranean and that only their main fleet can seriously interfere with our operating there. It established, I think, a certain degree of moral ascendancy since, although superior in battleships, our fleet was heavily outnumbered in cruisers and destroyers and the Italians had strong shore-based air forces within easy range compared to our few carrier-borne aircraft. On our side the action has shown those without previous war experience, how difficult it is to hit with the gun at long range, and therefore the necessity of closing in when this can be done in order to get decisive results. It showed that high level bombing even on the heavy and accurate scale experienced during these operations, yields few hits and that it is more alarming than dangerous.

"Finally, these operations and the action off Calabria produced throughout the fleet a determination to overcome the air menace and not to let it interfere with our freedom of manoeuvre, and hence our control of the Mediterranean."[50]

The Italian Official History contains a lengthy review of the operations. Much of it deals with topical and technical matters, and with Admiral Campioni's reasons for the decisions he took, all of which seem to have been approved by the Ministry of Marine. The latter in their remarks stress the value of the information received by wireless interception in the early stages of operation M.A.5, and from reconnaissance aircraft on 8th July. On the other hand failure of air reconnaissance on the 9th embarrassed Admiral Campioni in the early stages of the approach.

As regards the action, they were impressed by the advantage conferred on the British Fleet by the presence of an aircraft carrier: –

"English reconnaissance aircraft were able to follow our fleet undisturbed, providing valuable information all the time to their C.-in-C., because of our failure to stop them owing to our shore-based fighters being out of range, and not possessing an aircraft carrier with our fleet.

"The presence of an aircraft carrier with the English fleet, besides permitting them to fight off the activities of our aircraft, both bombers and reconnaissance, allowed the enemy to carry out attacks with torpedo aircraft which, although frustrated by ships' manoeuvring, interfered with the formations attacked and so delayed their rejoining the remainder of our forces."

Naturally, as Admiral Cunningham remarked, there was considerable disappointment in the Mediterranean Fleet that the Italians had managed to evade close action. Nevertheless, this first encounter set the tone, as it were, for the whole naval war in the Mediterranean and was the first step in establishing that moral ascendancy which Sir Andrew Cunningham – with numerically inferior forces – maintained against the Italians till their capitulation in 1943.

It was no doubt recognition of this aspect which in some measure prompted the message from the Admiralty received by the C.-in-C. on 17th July: –

"Their Lordships have read with great satisfaction your telegraphic report of operations carried out between 7th and 13th July, and wish to congratulate you and all concerned on the determined and efficient manner in which they were conducted."

Action off Cape Spada, Crete 19th July 1940

Plan for Operations in Aegean

Within a week of the conclusion of Operation M.A.5, a fortuitous encounter between H.M.A.S. *Sydney* with five destroyers and two Italian 6-inch gun cruisers resulted in the sinking of one of the latter, and must have accentuated Italian doubts as to their control of the Mediterranean which may have been engendered by the brief engagement off Calabria ten days previously.

It was Admiral Sir Andrew Cunningham's policy to use his light forces in periodic sweeps, as a means of countering the activities of Italian submarines in areas through which British convoys had to pass and at the same time attacking Italian shipping.

On 17th July 1940 orders were issued for such an operation, which was to consist of a submarine hunt towards the The Kaso Strait and round the north coast of Crete by four destroyers, combined with a sweep by a cruiser and one destroyer into the Gulf of Athens for Italian shipping. The cruiser was to be prepared to support the destroyers in case of need.[51] The forces for these operations were organised in two groups, viz., –

> **Force "A"** 3rd Division, 2nd D.F. under Commander (D2).
> *Hyperion* (four 4.7-inch) Commander H. St. L. Nicolson, D.S.O. (D2).
> *Ilex*, (four 4.7-inch) Lieutenant-Commander P. L. Saumarez, D.S.C.
> *Hero* (four 4.7-inch) Commander H. W. Biggs, D.S.O.
> *Hasty* (four 4.7-inch) Lieutenant-Commander L. R. K. Tyrwhitt.
> **Force "B"**
> *Sydney* (eight 6-inch, eight 4-inch, H.A.) Captain J. A. Collins, R.A.N.
> *Havock* (four 4.7-inch) Commander R. E. Courage, D.S.O., D.S.C.

Movements of Forces, 18th–19th July

Force "A" sailed from Alexandria at 0015, 18th[52], and swept towards the Kaso Strait. After passing through the strait at 2130, keeping well over towards the Cretan shore to avoid being sighted from Kaso Island,[53] the division steered westward at 18 knots between Ovo Island and the Cretan shore. Nothing was sighted, and at 0600, 19th, course was altered to 240° to pass through the Antikithera Channel, the destroyers spread in line abreast 1½ miles apart, carrying out the anti-submarine sweep at 18 knots.

Force "B" – the *Sydney* with the *Havock* in company – sailed from Alexandria at 0430, 18th, and after passing through the Kaso Strait at 2345, steered a mean course 295°, speed of advance, 18 knots, zig-zagging on account of full moon and improving visibility. Captain Collins seems to have found the double object given to him in the operation orders something of an embarrassment, for he subsequently wrote that in the morning of the 19th "I was ... proceeding on a westerly course about 40 miles north of Crete in accordance with my instructions to afford support to (D)2 and destroyers ... My instructions included the second object of the destruction of enemy shipping in the Gulf of Athens. I decided however that it was my duty to remain in support of [the] destroyers until 0800, by which time they should have cleared the Antikithera Strait, although this precluded the successful achievement of the second object."[54]

Meanwhile, unknown to the British, two Italian cruisers under Vice-Admiral F. Casardi, the *Giovanni delle Bande Nere*[55] (flag) and *Bartolomeo Colleoni* had sailed from Tripoli at 2200, 17th July, for the Aegean. Throughout the 18th they steered to the eastward for a point 30 miles north of Derna, which they reached at 2307, 18th, and then turned to the northward. At 0700, 19th, they were steering to enter the Aegean through the Antikithera Channel, just as Commander Nicolson's destroyers were approaching it from the E.N.E. (See Fig. 4).

Surface Contact (Plan 6)

At 0722, 19th July, two Italian cruisers were sighted ahead by the *Hero*, the second destroyer from the northward. The Italians had sighted the destroyers about five minutes earlier and apparently turned to head them off, as they seemed to the *Hero* to be steering 160°: but Admiral Casardi, suspecting from their formation that they were screening heavy craft, hauled round to port at about 0723 and steadied on 360°. However prudent this may have been, it lost him an opportunity of inflicting serious damage on the destroyers with his heavier armament.

On sighting the enemy at 0722, Commander Nicolson at once turned his division to starboard together to course 060°, and increased speed, the destroyers concentrating in sub-divisions on the *Hyperion*, in accordance with previous instructions.

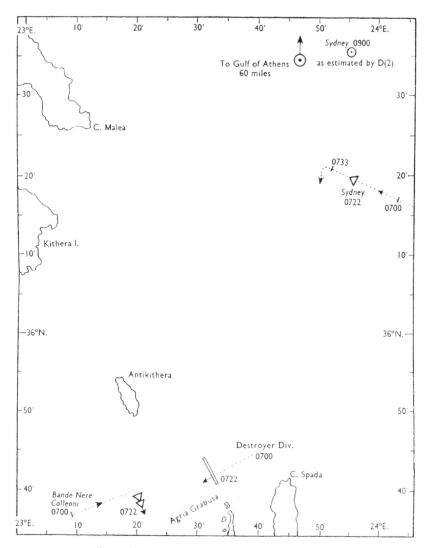

Fig. 4. POSITION OF FORCES, 0722, 19TH JULY 1940

It was estimated that the *Sydney* at 0900 would be in position 010°, 55 miles from Cape Spada[56], and while steering for this position Commander Nicolson endeavoured to work round to the northward. Actually, thanks to Captain Collins' decision to give precedence to supporting the destroyers, the *Sydney* was a good deal nearer, and when at 0733 she received Commander Nicolson's enemy sighting report (two enemy cruisers steering 160° bearing 255°, distant ten miles) her position was 010° Cape Spada 40 miles. The *Hyperion* gave her own position as

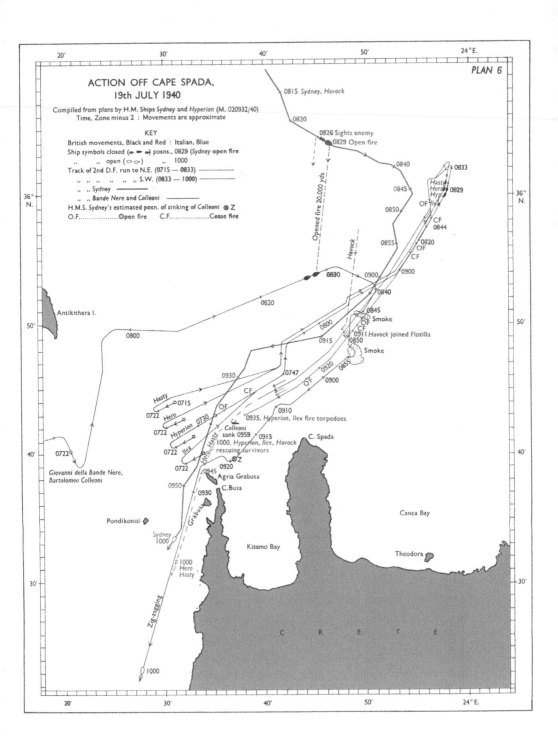

ACTION OFF CAPE SPADA,
19th JULY 1940

Compiled from plans by H.M. Ships *Sydney* and *Hyperion* (M. 020932/40)
Time, Zone minus 2 : Movements are approximate

KEY

British movements, Black and Red : Italian, Blue
Ship symbols closed (●—●—●) posns., 0829 (*Sydney* open fire
  "   "   open (○○)   "   1000
Track of 2nd D.F. run to N.E. (0715 — 0833) ————
  "   "   "   "   " S.W. (0833 — 1000) ————
  "   " *Sydney* ————
  "   " *Bande Nere* and *Colleoni* ————
H.M.S. *Sydney's* estimated posn. of sinking of *Colleoni* ⊗ Z
O.F. .... Open fire   C.F. .... Cease fire

340° Agria Grabusa[57] Light 3 miles. Acting on this information Captain Collins altered course at 0736 to 240° to close the destroyers but on receipt a minute later of an amplifying report giving the *Hyperion's* course as 060° and the enemy's as 360°, he hauled round to 190° and commenced to work up to full speed.

Destroyer Engagement with Italian Cruisers (Plan 6)

By this time (0737) Commander Nicolson's destroyers had been in action for 11 minutes. One of the enemy cruisers had opened fire at 0726 on the *Hyperion* and *Ilex*, and the latter returned the fire. With their engines working up fast, the speed of the destroyers reached 31 knots by 0735, and the *Hyperion* then opened fire with her after guns at maximum range, but ceased firing very soon as all her shots fell short. The enemy's shooting was erratic. His salvoes fell short, throwing up red, yellow and green splashes, possibly due to the use of identifiers. The Italian report stated that the destroyers were scarcely visible, either because of mist or the slanting rays of the sun, which was bearing about 070° at 11° elevation.

Although the range was opening rapidly, the enemy, instead of heading in chase of the destroyers, held on his course north – "manoeuvring so as to keep at the limit of enemy gun range and to avoid the chance of an effective torpedo attack".[58] These tactics again lost him a favourable chance of utilising his superior gun power. At 0738 the enemy bore 270°, 11 miles, and the *Hyperion* at 0740 ordered her division to cease firing as the enemy was out of range. Five minutes later the enemy's fire also ceased.

At 0747 the enemy, then bearing 270°, 14 miles, was still steering north. With the object of gaining ground and of identifying the class of the enemy cruisers, the destroyer division altered course to 360°. At 0753, when the enemy turned to close, course was altered back to 060°. A signal from the C.-in-C. to join the *Sydney* was received by the *Hyperion* at 0800, and four minutes later course was altered to 030°, with the enemy then bearing 265°, 17 miles, steering 090°. These positions were signalled to the *Sydney* at 0805, and course was altered a minute later to 060°. At about this time there was sighted ahead eight miles off a Greek steamer, which turned away quickly to the northward.

Still trying to work to the northward, the destroyers' course was altered to 040° at 0814 and to 030° at 0821. The enemy reopened fire at 0825, but again his shooting was very short and erratic. He ceased fire after five minutes, and was then observed to be altering course to the southward.

This was due to the sudden arrival of the *Sydney*. Commander Nicolson had kept her informed of his movements and those of the enemy. Captain Collins on the other hand had been careful to preserve W/T silence to avoid disclosing the presence of the Sydney.[59] In this he was entirely successful. He had altered course at 0800 to 150° and shortly afterwards signals arrived from the C.-in-C. directing the destroyers to join the *Sydney* and the latter to support them. Further alterations of course were made at 0815 to 160° and at 0820 to 120°; at 0826 the enemy ships, steering 090°, were sighted bearing 188°, range 23,000 yards, about 20° before the starboard beam, and three minutes later the *Sydney* opened fire on the *Bande Nere* at a range of 20,000 yards.

The gun flashes were seen away on the port beam of the *Hyperion* and at 0832 the *Sydney* and *Havock* could be seen bearing 290°, 10 miles – a welcome sight. Commander Nicolson by then steering 020° at once altered course, first to 240° then to 260° and formed the division in line ahead.[60] The enemy cruisers, then 17,400 yards distant, were by that time steaming fast to the south-eastward making heavy black smoke, and at 0836 the *Hyperion* led round to 170°, in order to get to a position of torpedo advantage on their bow.

H.M.A.S. *Sydney* Engages Enemy Cruisers (Plan 6)

When the *Sydney* opened fire on the *Bande Nere* at 0829, she took the Italians completely by surprise. They were then engaged with the destroyers on their other side and the first intimation they had of her presence was the arrival of her salvoes. Low-lying mist partially concealed the new enemy, which was thought to consist of two cruisers. Admiral Casardi at once altered course some 40° away steadying on about 1150, and at 0832 the Italians returned the fire, concentrating on the *Sydney's* gunflashes, which were all they could see. Their salvoes fell short at first, then over, with an occasional straddle.

The *Sydney* continued on a south-easterly course to meet the destroyer division and at the same time to close the enemy. At 0835 her fire appeared effective[61] and the enemy was seen to turn away, making smoke.

Three minutes later (0838) Commander Nicolson's destroyers hove in sight line on the port bow about six miles off, steering 170°; at that moment they opened fire in divisional concentration at extreme range on the left-hand cruiser, but ceased fire after five minutes as all their salvoes were falling short. The *Havock* at once proceeded to join Commander Nicolson and at 0841 Captain Collins ordered the destroyers to "Close and attack the enemy with torpedoes"; but by the time the signal got through (0844) a drastic alteration of course to the south-westward by the enemy at 0840 had rendered this impossible. Commander Nicolson therefore altered course together to 215° and forming the division on a line of bearing 350°, chased at his best speed. The *Sydney* also turned to 215° at 0845, a manoeuvre which brought her on the beam of the destroyers; from then onwards the action was a chase.

It was not until about this time that Captain Collins was able definitely to identify the class of his opponents and "was relieved"[62] to find they were not 8-inch gun ships. He had been " even more pleased"[62] to observe the enemy making smoke in the early stages, which implied that they were already thinking of evasive tactics.

At about 0846 the *Sydney's* original target was so obscured by smoke that fire was shifted to the rear cruiser (*Colleoni*), which was engaged by "A" and "B" turrets on bearing 203°, range 18,000 yards. The destroyer division also renewed its fire at extreme range for a couple of minutes. At 0851 the enemy altered course to port, and the *Sydney* conformed, which had the effect of opening her "A" arcs; but two minutes later the enemy, making vast quantities of smoke, altered course to starboard, 16 points in succession,[63] and the *Sydney*, observing them steadying on course 230° at 0856, resumed the chase in a south-westerly direction.

For a minute, at 0901, the *Sydney* checked fire while she shifted target again to the *Bande Nere*. When this ship, at 0908, again became obscured by smoke, fire was shifted back again to the *Colleoni* then bearing 210°, range 18,500 yards. At 0915 the *Sydney* altered course 30° to starboard to open her "A" arcs, and it was soon evident that her fire was having considerable effect. With the range down to 17,500 yards at 0919, the *Sydney* also came under an accurate fire, receiving her only hit at 0921. This projectile, bursting on the foremost funnel, blew a hole about three feet square in the casings, causing minor damage to three boats and some fittings, but only one slight casualty.

Throughout the chase, the destroyers steaming at 32 knots had made every effort to reduce the range, but until 0918, when the range of the *Colleoni* was down to 17,000 yards and closing rapidly, they were unable to do so.

The Sinking of the *Bartolomeo Colleoni*

At 0923 the *Colleoni* was seen to be stopped, apparently out of action in a position about five miles E.N.E. of Cape Spada. Survivors afterwards stated that she was brought to by a shell in the engine or boiler room. The electrical machinery failed, including the turret power hoists and steering gear. All her lights went out and ratings stationed in the magazines groped their way out by means of matches and cigarette lighters! The *Bande Nere*, after a tentative turn towards her wounded consort, left her to her fate, and made off at high speed to the southward, rounding Agria Grabusa Island at a distance of about a mile, with the *Sydney* in hot pursuit, leaving the destroyers to finish off the *Colleoni*.

Commander Nicolson altered course to 240° and opened fire in divisional concentration at a range of 14,500 yards. By 0930 the range was down to about

5,000 yards. The *Colleoni* was drifting and silent; for some minutes she had been hit repeatedly, chiefly below the bridge; her control had been put out of action and some H.A. ammunition set on fire. The whole bridge structure was soon in flames. But she was still afloat, and at 0933 the *Sydney* signalled the one word "Torpedo." Ordering Commander Biggs of the *Hero* to take charge of the other destroyers and follow the *Sydney*, Commander Nicolson in the *Hyperion* with the *Ilex* approached his quarry. By then the *Colleoni* was on fire amidships, her colours on the mainmast had been shot away or, as some thought, struck, and a heavy explosion had occurred forward.

At 0935 the *Hyperion* fired four and the *Ilex* two torpedoes at a range of 1,400 yards. One torpedo from the *Ilex* hit the *Colleoni* forward, blowing away about 100 feet of her bows and her aircraft. The *Hyperion's* torpedoes, owing to too great a spread, passed two ahead and two astern, and ran on to explode ashore on Agria Grabusa Island. The *Hyperion* then closed in, and observing the *Colleoni* more or less abandoned, but not sinking or too heavily on fire, Commander Nicolson decided as he passed down her starboard side to go alongside and see if anything could be salved. Barely two minutes elapsed, however, before a large fire broke out in the forward superstructure which was followed by an explosion which blew the whole bridge away in a cloud of smoke. The *Hyperion* then fired another torpedo at short range, which hit the doomed ship amidships at 0952, and seven minutes later the *Colleoni* heeled over and sank bottom up in position 029° Agria Grabusa Light 4.5 miles.

The *Hyperion* and *Ilex* immediately began to rescue survivors, in which work they were joined by the *Havock*, which had been too far off to read Commander Biggs' signal to join him and had apparently missed a signal from Captain Collins at 0943 to Commander Nicolson to leave one destroyer to deal with the *Colleoni*, and follow him with the rest. According to survivors' accounts, the men of the *Colleoni* had started to jump overboard as soon as the ship stopped, and many of them were in the sea before the *Ilex's* torpedo struck the ship. She had suffered many casualties forward, on the upper deck and round the bridge, among them her Captain seriously wounded.[64] There seems to have been little or no attempt to launch any boats or rafts, but all the crew had life belts.

The Italians were much impressed by the rate and accuracy of the British gunfire, as well as the tactical superiority of the British Commanders. Some prisoners even insisted that the calibre of our guns must be more than 6-inch.

During the rescue work several signals were received from Captain Collins, directing the destroyers to join him as soon as possible, but it was not till 1024 that the *Hyperion* and *Ilex* proceeded at high speed to do so,[65] leaving the *Havock* to continue picking up survivors. The *Ilex* had some 230 prisoners on board. Most of them were naked and 58 wounded, 25 seriously, three of whom died that night.

At 1138 the *Havock* signalled to the *Sydney* that survivors stated that the Italian cruisers had expected to meet strong supporting forces that morning.[66] At 1237, when she had picked up some 260 survivors, six Savoia bombers were sighted, approaching from the southward. Thus threatened with attack, the *Havock* was forced to abandon her humane task and proceeded at full speed for Alexandria.

Altogether, 525 survivors out of a complement of 630 had been picked up by the three destroyers, and it was afterwards learned from the Naval Attaché, Athens, that seven others were rescued off Crete, after swimming for 26 to 42 hours.

Chase of the *Bande Nere*

Meanwhile the *Bande Nere*, after passing between the island of Pondiko Nisi and the Cretan mainland, at 0945 bore 192° at a range of 20,000 yards from the *Sydney*. At 0950 the Italian received a second hit; a shell penetrated the quarter deck and exploded on a bulkhead, killing four and wounding 12 ratings. But ammunition in "A" and "B" turrets was running low and the *Sydney* checked fire; the *Bande Nere*, however, continued firing her after guns, the shots from which fell consistently 300 yards away on the *Sydney's* quarter. At 0955 Captain Collins repeated his signal to Commander Nicolson to finish off the *Colleoni* and rejoin him, and three minutes later reopened fire on the *Bande Nere*, still 20,000 yards distant, but checked fire again at 1011. By this time, the range was increasing and the visibility of the target and the fall of shot becoming more indistinct. A final couple of salvoes at 1022, range 21,000 yards, could not be observed; the Mediterranean haze combined with the enemy's smoke had rendered spotting impossible. The *Sydney* then had remaining only four rounds per gun in "A" turret and in "B" turret one round per gun of C.P.B.C. shell. Shortly afterwards, the Bande Nere, 11 miles off, disappeared in the haze, going 32 knots on course 200°.

The *Hero* and *Hasty*, gradually drawing further ahead of the *Sydney*, had continued the chase at 31 knots, firing ranging salvoes at intervals in the hope that the enemy's frequent alterations of course would bring him in range, but they all fell short. At 1020 the *Hero* signalled to the *Sydney* "Regret, I am not catching her", and eight minutes later in compliance with a signal from Captain Collins, she and the *Hasty* dropped back to form a close screen on the *Sydney*. At 1037 Captain Collins reluctantly abandoned the chase, and altered course to 150° for Alexandria, reducing speed to 25 knots to allow the *Hyperion* and *Ilex* to come up. The last seen of the *Bande Nere* was from the *Hero* at 1044 – a smudge on the horizon bearing 177°, 15 miles away.

General Situation, 1100, 19th July

While the *Sydney* and the destroyers had been fighting their eminently satisfactory action, the C.-in-C. at Alexandria, acting on their reports and in view of the possibility that there might be other enemy forces at sea had decided to take the Fleet to sea.[67]

The general situation at 1100, 19th July – shortly after the *Bande Nere* had been lost to view – was as follows: Vice-Admiral Tovey in the *Orion* with the *Neptune* had sailed at 0915 and was sweeping to the north-westward at 30 knots. The C.-in-C. in the *Warspite* with destroyer screen was just leaving harbour, to be followed at 1230 by the 1st Battle Squadron (less *Royal Sovereign*), *Eagle* and screen for a sweep to the westward. An air reconnaissance by flying boats of 201 Group R.A.F. was arranged to search for the *Bande Nere*, but as it was clear that she could not be intercepted before reaching Tobruk if making for that port, the *Eagle* was ordered to prepare a striking force to attack Tobruk harbour and 201 Group was requested to make a dusk reconnaissance.

Actually, the *Bande Nere* then (1100, 19th) some 40 miles due west of Gavdos Island, and steering for Tobruk, altered course for Benghazi about an hour after shaking off the pursuit, where she arrived that afternoon.

The *Sydney, Hero* and *Hasty* some five miles south of Elaphonisi Light (the south-west point of Crete) were steering 150°, 25 knots, and the *Hyperion* and *Ilex*, about 18 miles astern of them, were steering to overtake them at 30 knots. Off Agria Grabusa the *Havock* was still picking up the *Colleoni*'s survivors.

H.M.S. *Havock* Damaged by Air Attack

Commander Courage in the *Havock*, as already mentioned, continued rescue work till 1237, when on the appearance of enemy aircraft he steered at full speed for Alexandria. At 1245 and 1250 the bombers in formations of three attacked her without success, doing no more than deluge her with water from near misses. A couple of hours later (1455), nine more aircraft attacked her off Gavdos Island in flights of three, the second flight scoring a near miss, splinters from which penetrated and flooded No. 2 boiler room. Two ratings received minor injuries. These attacks, which were made from levels between 3,000 and 4,000 feet, were countered with effective gunfire, which in two instances broke up the formations. The bomb that caused the damage appeared to be one of 250lb., which burst six feet under water about ten feet from the ship's side. After losing way for five minutes the *Havock* picked up speed again and was able to proceed at 24 knots.

Captain Collins, on receiving the *Havock*'s signal reporting her damage at about 1500, and finding to his surprise that she was some 75 miles to the northward,[68] turned back in the *Sydney* in support, after ordering the *Hero* and *Hasty* to continue on their course for Alexandria and informing the C.-in-C., who detached the *Liverpool* to join the *Sydney*. Shortly after turning northward, a heavy bombing attack was made on the *Sydney* without success. Realising as he proceeded north the danger of submarine or possibly surface attack, Captain Collins ordered the *Hyperion* and *Ilex* to join the *Havock* at sunset. The *Sydney* made contact with the *Havock* at about 1640 and took station a mile astern of her; as she did so, Commander Courage signalled: "Thank you. I hope your H.A. is as good as your L.A." – a happy allusion to the *Sydney's* prowess in the surface action combined with a heartfelt desire in the present circumstances.

Meanwhile the *Hyperion* and *Ilex*, having been unable to rendezvous with the *Sydney* (they had been steering further to the eastward than the cruiser) were proceeding to Alexandria. When the *Havock's* report of being damaged was received, Commander Nicolson turned back to her assistance, but later (1545) learning that the *Sydney* had also turned back, resumed his former course until 1608, when he received Captain Collins' signal to join the *Havock* at sunset. After the junction was effected at 1840, the *Hyperion* and *Ilex* formed a screen ahead of the *Havock* on course 150°, speed 20 knots. The last bombing attacks of the day occurred between 1845 and 1848, doing no damage. At 2100 the *Sydney* parted company to rendezvous with the 7th Cruiser Squadron, the destroyers continuing for Alexandria.

Return to Alexandria

Little remains to be told.

As no further information of the *Bande Nere* came in during the afternoon of the 19th July, the C.-in-C. decided that at 2100 all forces should return to Alexandria. The *Warspite's* aircraft was catapulted at 1700 to search the Tobruk area, but was obliged to make a forced landing to the eastward of the port, and the *Jervis* was detached to search for it.

Tobruk spent a disturbed night. Aircraft of Nos. 55 and 211 Squadrons, R.A.F., carried out bombing attacks on the shipping there and claimed several hits. At 0240, 20th, six aircraft of No. 824 Squadron, F.A.A., from the *Eagle* made a successful moonlight torpedo attack, encountering heavy barrage fire from all sides of the harbour, which damaged three aircraft, wounded an observer seriously and slightly wounded a pilot. Hits were claimed on three ships, and a sheet of flame from an oiler indicated that she carried petrol. Reconnaissance of Tobruk after the night raids showed the following ships were absent: one large cruiser, one destroyer and two merchant vessels.

Search for the *Warspite*'s aircraft was continued by flying boats of 201 Group after dawn on 20th July without success.[69]

The Fleet entered harbour at Alexandria during the morning of the 20th, where all ships cheered the *Sydney* and Commander Nicolson's destroyers on their arrival. Immediate recognition[70] of the successful issue of this action was conveyed in a signal from the First Lord of the Admiralty, saying that His Majesty the King had awarded the C.B. to Captain Collins and a bar to the D.S.O. to Commander Nicolson, and "His Majesty has also asked me to send his personal congratulations to all concerned in this splendid achievement."

In his covering letter, dated 21st September, 1940, to the Admiralty, Sir Andrew Cunningham wrote: –

"The credit for this successful and gallant action belongs mainly to Captain J. A. Collins, C.B., R.A.N., who by his quick appreciation of the situation, offensive spirit and resolute handling of H.M.A.S. *Sydney*, achieved a victory over a superior force which has had important strategical effects. It is significant that, so far as is known, no Italian surface forces have returned into or near the Aegean since this action was fought."

Remarks on the Action off Cape Spada

The action off Cape Spada was practically a duel between the *Sydney* and two adversaries, each of which was her equal in force, though the presence of the British destroyers undoubtedly influenced Admiral Casardi's tactics. Several points of interest emerge from the narrative.

It will be noted that this was one of the few surface actions of the war in which aircraft – either for reconnaissance, spotting or attacking – played no part. Admiral Casardi had not catapulted any of his aircraft in the early morning because he considered it too rough, and he also thought it certain that reconnaissance by shore-based aircraft over the area of the Aegean he had to pass through, would have been arranged by Headquarters at Rhodes. The *Sydney* had no aircraft embarked – a circumstance characterised by Captain Collins as "unfortunate"; she had lost her aircraft at the bombardment of Bardia on 21st June, and a replacement had been damaged by bomb splinters before it could be embarked.

The initial mistake of the Italian Admiral in steering north and engaging the destroyers at long range instead of immediately chasing them and trying to overwhelm them with his superior weight of metal has been remarked on. It is true that the formation of the destroyers may well have looked like a screen for heavier craft; but if a superior force were always to hold off till perfectly certain of what *might* be out of sight beyond the enemy, few surface actions would ever take place.[71] *Per contra* Captain Collins' unhesitating attack on a force practically double his strength, after having duly gauged the risks and taken steps to minimise them by keeping wireless silence and skilfully exploiting the advantage of surprise, achieved the success it deserved. The effect of the surprise was helped by the presence of the *Havock* which, as he suspected, was mistaken by the enemy for a cruiser in the first shock of the attack. It is also of interest to note the encouragement Captain Collins derived from the Italians' early use of smoke, which he immediately recognised as evidence that his enemy was fighting with one eye over his shoulder.

Perhaps the Italians were particularly unfortunate in meeting the *Sydney*, which had been in action twice during the preceding three weeks. "I was thus," wrote Captain Collins, "in the happy position of taking a ship into action that had already experienced two successful encounters with the enemy." The superiority of the *Sydney*'s gunfire, both for accuracy and rate, was most marked throughout the action.[72]

The shooting of the Italians was poor. Though described as accurate for range at first, it was slow, erratic and spasmodic, and fell off under punishment. It is remarkable that between them, the two enemy ships only succeeded in scoring a single hit. Any advantage they might have had from superior speed was discounted by their violent zig-zagging, which enabled the *Sydney* to keep the range steady, while opening her "A" arcs.

"The destroyers also were ably handled and fought"[73] both in retirement and on turning back immediately after sighting the *Sydney* at right angles to the enemy's course – a movement that possibly prevented the Italians from trying to escape to the eastward.[74]

To sum up, this little action well illustrates the value and application of almost all the principles of war. The importance of having the aim clearly defined comes out in Captain Collins' deliberate decision the night before the action as to his principal aim – which the operation orders issued to him had left a little ambiguous – and his adherence to it, viz., the support of the destroyer division. Thus, when the enemy cruisers were reported, he was in a position to fulfil his aim, and lost no time in steering to do so. As events developed, the destruction of the enemy cruisers became the immediate object. Incidentally, this was the surest way of achieving the original aim. He had exceptional reason to be satisfied with the morale of his ship's company; and – though he does not specifically state it in his report – he was probably equally satisfied from past experience that the aim of the enemy was not too good. Offensive action (which seems to have been rather lost sight of by the Italians) was the keynote of his tactics; but he did not forget security. He was about to attack a very superior force, and he "determined to make full use of *Surprise*"[75] in order to redress the balance – so far as might be – in his favour. Such weight did he give to the importance of surprise that he deliberately accepted some risk of failing to concentrate with the destroyers, through their ignorance of his position. This risk – which was much felt by Captain Collins at the time – was more apparent than real, and as things turned out, thanks to the intelligent co-operation of Commander Nicolson, concentration of force was effected most efficiently at the critical moment.

Thereafter, the action became a chase, in which the Italians had the legs of the British, and were bound to get away, except for a speed-reducing hit such as happened to the *Colleoni*; but it is worth noting that after she had been winged, Captain Collins left her to be finished off by some of the destroyers and he himself with the others at once followed up his success by pressing on in chase of the *Bande Nere* (economy of effort and maintenance of the aim). Nor did he abandon the chase till lack of ammunition and his obvious inability to catch her rendered further pursuit useless.

Action off Cape Spartivento, Sardinia, 27th November 1940

Introductory Remarks

Prior to the action off Cape Spartivento, a highly significant air attack by British forces on the Italian Fleet took place at Taranto. Within the following fortnight, there occurred an action in the Western Mediterranean, off Cape Spartivento, Sardinia, between British forces under Vice-Admiral Sir James Somerville and units of the Italian Navy under Admiral I. Campioni. The encounter took place during operations to ensure the passage of very important military stores and personnel through the Mediterranean to the Middle East. The safe passage of these reinforcements was Sir James Somerville's paramount consideration throughout and it is in the light of this liability that the action must be studied.[75]

Once again the Italians, availing themselves of their superior speed, withdrew almost before action was joined, and little material damage was suffered by either side. But the British were thereby left free to pass the convoy through according to plan, and the operations contributed another nail in the coffin to Italian supremacy in the Mediterranean.[76]

Plan of Operation "Collar"

The British units taking part in the operation, which was known as "Collar", were organised in three groups[77] as follows: –

Force **"B"** consisting of the battle-cruiser *Renown* (Flag Officer Commanding Force "H", Vice-Admiral Sir James F. Somerville), the aircraft carrier *Ark Royal*, cruisers, *Sheffield* and *Despatch*, and nine destroyers of the 8th and 13th Flotillas.

Force **"F"** composed of the cruisers *Manchester* (Flag, Vice-Admiral L. E. Holland) and *Southampton*, each carrying about 700 R.A.F. and military personnel, the destroyer *Hotspur*, four corvettes on passage to the Eastern Mediterranean, and three merchant vessels carrying mechanical transport.

Force **"D"** from the Eastern Mediterranean, consisted of the battleship *Ramillies*, the cruisers *Newcastle*, *Berwick* and *Coventry* (A.A.) and five destroyers.[78]

The general plan of the operation was that Forces "B" and "F" should escort and cover the passage of the transports and corvettes from Gibraltar through the Western Mediterranean, and should be met by Force "D" to the south of Sardinia at approximately noon,[79] 27th November. All three forces were then to make for a position between Sicily and Cape Bon (latitude 37° 40' N., longitude 10° 50' E.) which they would reach at dusk. After dark, Vice-Admiral Holland with Force "F", reinforced by the *Coventry* and destroyers of Force "D" was to pass through the Narrows to the Eastern Mediterranean, where he would be met the next day by the Mediterranean Fleet. Force "B" with the *Ramillies*, *Newcastle* and *Berwick* would then return to Gibraltar.

Preliminary Considerations and Enemy Intelligence

The condition of the ships taking part in the operation was not wholly satisfactory. The *Renown*, *Ark Royal* and *Sheffield* were in good fighting condition, but the *Ark Royal* had a number of inexperienced pilots and observers, and the efficiency of her torpedo striking force was low, owing to the lack of opportunities for exercise. The destroyers of the 8th and 13th Flotillas had been running very hard, though there was no reason to anticipate the development of any definite defects. These ships comprising the permanent nucleus of Force "H", were the only vessels in the whole force which had ever worked together as a squadron[80]. Some of the cruisers were handicapped by defects. The *Berwick* could not steam more than 27 knots, owing to the removal of some rows of turbine blades, and *Newcastle*'s boilers were not entirely reliable.

The *Hotspur* had just undergone temporary repairs and her speed was limited to about 20 knots; she was also without Asdic. The corvettes could not be relied upon for a speed of advance of more than 14 knots.

The *Manchester* and *Southampton* were each to carry some 700 R.A.F. and military personnel, to the detriment of their fighting efficiency, and doubts were expressed by Vice-Admiral Holland as to the advisability of including them in Force "F". As extreme importance was attached to the safe and timely arrival of these reinforcements at Alexandria, he decided that the cruisers should proceed independently, relying on their high speed and mobility; for with so many additional men on board, the ships were not in a condition to fight and if compelled to do so, the casualties among the R.A.F. might be heavy. Vice-Admiral Somerville on the other hand, was of the opinion that the complete object of the operation, which included the safe passage of the transports and corvettes, was more likely to be achieved by a show of force sufficiently powerful to deter the Italians from attempting to interfere.[81]

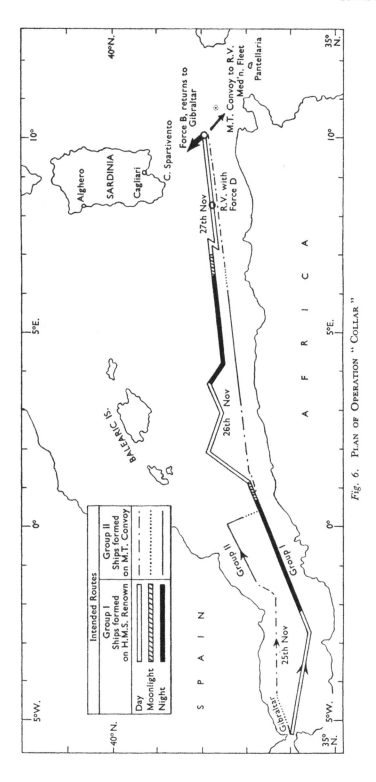

Fig. 6. PLAN OF OPERATION " COLLAR "

No very definite intelligence with regard to the Italian Naval Forces seems to have been available,[82] but Vice-Admiral Somerville considered it very probable, in view of the Taranto episode,[83] that the enemy would attempt some operation in the Western basin of the Mediterranean. There they could achieve a considerable superiority over Forces "B" and "F" (1 bc., 1 ac., 4 cr., 10 dr.) which would be forced to stand and fight owing to the presence of the slow transports (16 knots). He estimated that a concentration of three battleships, five to seven 8-inch cruisers, and several 6-inch cruisers with other light forces could be effected by the enemy for this purpose.[84] For this reason, he asked for the battleship *Royal Sovereign*, then undergoing repairs at Gibraltar, to be included in the operation; this was approved by the Admiralty, but her defects could not be completed in time.

British and Italian Movements, 25th–27th November

The transports passed through the Strait of Gibraltar during the night of 24th/25th November, and were joined by the four corvettes to the eastward of Gibraltar a.m., 25th. The remainder of Forces "B" and "F" sailed at 0800 that morning, and the operation proceeded according to plan without any particular incident until the morning of 27th November.

These movements and the departure of Force "D" from Alexandria did not escape the notice of the Italians and at 1200, 26th November, strong forces under Admiral Campioni, the C.-in-C. Afloat, left Naples and Messina and steered to pass to the southward of Cape Spartivento, Sardinia (a distance of about 350 miles) with the intention of intercepting Force "H". The Italians were organised in two Squadrons, viz: –

> **First Squadron**, consisting of the battleships, *Vittorio Veneto* (flag, C.-in.-C.), *Cesare*, and eight destroyers.
> **Second Squadron**, under Vice-Admiral Iachino, six 8-inch gun cruisers, *Pola* (flag, Vice-Admiral Iachino), *Fiume, Gorizia* (1st division), *Trieste* (flag, Vice-Admiral Sansonetti), *Trento, Bolzano* (3rd division) and eight destroyers.[85]

Throughout the afternoon of 26th November and the night 26th/27th, the fleet made to the westward without incident. No further news of the British came in, except a report shortly after midnight from the torpedo boat *Sirio*, which had sighted seven warships (types unspecified) on a north-westerly course off Cape Bon; to these ships (Force "D"), Admiral Campioni correctly assigned the intention of joining the group coming from Gibraltar.

Situation at 0800, 27th November (Plan 9)

At 0800, 27th November, about half an hour before sunrise,[86] the situation was as follows. The Italian battlefleet was about 30 miles E.S.E. of Cape Spartivento, steering 260° at 16 knots with the 1st Cruiser Division some 11 miles ahead and the 3rd Division disposed 180°, five miles from the 1st Division.

Vice-Admiral Somerville in the *Renown*, with the *Ark Royal, Sheffield* and four destroyers, was about 90 miles south-west of Cape Spartivento, steering 083°, 16 knots.

Some 30 miles to the W.S.W. of him, the Vice-Admiral, 18th Cruiser Squadron in the *Manchester*, with the *Southampton, Despatch* and five destroyers, was in company with the convoy. The four corvettes had been unable to keep up with it and were about 10 miles to the westward.

The visibility was excellent, the wind south-easterly, force 3 to 4, and the sea calm. Neither British nor Italian forces were aware of the presence of each other.

At this time, the *Ark Royal* flew off a section of fighters, one A/S Patrol, one meteorological aircraft and seven T.S.R.s designed to cover the area to the west of Sardinia, and between Sardinia and Africa. The depth of this reconnaissance to the eastward was sufficient to cover Force "D" (1 bs., 3 cr., 5 dr.) which was approaching from Skerki Bank.

Vice-Admiral Somerville continued on an easterly course, in order to concentrate with Force "D" should the air reconnaissance reveal the presence of important enemy units in the vicinity of that force.[87] At 0900, having received no such report, he altered course to the south-westward to join the convoy and give it additional A.A. defence against the earliest bombing attacks from the Sardinian airfields.

Reconnaissance Aircraft Report Enemy Forces at Sea

Just about this time, at 0852, one of the *Ark Royal's* reconnaissance aircraft had sighted a group of warships about 25 miles to the southward of Cape Spartivento, and closing to investigate, at 0906, sent an alarm report of four cruisers and six destroyers, which, however, was not received by any ship of the British Forces. Sighting the convoy at 0920, the *Renown* manoeuvered to pass astern of it and take station to the southward and up sun, in the probable direction of air attack. At 0956, while still on the port quarter of the convoy, Vice-Admiral Somerville received from the *Ark Royal* an aircraft report, timed 0920, of five cruisers and five destroyers some 65 miles to the north-eastward of him.[88]

Though it seemed possible that this report referred to Force "D" steam was at once ordered for full speed, and screens of two destroyers each were detailed for both the *Ark Royal* and the convoy. Further reports from aircraft, confirmed by the

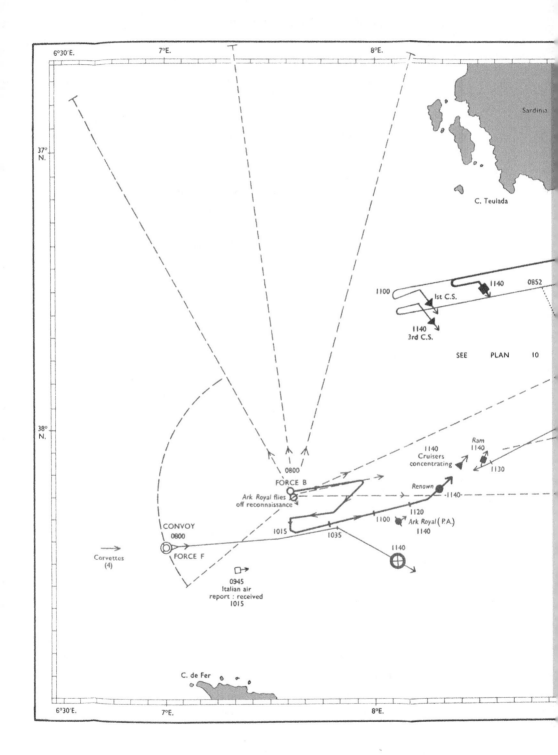

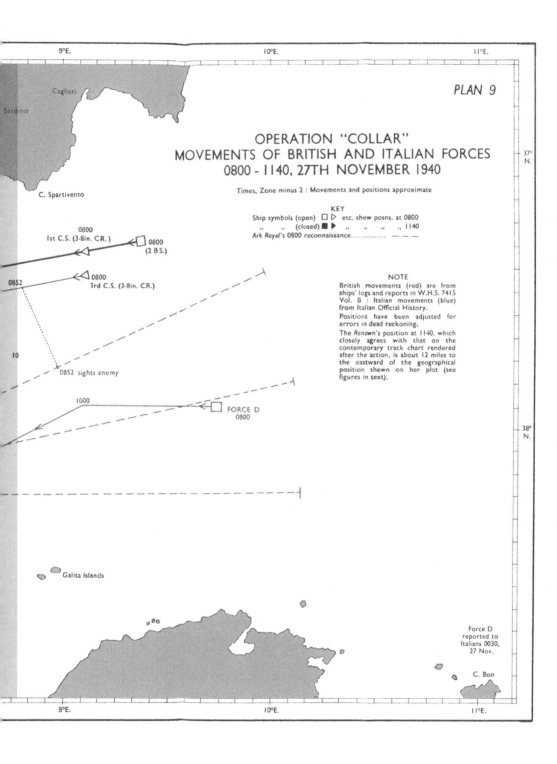

PLAN 9

OPERATION "COLLAR"
MOVEMENTS OF BRITISH AND ITALIAN FORCES
0800 - 1140, 27TH NOVEMBER 1940

Times, Zone minus 2 : Movements and positions approximate

KEY

Ship symbols (open) □ ▷ etc. shew posns. at 0800
       ,,   ,,   (closed) ■ ▶ ,, ,, ,, ,, 1140
Ark Royal's 0800 reconnaissance.............. — — —

NOTE

British movements (red) are from ships' logs and reports in W.H.S. 7415 Vol. B : Italian movements (blue) from Italian Official History.

Positions have been adjusted for errors in dead reckoning.

The *Renown's* position at 1140, which closely agrees with that on the contemporary track chart rendered after the action, is about 12 miles to the eastward of the geographical position shewn on her plot (see figures in text).

9°E.

Cagliari

Sardinia

C. Spartivento

0800
1st C.S. (3-8in. CR.)

0800
(2 B.S.)

0852

0800
3rd C.S. (3-8in. CR.)

10

0852 sights enemy

1000

FORCE D
0800

Galita Islands

Force D
reported to
Italians 0030,
27 Nov.

C. Bon

10°E.

11°E.

37°
N.

38°
N.

Ark Royal, established by 1015 the presence of enemy battleships and cruisers, and the *Renown* altered course to 075° to join the *Ramillies*, increasing speed as rapidly as possible to 28 knots.

Measures to Safeguard Convoy and to Join Force "D" (Plan 9)

Twenty minutes later, though the plot at 1035 clearly showed enemy forces to the north-east, their composition and relative position was still in doubt. In these circumstances, the Vice-Admiral decided that the convoy should continue towards its destination, steering a south-easterly course (120°) in order to keep clear of any action which might develop. It was given an escort of two cruisers, the *Despatch* (Commodore C. Douglas-Pennant) and *Coventry* and two destroyers.[89] The remainder of the cruisers and destroyers of Force "F" (2 cr., 3 dr.) were ordered to join Force "B" (1 bc., 1 ac., 1 cr., 4 dr.,) which steered to concentrate with Force "D" (1 bs., 3 cr., 5 dr.) prior to attacking the enemy. At the same time, Malta was told the position of two enemy battleships, and the *Ramillies* was told the position of the *Renown*. The *Ark Royal* was ordered to prepare and to fly off a T/B striking force, acting independently under cover of the battlefleet.

At 1058 a Sunderland flying-boat closed the Renown and reported Force "D" bearing 070° 34 miles. As the junction of the two forces seemed to be assured, the speed of the *Renown* was reduced to 24 knots, in order to maintain a position between the convoy and the enemy force. Its estimated position was 025° 50 miles distant and the flying-boat was ordered to shadow and report its composition.

The cruisers *Manchester, Sheffield* and *Southampton* had meanwhile concentrated with the destroyers in the van, bearing five miles from the *Renown* in the direction of the enemy.

Reports from the reconnaissance aircraft of the *Ark Royal* contained a number of discrepancies which made it impossible to obtain a clear picture of the situation. Two groups of cruisers had been reported, as well as two battleships; it seemed certain that five or six cruisers were present, but the number of battleships remained in doubt; it might be one, or two or three. "But whatever the composition of the enemy force", it was clear to Vice-Admiral Somerville that "in order to achieve his object – the safe and timely arrival of the convoy at its destination – it was essential to show a bold front and attack the enemy as soon as possible."

At 1115, the enemy originally steering to the westward, were reported to be altering course to the eastward.[90]

All this time Force "D" had been coming westward, and at 1120[91] was sighted in the *Renown*, approximately 24 miles distant. The *Ramillies* sighted Force "H", bearing 239°, five minutes later.

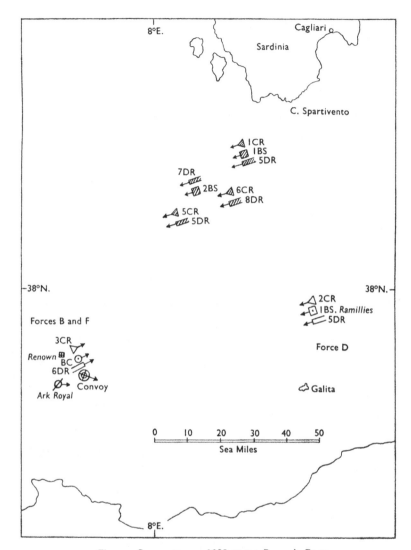

Fig. 7. SITUATION AT 1035 FROM *Renown's* PLOT

The aircraft reports indicated that the enemy force consisted of two battleships, six or more cruisers and a considerable number of destroyers. The action appeared likely to develop into a chase and the *Ramillies* was therefore ordered to steer 045°, so as not to lose ground. Vice-Admiral Holland was placed in command of all the cruisers in the van, and the *Berwick* and *Newcastle* from Force "D" were ordered to join him. It was shortly after this that the *Ark Royal* flew off the first T/B striking force.[92]

107

The Approach (Plans 9, 10)

At 1134, Vice-Admiral Somerville increased to 28 knots, and six minutes later altered course to 050° to close the enemy. The position of the British forces was as follows: Fine on the port bow of the *Renown* were the cruisers *Manchester*, *Southampton* and *Sheffield* in single line ahead; the *Berwick* and *Newcastle* were coming from the eastward to join them. Two miles astern of the cruisers, Captain de Salis (D.8) in the *Faulknor* was gradually collecting the *Encounter* and the 8th Flotilla, some of which had been screening the convoy. The five destroyers of Force "D" were also coming west to join the *Faulknor*, and were eventually stationed three miles 270° from her.

Ten miles fine on the starboard bow of the *Renown*, the *Ramillies* was altering to a parallel course. The *Ark Royal* had dropped some distance astern, and was carrying out flying operations between the main force and the convoy, which was now about 22 miles S.S.W. from the Admiral.

At 1154, the Sunderland flying-boat returned, and reported six cruisers and eight destroyers, bearing 330°, 30 miles from the *Renown*. Her report unfortunately gave no course or speed of the enemy, and she disappeared from sight before this could be obtained. This information – the first visual link received – indicated that one group of the enemy forces was considerably further to the west than those previously reported, and moreover that it was in a position to work round astern and attack the *Ark Royal* and the convoy. Vice-Admiral Somerville accordingly altered course to north in order to avoid getting too far to the eastward.[93]

Vice–Admiral Somerville's Appreciation, Noon, 27th November

The situation as it appeared from the *Renown's* plot just before noon is shown in Fig. 8 overleaf. The prospects of bringing the enemy to action appeared favourable. The composition of the Italian forces was not definitely established, but there did not appear to be more than two battleships with them.

The British forces had effected their concentration, of which the enemy seemed to be unaware, since no shadowers had been sighted or detected by radar. His speed was reported as between 14 and 18 knots, which suggested that his reconnaissance was not completed. The sun was immediately astern of the British forces, giving them the advantage of light, and, if the nearest reported position of the enemy was correct, there seemed every possibility of bringing off a simultaneous surface and T/B attack, providing he did not retire immediately at high speed.

Vice-Admiral Somerville's intentions were: –

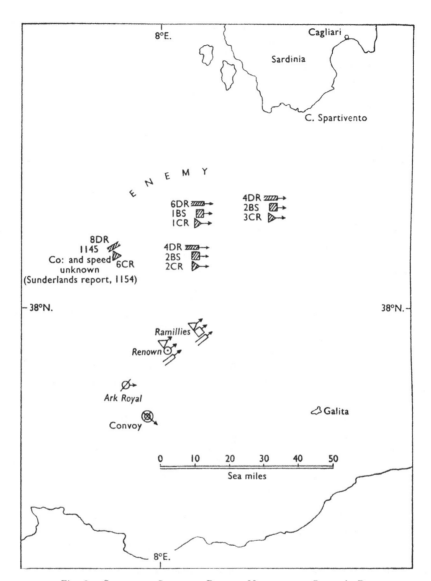

Fig. 8. SITUATION SHORTLY BEFORE NOON FROM *Renown's* PLOT

(i) To drive off the enemy from any position from which he could attack the convoy.

(ii) To accept some risk to the convoy, providing there was reasonable prospect of sinking one or more of the enemy battleships.

To achieve the second of them, he considered that the speed of the enemy would have to be reduced by T/B attacks to 20 knots or fewer, and that the enemy battleships must be engaged by the *Renown* and *Ramillies* in concert.

Admiral Campioni's Appreciation, Noon, 27th November (Plans 9, 10)

It was not till 1015, 27th November that the Italian C.-in-C., received any further news of the British. This came from an aircraft catapulted from the *Bolzano* – a report of one battleship, two light cruisers and four destroyers in position 20 miles north of Cap de Fer (135 miles S.W. of Spartivento) steering 090° at 0945.[94] Admiral Campioni, for a time, thought this was the Cape Bon force (Force "D"), as the numbers coincided with the group reported during the night, though the position was further to the west than was to be expected, even if the ships had only just reversed course.

A second sighting report, received from the *Gorizia*'s aircraft at 1144, confirmed the position given in the 1015 report, but did not mention "two cruisers," an omission possibly explained by the fact that the cruisers of Force "B" had by then moved on ahead of the *Renown* to join the cruisers of Force "D". (See Plan 9.).

Acting on the *Bolzano*'s report, Admiral Campioni led the First Squadron round to course 135° at 1128. Both divisions of cruisers of the Second Squadron conformed to his turn to the S.E. He then envisaged an encounter between the whole of his forces and the *Renown*, with possibly two cruisers and some destroyers; this view was upheld by the *Gorizia*'s aircraft report at 1144. He had not, at that time, appreciated that Forces "B" and "D" had joined, nor that the *Ark Royal* was in the offing, although he knew the aircraft-carrier had left Gibraltar with the other ships. His report reads as follows:

"The sighting report (at 1015) persuaded me to alter course to 135° in order to close the English forces, and if possible intercept them. This appeared possible at the time, also I had in mind that the English forces were inferior to the Italian. Furthermore the encounter would be brought about in waters closer to Sicily than Sardinia, which is in conditions favourable to us.

"But whilst our forces were taking up station on the new course I received at 1155 a signal, originally made at 1110 by an aircraft from Armera, giving the position of the *Renown*'s group. This position was 20 miles nearer to the *Vittorio Veneto* than the one shown by the plot based on previous sighting reports, and was near enough to the other British forces to render their meeting very easy.

"A state of affairs was thus created which on the best hypothesis was unfavourable to us numerically[95] and qualitatively. Particularly important was the presence of an

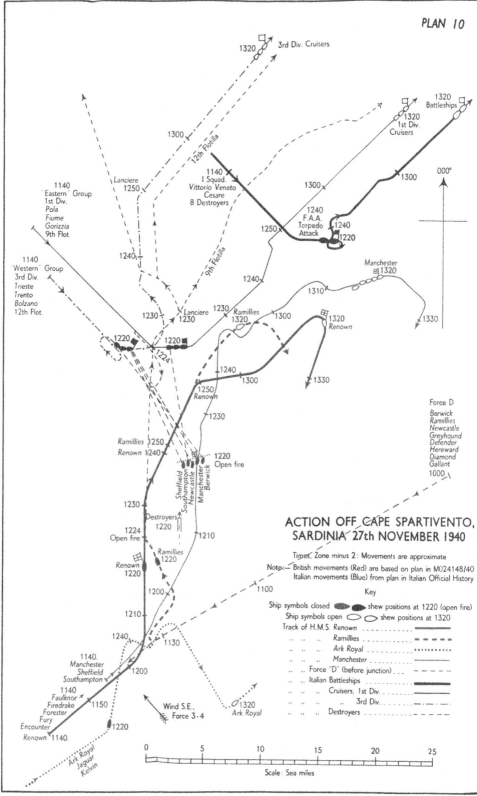

PLAN 10

1320 3rd Div. Cruisers

1320 Battleships

1300

12th Flotilla

1320 1st Div. Cruisers

1300

000°

1140 "Eastern" Group 1st Div. Pola Fiume Gorizzia 9th Flot.

Lanciere 1250

1140 I Squad. Vittorio Veneto Cesare 8 Destroyers

1300

1240 F.A.A. Torpedo Attack 1240 1220

1250

1240

Manchester 1320

1310

1330

1140 "Western" Group 3rd Div. Trieste Trento Bolzano 12th Flot.

1240

9th Flotilla

1240

1230 Lanciere 1230

1230 Ramillies 1320

1300

1320 Renown

1220 1224 1220

1250 Renown

1240 1300

1330

Ramillies 1250 Renown 1240

1230

Force D
Berwick
Ramillies
Newcastle
Greyhound
Defender
Hereward
Diamond
Gallant
1000

1220 Open fire

Sheffield Southampton Newcastle Manchester Berwick

1230

Destroyers 1220

1224 Open fire

1210

Renown 1220

Ramillies 1220

1200

**ACTION OFF CAPE SPARTIVENTO,
SARDINIA 27th NOVEMBER 1940**

Times, Zone minus 2: Movements are approximate

Note:— British movements (Red) are based on plan in M024148/40
Italian movements (Blue) from plan in Italian Official History

1210

1100

Key

1240

1130

Ship symbols closed ●●●● shew positions at 1220 (open fire)
Ship symbols open ◯◯ ◯ shew positions at 1320

Track of H.M.S. Renown ——————
"   "   "   Ramillies - - - - - -
"   "   "   Ark Royal ••••••••
"   "   "   Manchester ————
"   " Force "D" (before junction) – – –
"   " Italian Battleships ——————
"   "   "   Cruisers, 1st Div. ——————
"   "   "   "   3rd Div. —·—·—·—
"   "   "   Destroyers - - - - - -

1140 Manchester Sheffield Southampton

1200

1140 Faulknor Firedrake Forester Fury Encounter Renown 1140

1150

1220

Wind S.E. Force 3-4

1320 Ark Royal

Ark Royal Jaguar Kelvin

0   5   10   15   20   25

Scale: Sea miles

C.B.H. 22724

aircraft-carrier, which with well-directed action properly synchronized with action of their ships, that were certainly not inferior to ours, would have brought about a situation of the utmost gravity.

"It was a situation not only at variance with the directive given to me by the Ministry of Marine, but with that, imposed by military necessity." – The Admiral then explains that in this latter term he was referring to the effect on the Italian navy of the F.A.A. attack on Taranto on 11th November, and the fact that the battleship *Andrea Doria* was not yet ready.

"Under these conditions," continued Admiral Campioni, "in conformity with the spirit and letter of the orders received and with what at that moment I deemed to be my duty, I decided not to become involved in a battle. In theory I should have been able to take into calculation an effective intervention by our shore-based aircraft, but my previous experience discouraged me from putting too much faith on such intervention, having learnt from experience what to expect."[96]

At 1215, 27th November, the Italian admiral's appreciation and decision amounted briefly to this:

"The British aircraft will damage our ships, the Italian aircraft will not damage theirs, the enemy are not inferior in numbers or quality to us, and at present we cannot afford any further reduction in capital ship strength."

He therefore hoisted the signal not to become involved in action, "course 090°; increase speed of engines."

Surface Contact (Plan 10)

Meanwhile, Admiral Somerville was steering to the northward at his best speed to close the enemy.

At 1207, the *Renown* developed a hot bearing on one shaft, which limited her speed to 27½ knots. At the same time, puffs of smoke were observed on the horizon bearing 006°, and the cruisers in the van sighted masts and ships between the bearings of 006° and 346°. Six minutes later (1213, 27th), a signal (timed 1147) came in from the *Ark Royal*, reporting the composition of the enemy as two battleships and six cruisers, accompanied by destroyers. This report did not nullify that of the Sunderland. There still remained the possibility that the Sunderland's reported group of six cruisers and destroyers was a separate force further to the westward. The British cruisers by this time were concentrated in the van, and had formed a line of bearing 075°-255° in the sequence from west to east, *Sheffield, Southampton, Newcastle, Manchester, Berwick.*[97]

The nine destroyers were stationed five miles 040° from the *Renown*, in order to be placed favourably to counter-attack any destroyers attempting a torpedo attack on the *Renown* or *Ramillies*.[98]

The situation as seen by the cruisers immediately before the action commenced was as follows: Between the bearings of 340° and 350° three enemy cruisers and some destroyers were visible at a range of about 11 miles, steering a northerly course.[99] This force will be referred to as the "Western group".

A second group of cruisers, also accompanied by destroyers, which will be referred to as the "Eastern group" bore between 003° and 013°. This group was further away and was steering approximately 100°.

The Action (Plan 10)

At 1220, 27th the enemy in the Western group[100] opened fire, and the British advanced forces immediately replied. The enemy's first salvo fell close to the *Manchester*, exact for range, but 100 yards out for deflection. As soon as fire was opened by the British cruisers, the Italians made smoke and retired on courses varying between north-west and north-east. Behind their smoke screen they seemed to be making large and frequent alterations of course, judging from glimpses which were obtained.

Actually, the cruisers had just received the C.-in.-C.'s orders to steer to the eastward, followed at 1224 by a signal "Do not join action". At 1222 the Eastern group[101] had altered to 050°, 28 knots, increasing to 30 knots at 1230. At the same time Vice-Admiral Iachino ordered the Western group to keep further away from the enemy. "The Third Division," he subsequently wrote, "being the target of the English fire and realising that at any moment a salvo of 15-inch shells might hit them, increased to their maximum speed and presented their sterns to the enemy".

It was at 1224 that the *Renown* opened fire at the right-hand ship of the Western group (identified as an 8-inch cruiser of the *Zara* class) at a mean range of 26,500 yards. After six salvoes, the target was lost in smoke. The *Ramillies* also fired two salvoes at maximum elevation to test the range, but both fell short; she then dropped astern following in the wake of the *Renown* at her best speed, 20.7 knots, throughout the action.

Just before opening fire, the *Renown* had sighted two ships which were not making smoke, bearing 020° at extreme visibility. They were thought at the time to be the Italian battleships, though they proved later to be cruisers of the Eastern group. On losing her first target, the *Renown* altered course to starboard to close these supposed battleships and to bring the cruisers of the Western group broader on the bow. She had hardly done so when the centre ship of the latter group appeared momentarily through the smoke, and was given two salvoes. Again course was altered to open "A" arcs on the left-hand ship, at which eight salvoes were fired at a range of about 30,700 yards before she too disappeared in the smoke at 1245. At this moment, two large ships steering to the westward emerged from the smoke cloud; the *Renown's* turrets were trained on this new target, but before fire could be opened, they were fortunately identified as French liners.

The enemy were by this time on the run, and had passed outside the range of our capital ships, though at 1311, the *Renown* fired two ranging salvoes, which fell short, at two ships of the Eastern group.

Meanwhile the British cruisers had been hotly engaged at ranges varying between 23,000 and 16,000 yards. Many straddles were obtained, but smoke rendered spotting and observation exceedingly difficult. No concentration of fire was ordered, owing to the rapidly changing situation, and the large number of targets.[102]

The *Manchester, Sheffield* and *Newcastle* all opened fire at first on the right-hand ship of the Western group; the *Berwick* engaged the left-hand ship of the same group, whilst the *Southampton* chose the left-hand ship of the Eastern group. The *Manchester* and *Sheffield* continued firing at the same ships for about 20 minutes (until 1236 and 1240 respectively), but the *Newcastle*, after firing 18 broadsides, shifted to the *Berwick's* target. The *Southampton*, after five salvoes at her original target, engaged a destroyer which was seen to be hit. At least one other destroyer was believed to have been hit during this phase and the *Faulknor* at 1227 and *Newcastle* at 1233½ thought they saw hits on a cruiser by large calibre shell.

The enemy's fire was accurate during the early stages but, when fully engaged, it deteriorated rapidly, and the spread became ragged. Their rate of fire, is described as "extremely slow." The only casualties on the British side occurred in the *Berwick*, which received a hit from an 8-inch shell at 1222, which put "Y" turret out of action.[103] The *Manchester* was straddled several times, but though under continuous fire from 1221 till about 1300, escaped unscathed.[104]

By 1234, 27th, the ships in the Western group were almost lost in smoke. At this time the course of the British cruisers was 020°, and the Eastern group of the enemy was passing across their front from left to right. Vice-Admiral Holland therefore altered course to 360°, with the intention of separating the two enemy groups, and then concentrating on one or other of them. This manoeuvre was successful, and he selected the Eastern group as his target,[10] the *Manchester* shifting her fire to the left-hand ship of this group, then 30° on her starboard bow, at a range of 21,000 yards. This ship she engaged for between three and four minutes, and then shifted her fire to a destroyer making a smoke screen 17,000 yards on the port bow, which after being straddled several times, turned away behind her own smoke.[106] By 1240, all ships of the 18th Cruiser Squadron were firing at this group. The *Berwick* received another hit at 1235, which wrecked some cabins without causing any casualties. She had just started to engage a ship thought to be an 8-inch cruiser of the *Pola* class at which she fired 47 salvoes during the next 20 minutes.[107]

At 1245 the cruisers altered course to 090° to prevent the enemy working round ahead and attacking the convoy. This brought the relative bearing of the Eastern group to Red 40, and the *Manchester* once more engaged the left-hand ship. Five minutes later a further alteration to the southward was made to counter what appeared to be an attempt to "cross the T" of the 18th Cruiser Squadron. The enemy, however, at once resumed their north-easterly course, and Vice-Admiral Holland led back to 070° at 1256 and 030° at 1258. The rear ship of the enemy line was heavily on fire aft;[108] between 1252 and 1259, she appeared to lose speed, but picked up again and drew away with her consorts.

At 1301, the masts of a fresh enemy unit steering to the south-west were sighted at extreme visibility right ahead of the *Manchester*. It bore 045° and two minutes later, two battleships were identified in it; their presence was quickly corroborated by large splashes which commenced to fall near the *Manchester* and *Berwick*, and an enemy report was made to the Admiral. The end on approach resulted in the range decreasing very rapidly, and at 1305 Vice-Admiral Holland turned the cruisers to 120°, with the dual purpose of working round the flank of the battleships and closing the gap to the *Renown*. The enemy battleships were not prepared to close and altering course to the north-eastward, presumably joined their 8-inch cruisers. Vice-Admiral Holland therefore altered back to 090° at 1308, and steadied on a course of 050°. The enemy were by now rapidly running out of range, and ten minutes later the action came to an end.

First Attack by H.M.S. *Ark Royal's* T/B Striking Force (Plan 10)

Meanwhile, a T/B striking force consisting of 11 aircraft of No. 810 Squadron had been flown off from the *Ark Royal* at 1130, with orders to attack the Italian battleships reported by reconnaissance aircraft. At 1216 they sighted two battleships between 25 and 30 miles to the eastward, and altered course so as to approach from the direction of the sun. The ships were identified as one of the *Littorio* (*Vittorio Veneto*) and one of the *Cavour* (*Cesare*) class; they were screened by seven destroyers, one ahead, and three in line ahead about 1,000 yards on each beam of the heavy ships. The enemy's course was easterly, and their speed about 18 knots; this course was altered in succession to the westward some five minutes before the attack developed and almost immediately afterwards back again to the eastward together.

The aircraft were unobserved by the battleships until the leader was about 1,500 ft., although the cruisers to the westward had opened fire on them, evidently only as a warning to the battleships, for the bursts were very short.

The leading battleship *Veneto* was selected as the target, and all torpedoes were dropped inside the screen at about 700 to 800 yards range. One hit was claimed just abaft the after funnel,[109] and an explosion also occurred just astern of her; another explosion was seen ahead of the *Cesare*. No other hits were seen. A very heavy concentration of light A.A. fire from both heavy ships and screening destroyers was opened on the aircraft; during the getaway, heavier weapons were used, and the cruisers, which by then were about five miles to the west, also joined in. The aircraft in passing machine-gunned the bridges of the battleships and destroyers; all returned safely to the *Ark Royal*.[110]

The Italian views on this attack are now available, and are of interest. After remarking that the attack was carried out with resolution, Admiral Campioni stated that it "was successfully staved off by the manoeuvring and gunfire of our ships, and through the presence of a close escort of destroyers.

"The fact that the battleship group had, as it happened, inverted their course just previous to the attack developing,[111] must have had a marked effect as well. The aircraft could not pass over the destroyer lines except with extreme difficulty and suffering a loss of control; which confirms the great usefulness of a close escort in the special case of air-torpedo attacks. It is essential that the close escort should be left in position up to the last moment, and removed only when the gun action renders their presence no longer possible. Furthermore, I wish to confirm the great advantage of distant A.A. escorts, although the tasks of our smaller naval units does not usually permit of such employment."

In this connexion Vice-Admiral Iachino, in his summing-up, recommended that in future 6-inch cruisers of the *Di Giussano* class should accompany the Squadrons to act as A.A. cruisers.

Vice-Admiral Somerville's Appreciation, 1315, 27th November

The relative positions of the opposing forces at 1315 are shown in Fig. 9. Firing had practically ceased, owing to the enemy drawing out of range. The heavy smoke made by the Italians during the chase had prevented accurate fire, and so far as was known, no serious damage had been inflicted on them. The British striking force had attacked, but no report of the results had been received. It seemed evident that the speed of the enemy had not been materially reduced.[112]

The British forces, meanwhile, were rapidly approaching the enemy coast, and

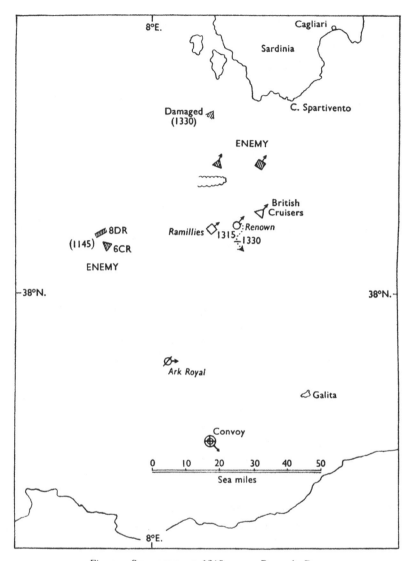

Fig. 9. SITUATION AT 1315 FROM *Renown's* PLOT

it was a question whether a continuance of the chase was justified, and likely to be profitable.

The main object of the whole operation was still the safe passage of the convoy. The enemy's principal units had been driven off far enough to ensure that they could no longer interfere with it, even if the cruisers reported to the north-westward by the *Sunderland* had been working towards it round the western flank of the British forces. It was also important to provide the fullest possible scale of

117

defence for the transports against attacks by torpedo bombers and light surface forces at dusk,[113] and in order to reach the convoy in time to do this, it would be necessary for the British main forces to shape course for it before 1400. In any case, the enemy's superiority of speed rendered it most improbable that he could be brought to action by the *Renown* and the *Ramillies*. Under these circumstances, Vice-Admiral Somerville decided to abandon the chase and rejoin the convoy as soon as possible.[114]

At 1312 Vice-Admiral Somerville accordingly ordered his forces to retire, course 130°. Half an hour later, he received a report of an enemy damaged cruiser stopped in a position 30 miles from the *Renown* and ten miles from the coast of Sardinia. The question of detaching the *Berwick* and *Newcastle*[115] to search for and attack this ship was carefully considered. It would, however, have involved the main British forces remaining in a position to support these cruisers, which would cause unacceptable delay in rejoining the convoy. There was the further possibility of isolated ships in such close proximity to the enemy coast being singled out for air attack; the *Berwick* was most vulnerable to this form of attack, and her disablement would have involved the whole British force in the task of effecting her extrication. There was nothing to indicate that the damaged enemy would remain stopped, and she might well affect her escape before she could be overtaken.[116]

Instructions were therefore sent to the *Ark Royal* to attack the damaged cruiser with aircraft if it was considered feasible; all the rest of the force continued to the southward, the Vice-Admiral, 18th Cruiser Squadron, being ordered to join the convoy with the *Manchester* and *Southampton*.

Further Attacks by H.M.S. *Ark Royal*'s Aircraft

The signal directing an attack to be made on the damaged cruiser was received in the *Ark Royal* at 1351. The Second Torpedo Bomber striking force was just ready to fly off. Captain Holland, considering that the signal he had sent at 1339 reporting the hit believed to have been scored on the *Veneto* by the First striking force had not reached Vice-Admiral Somerville, and that he would have ordered the second attack to be made on the battleships had the Admiral received it[117], decided to send the torpedo bombers against them and to dive-bomb the damaged cruiser with seven Skuas, which were then arming with 500-lb bombs.

The T/B striking force consisting of nine Swordfish, was flown off at 1410. The Squadron Leader was given the enemy battleships as his objective, but with full liberty to change it at his discretion as he alone would be in a position to judge the possibility or otherwise of achieving a successful attack.

The aircraft sighted three cruisers screened by four destroyers about 12 miles off the south-east coast of Sardinia, steering to the eastward at high speed. These were the *Pola*, *Fiume* and *Gorizia*. Some eight miles ahead of the cruisers were the two battleships, heavily screened by ten destroyers. There was a total absence of cloud cover, and it was considered essential to attack from the direction of the sun, if any degree of surprise were to be achieved. As any attempt, however, to gain such a position with regard to the battleships would inevitably have led to the striking force being sighted by the cruisers, it was decided to attack the latter.

The attack was carried out at 1520 and was not sighted till very late, only two salvoes being fired before the first torpedo was dropped. As the first Swordfish reached the dropping position, the cruisers turned together to starboard. This caused several of the following aircraft, who were already committed to their "drop", to miss their targets, but one hit was claimed on the rear cruiser, and another possible hit on the leading cruiser.

The enemy gunfire then became intense, apparently quite regardless of direction or of danger to their own ships. One large projectile was seen to hit the water close to the rear cruiser, and shells from close-range weapons-were seen to burst close alongside all ships. Two of the British aircraft were struck by shrapnel, but all returned safely to the *Ark Royal*.

Describing the attack, Vice-Admiral Iachino reported that it was carried out by eight or nine aircraft, who "launched three torpedoes at the *Pola*, and five or six against the *Fiume* and *Gorizia*. One torpedo was seen to break up on reaching the water and some of the others may not have run since their tracks were not seen. The *Fiume*, however, observed four or five tracks which passed rather close, and one torpedo exploded at the end of its run. One of the aircraft was definitely brought down; and another when passing over the bridge of the *Libeccio* machine-gunned her with negative results.

"The ships manoeuvred repeatedly to prevent the attacks and to avoid the torpedoes, which were dropped at an inclination of between 30° and 50° and at a distance of 1,700 to 2,200 yards, coming in by groups always from the same side, i.e., 'down sun' ... It remains to be said that our A.A. fire was not brilliantly controlled."

Meanwhile, the striking force of seven Skuas had flown off at 1500. They failed to locate the damaged cruiser but carried out an unobserved attack on three cruisers identified as *Condottieri* class, steering north off the south-west corner of Sardinia. These were actually the *Trieste*, *Trento* and *Bolzano*, which had been sent by Vice-Admiral Iachino to cover the retirement of the damaged *Lanciere*. No hits were obtained, but according to the Italian report five bombs fell very close to the *Trento*.

On the way back to the *Ark Royal* the Skuas encountered and shot down an Italian R.O.43.

Enemy Air Attacks on British Forces

While these British flying operations had been taking place, Vice-Admiral Somerville had been steering to the southward in accordance with his decision to close the convoy. The *Ark Royal* had lost sight of the *Renown* to the north-eastward at about 1250, but since the receipt of the signal ordering the retirement of British forces, Captain Holland had been making good a course of 090°, so far as his flying operations permitted, in order to rejoin the Flag. The first radar indications of the presence of enemy aircraft were received in the *Renown* at 1407, and the line was staggered. Shortly afterwards, bomb splashes were observed on the horizon – the result of an attack by the *Ark Royal's* Fulmars, which caused several of the Italians to jettison their bombs.

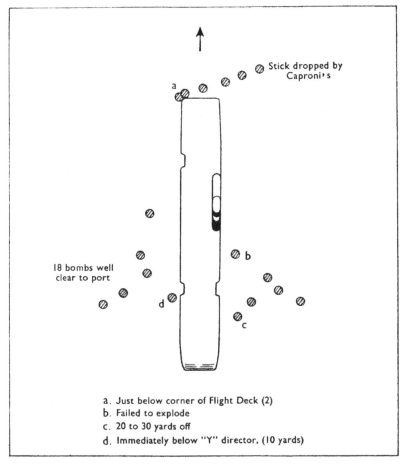

a. Just below corner of Flight Deck (2)
b. Failed to explode
c. 20 to 30 yards off
d. Immediately below "Y" director, (10 yards)

Fig. 10. BOMBING ATTACK ON H.M.S. *Ark Royal*

As soon as the enemy aircraft, consisting of ten S.975 in "V" formation, were sighted by the *Renown* a turn by blue pendant was made by the British ships in order to bring all guns to bear.

The enemy maintained a steady course, and their bombs fell well clear of the heavy ships, but close to the screening destroyers.

Two further attacks were made at about 1645, each by squadrons of five aircraft. These attacks were concentrated on the *Ark Royal*, which by this time was in company with the fleet, but owing to flying operations, not actually in the line. Apart from a few bombs which were jettisoned as the result of interception by our fighters, the high level bombing performed from a height of about 13,000 ft. was most accurate. Some 30 bombs fell in her vicinity – two at least, within ten yards of the ship – and she was completely obscured from view by the splashes.

About 1 ½ minutes after this attack, a stick of bombs fell unexpectedly just ahead of the ship. These were dropped by four Caproni bombers, which had succeeded in approaching unobserved under cover of the first attack and missed by a very narrow margin.

The *Ark Royal* fortunately suffered no damage, nor, so far as is known, did the enemy bombers.[118] Vice-Admiral Somerville remarked that the complete failure of either fighter attack or gunfire to break up the formation of the Italian Squadrons was most noteworthy.

No further bombing attacks took place; the convoy[119] was sighted at 1700, and the operation proceeded subsequently according to plan.

Composition of and Damage to Italian Forces

Owing to the long ranges at which the action was fought, the use of smoke by the Italians, and also to somewhat confusing air reconnaissance reports, there was considerable speculation after the action as to what enemy forces had actually been present. The composition of the battlefleet and the Eastern group of cruisers was correctly assessed. These cruisers had closed to about eight miles from the battleships by 1240, and were thought to have followed astern of them. Immediately after the surface action ceased, the battlefleet steered for Cagliari at about 25 knots; at about 1500 it turned to the eastward and when last seen was steering north up the east coast of Sardinia. The composition of the Western group was doubtful; the *Newcastle* considered that all these cruisers were 6-inch gun ships, but other ships were of the opinion that one or more 8-inch cruisers were included in it. After the action, their movements were very uncertain; it was thought probable that they rejoined the battlefleet, but it was recognised that they might have been the cruisers attacked by the Skuas at 1530 (as was actually the case). Whether a third group of cruisers was operating, as suggested by the report of the Sunderland at 1154, was still more doubtful. After analysing all the available evidence, Admiral Somerville considered that it was not possible to state definitely whether the enemy forces included six or nine cruisers.

With regard to the damage inflicted on the Italians, the estimate was considerably in excess of that actually suffered. It was thought that the rear cruiser of the Eastern group and two destroyers in the Western group were certainly hit; some observers in the *Southampton* considered that one of the latter was sinking, and Vice-Admiral Holland suggested that it was not unlikely that the Western group received other damage which prompted the dense smoke screen into which it retired. Actually, according to the Italian Official History, the only ships hit in the gun action were the destroyer *Lanciere* (seriously) and the cruiser *Fiume*; in this case the shell failed to explode and the damage was negligible. One battleship and one cruiser or possibly two were believed to have been hit by torpedoes in the F.A.A. attacks, and one cruiser might have been damaged by the Skuas' bombs; but in fact none of these attacks achieved success. Despite this meagre material damage, however, the resolute attitude of Vice-Admiral Somerville's force was sufficient to deter the enemy from any serious attempt on the convoy.

The Vice-Admiral, Force "H" 's Remarks on the Action

In commenting on the action, Vice-Admiral Somerville remarked that the fact that ships carried out their action duties correctly with the minimum of signalled instructions, and despite the fact that many of them were working together for the first time, is a tribute to the soundness of our tactical training in peace and to the Fighting Instructions. On the other hand, in many important respects the standard of fighting efficiency obtained in peace considerably exceeded that reached in war; this he attributed to lack of systematic practices and exercises, and instanced the reluctance of Vice-Admiral Holland to attempt a concentration of fire by the recently re-united cruisers of his squadron.

This lack of opportunities for training during war time made itself felt in several directions in this action. Many of the young observers of the *Ark Royal* had little or no experience of reporting enemy formations, and owing to the necessity of maintaining wireless silence, except in the immediate neighbourhood of Gibraltar, had had but little opportunity of exercising communications in the air.[120]

The results too of the torpedo attacks by the air striking force were disappointing when compared with peace-time practices. In each case, the approaches were skilful, unobserved and the attacks were pressed home with courage and resolution, but the results fell far short of what might have been hoped for. This was attributed entirely to lack of initial training and subsequent "runner" practices.

Spotting aircraft did not give much assistance. This was partly due to the fact that in almost every case they were flown off too late, owing to wrong estimates of the probable time of contact with the enemy. In the *Berwick*, the aircraft was damaged by the blast of the first salvo, which was fired just as it was about to be launched, and it had to be jettisoned.

The Admiral pointed out that it was better to fly off spotting aircraft too soon rather than too late, especially when an aircraft carrier on which they can land in an emergency is present. Difficulties were experienced by them in obtaining communication and in observing the fall of shot owing to the dense smoke surrounding the targets. Most ships commented on the difficulty of target identification and observation due to this smoke. Apart from this, difficulties were experienced in maintaining line, due in part to "canted trunnion" error, and in part to evasive action of the enemy coupled with a long time of flight.

The initial accuracy of the Italian fire and its rapid deterioration when replied to has already been mentioned. Vice-Admiral Holland suggested on this account, that it might be worthwhile in future to open fire before the Italians.[126]

This initial accuracy was attributed to the stereoscopic range-finders in use in the enemy ships, and both Vice-Admiral Holland and Vice-Admiral Somerville expressed the opinion that further experiment with this type of range-finder was desirable in the British Fleet.

From the tactical point of view, Vice-Admiral Somerville pointed out that on this occasion the first consideration was to force the enemy away from the direction of the convoy as soon as possible, and that immediate attack by the cruisers proceeding at their maximum speed, and with the *Renown* in as close support as her speed permitted, appeared to offer the best prospects of achieving this object.

He suggested, however, that when dealing with enemy forces which have superior speed, ineffective air reconnaissance and a pronounced inclination to retire as soon as engaged, it might prove advantageous for our heavy and light forces to remain concentrated until contact is made – provided our Air reconnaissance is accurate and reliable. This might enable a heavy long range fire concentration to be brought on the whole or part of the enemy forces before he could retire out of range.

With regard to the operation of carrier-borne aircraft, Vice-Admiral Somerville remarked that it is most desirable that the carrier should act independently, provided her commanding officer is fully aware of the Admiral's view as to how his aircraft are to be employed. Not only do signalled instructions concerning striking forces, reconnaissances and so forth add to wireless congestion, but they may be impracticable to carry out precisely without dislocating the intricate flying on and off programme. Special circumstances may arise which call for special instructions, but the policy should be for the commanding officer of the carrier to act in accordance with the general situation and with what he knows to be the Admiral's views.

Epilogue

Vice-Admiral Somerville arrived back at Gibraltar with Force "H" in the afternoon of 29th November. Ships in harbour paraded bands and received him with cheers. Though naturally disappointed that the speed of the Italian ships had robbed him of the opportunity of forcing them to a close action, he could congratulate himself on the complete success of the operation in passing the reinforcements unscathed through to their destination.

Early next morning there arrived a signal from the Admiralty informing him that a Board of Enquiry, consisting of Admiral-of-the Fleet Lord Cork and Orrery (President), Vice-Admiral Sir G. H. D'Oyly Lyon and Captain R. G. Duke had been ordered to Gibraltar to enquire into his conduct in breaking off the action and the reasons why the second flight of the *Ark Royal's* Swordfish had not attacked the enemy's battleships.

No report from him (except a signal containing a brief, general account of the action made before arrival in harbour) had reached the Admiralty, and he was consequently surprised that his conduct and that of officers serving under him "should be called to account before any information could have been received on which to base a considered opinion of our actions."[122] Though he realised that the summoning of a Board of Enquiry did not necessarily imply criticism, he felt that it might in some measure compromise his prestige with Force "H". The C.-in.-C., Mediterranean, agreed with this view and refers to the matter in his book.[123]

The Board of Enquiry sat from 3rd to 7th December, and upheld Sir James. Somerville's actions throughout.

Appendix A

Italian Naval Forces: Operations 7th–10th July 1940

C.-in-C. and Commanding First Squadron, Admiral I. Campioni

First Squadron:
2 Battleships, six 6-inch Cruisers, 16 Destroyers.
Admiral Campioni (flag in *Cesare*)

In Support of convoy operations
5th Division: Battleships
Vice-Admiral Brivonesi

Name of Ship: *Giulio Cesare*
Main Armament: Ten 12.6-inch, twelve 4.7-inch
Speed: 26 knots
Name of Ship: *Conti di Cavour*
Main Armament: Ten 12.6-inch, twelve 4.7-inch
Speed: 26 knots

4th Division (6-inch Cruisers), Vice-Admiral Moriondo
Name of Ship: *Da Barbiano*
Main Armament: eight 6-inch, six 4-inch A.A.
Speed: 40 knots
Name of Ship: *Cadorna
Main Armament: eight 6-inch, six 4-inch A.A.
Speed: 39 knots
Name of Ship: *Da Giussano*
Main Armament: eight 6-inch, six 4-inch A.A.
Speed: 40 knots
Name of Ship: *Diaz
Main Armament: eight 6-inch, six 4-inch A.A.
Speed: 39 knots

8<u>th</u> Division (6-inch Cruisers), Vice-Admiral Legnani
Name of Ship: *Duca delgi Abruzzi*
Main Armament: ten 6-inch, six 4-inch A.A.
Speed: 35 knots
Name of Ship: *Garibaldi*
Main Armament: ten 6-inch, six 4-inch A.A.
Speed: 35 knots

<u>With battlefleet</u>
7<u>th</u> Destroyer Flotilla
Name of Ship: *Freccia*
Main Armament: four 4.7-inch, six 21-inch torpedo tubes
Speed: 36 knots
Name of Ship: **Dardo*
Main Armament: four 4.7-inch, six 21-inch torpedo tubes
Speed: 36 knots
Name of Ship: *Saetta*
Main Armament: four 4.7-inch, six 21-inch torpedo tubes
Speed: 36 knots
Name of Ship: **Strale*
Main Armament: four 4.7-inch, six 21-inch torpedo tubes
Speed: 36 knots

8<u>th</u> Destroyer Flotilla
Name of Ship: **Folgore*
Main Armament: four 4.7-inch, six 21-inch torpedo tubes
Speed: 36 knots
Name of Ship: **Fulmine*
Main Armament: four 4.7-inch, six 21-inch torpedo tubes
Speed: 36 knots
Name of Ship: **Baleno*
Main Armament: four 4.7-inch, six 21-inch torpedo tubes
Speed: 36 knots
Name of Ship: *Lampo*
Main Armament: four 4.7-inch, six 21-inch torpedo tubes
Speed: 36 knots

14th Destroyer Flotilla
Name of Ship: *Vivaldi*
Main Armament: six 4.7-inch, four 21-inch torpedo tubes
Speed: 38 knots
Name of Ship: *Da Noli*
Main Armament: six 4.7-inch, four 21-inch torpedo tubes
Speed: 38 knots
Name of Ship: *Pancaldo*
Main Armament: six 4.7-inch, four 21-inch torpedo tubes
Speed: 38 knots

15th Destroyer Flotilla
Name of Ship: *Pigafetta*
Main Armament: six 4.7-inch, four 21-inch torpedo tubes
Speed: 38 knots
Name of Ship: *Zeno*
Main Armament: six 4.7-inch, four 21-inch torpedo tubes
Speed: 38 knots

With 4th and 8th Division (6-inch Cruisers)
16th Destroyer Flotilla
Name of Ship: *Da Recco*
Main Armament: six 4.7-inch, four 21-inch torpedo tubes
Speed: 38 knots
Name of Ship: *Usodimare*
Main Armament: six 4.7-inch, four 21-inch torpedo tubes
Speed: 38 knots
Name of Ship: *Pessagno*
Main Armament: six 4.7-inch, four 21-inch torpedo tubes
Speed: 38 knots

Second Squadron:
Six 8-inch Cruisers, six 6-inch Cruisers, 20 Destroyers.
Admiral R. Paladini (flag in *Pola*)

Distant Cover East of Convoy Route
Name of Ship: *Pola*

Main Armament: eight 8-inch, twelve 4-inch A.A.
Speed: 33 knots

1st Division (8-inch Cruisers), Vice-Admiral Matteuchi
Name of Ship: *Zara*
Main Armament: eight 8-inch, twelve 4-inch A.A.
Speed: 33 knots
Name of Ship: *Gorizia*
Main Armament: eight 8-inch, twelve 4-inch A.A.
Speed: 33 knots
Name of Ship: *Fiume*
Main Armament: eight 8-inch, twelve 4-inch A.A.
Speed: 33 knots

3rd Division (8-inch Cruisers), Vice-Admiral Catteneo
Name of Ship: *Trento*
Main Armament: eight 8-inch, six 4-inch A.A.
Speed: 36 knots
Name of Ship: *Bolzano*
Main Armament: eight 8-inch, six 4-inch A.A.
Speed: 36 knots

Appendix B

Action off Calabria: Comparison of British and Italian Forces

British:

3 Battleships: mounting twenty-four 15-inch, thirty-two 6-inch

1 Aircraft: carrier mounting nine 6-inch, 17 T.S.R., 3 fighters

5 Light cruisers mounting forty-eight 6-inch

16 Destroyers mounting sixty-nine 4'7-inch, eight 4-inch

Italian:

2 Battleships: mounting twenty 12'6-inch, twenty-four 4'7 inch

6 Heavy cruisers: mounting forty-eight 8-inch

8 Light cruisers: mounting sixty-eight 6-inch

24 Destroyers: mounting one hundred 4'7-inch

In speed the Italian battleships had an advantage of 2-3 knots over the *Warspite* and *Malaya*, and 5-6 knots over the *Royal Sovereign*. With the exception of the four *Zara* class 8-inch cruisers, the Italian cruisers were from two to four knots faster than the British. The destroyers were practically equally matched for speed and armaments.

While the British Fleet had an advantage in having present an obsolescent aircraft carrier, the Italians had, at short range, numerous shore air bases affording a potentially vast aerial superiority.

Within easy distance too, were the naval bases of Taranto, Messina, Port Augusta, Syracuse, Palermo and Naples. any one of which offered secure shelter to damaged ships. All these ports were submarine bases, from which a strong concentration of submarines could operate at short notice.

Appendix C

Italian Air Bombing

The Commander-in-Chief made the following report to the Admiralty: –
"Following is my summary of Italian air bombing threat as seen before detailed reports from units have been scrutinised.

1. All units of the Fleet have been bombed several times a day for five days. As an example force with *Warspite* on 12th July was attacked 22 times, 260 to 300 bombs being dropped. Only period of immunity was when Fleet was unlocated South of Malta on 10th July and during hours of darkness.

2. Attacks have all been high level bombing in daylight, average height 12,000 feet by formations varying from nine to single aircraft but generally in sub flights of three. Bombs have been dropped in sticks varying from six heavy bombs to 18 or 27 light bombs per formation. Majority of bombs appear to be light case H.E.

3. Single aircraft have generally shied off when fired at, but formations have generally flown steadily on with surprising determination.

4. Most unpleasant attack on *Warspite* at 1550 12th July resulted in 24 bombs along port side and 12 across starboard bow simultaneously, all within one cable but slightly out for line.

5. A.A. fire with exception of one or two ships has been below pre-war standard but is improving under stress. It has been disappointing that I have not seen any enemy aircraft directly hit and fall into the sea. I am however satisfied that an appreciable number of Italians have failed to return. Naval Attaché, Athens reports one forced landed in Crete. Intercepted Italian reports show one forced landed off Cephalonia and one off Benghazi. Italians admit loss of two in Fleet engagement on 9th July. Three aircraft have been seen to leave formation after close burst by A.A. gunfire. *Warspite* has seen airmen getting out by parachute on two occasions.

6. Ammunition expenditure has been very heavy and Fleet has returned to harbour with less than half long range outfit remaining.

My summing up is: –

- Intensive high level bombing is to be expected on each occasion of a Fleet operation in the Central Mediterranean.
- The accuracy of Italian bombing entitled them to one per cent of hits and the Fleet were extremely lucky that this number was not obtained.
- This probable percentage of hits rising to two per cent as the Italians get more practice must be carefully weighed in considering the employment of valuable ships in the Central Mediterranean.
- That provided proper antidotes are supplied this scale of bombing attack can be accepted as a reasonable war risk like mines or submarines.
- Prolonged bombing is very wearing to personnel and system started by my predecessor of having at least two complete reliefs for whole A.A. armament in battleships and cruisers has been shown to be essential for prolonged operations."

(*Med. War Diary* 15th July 1940).

Appendix D

Action off Cape Spada: Comparison of the Opposing Forces, 19th July

The comparative force of the ships engaged in the action of 19th July off Cape Spada was:–

British

Sydney:
Tons: 6,980
Knots: 32.5
Guns: eight 6-inch and eight 4-inch

Hyperion:
Tons: 1,340
Knots: 36
Guns: four 4.7-inch

Hasty:
Tons: 1,340
Knots: 36
Guns: four 4.7 inch

Havock:
Tons: 1,340
Knots: 36
Guns: four 4.7-inch

Hero:
Tons: 1,340
Knots: 36
Guns: four 4.7-inch

Ilex:
Tons: 1,370
Knots: 36
Guns: four 4.7-inch

Total British guns:
Eight 6-inch
Eight 4-inch
Twenty 4.7-inch

Italian

Giovanni delle Bande Nere:
Tons: 5,069
Knots: 34
Guns: eight 6 inch-and six 4-inch

Bartolomeo Colleoni:
Tons: 5,069
Knots: 34
Guns: eight 6-inch and six 4-inch

Total Italian guns:
Sixteen 6-inch
Twelve 4-inch

Appendix E

Action off Cape Spada: Expenditure of Ammunition by the British Ships, 19th July

The expenditure of ammunition by the *Sydney* was 935 rounds C.P.B.C and 21 rounds H.E., in 181 salvoes. The destroyers expended: –

Hyperion: 150 rounds
Hero: 170 rounds
Havock: 55 rounds
Ilex: 213 rounds
Hasty: 150 rounds

Appendix F

Commander-in-Chief's Memorandum: Rescue of Survivors from Enemy Ships

As a result of the bombing attack on the *Havock* while engaged in picking up survivors, the Commander-in-Chief on 22nd July issued the following memorandum: –

1. "Whilst the instincts of the British race and the traditions of the sea produce in us all a powerful urge to rescue survivors of sinking ships, it must be remembered that there are other considerations to be weighed against this humane work.

2. We are waging a relentless war against odds, and here in the Mediterranean not only are we competing against numerically naval superior forces, but we have also against us very considerable air forces which our own Air Force is not yet in a position to attack, except in eastern Libya.

3. It follows that no favourable opportunity must be lost of destroying enemy forces, and the rescue of survivors must never be allowed to interfere with the relentless pursuit of enemy ships.

4. It must also be borne well in mind that practically the whole of the area of our operations is subject to enemy bombing. Therefore ships cannot usually afford to hang about picking up survivors, for not only do they thus expose themselves to bombing attack under very disadvantageous conditions, but also subsequent operations are liable to be delayed. Moreover a destroyer with a large number of prisoners on board is bound to be considerably reduced in fighting efficiency.

5. Difficult and distasteful as it is to leave survivors to their fate, Commanding Officers must be prepared to harden their hearts, for, after all, the operations in hand and the security of their ships and ships' companies must take precedence in war."

Appendix G

Operation "Collar": H.M. Ships, with Main Armament and Commanding Officers

Force "B"

Renown
(Flag, Vice-Admiral Sir James F. Somerville, K.C.B., D.S.O. (ret.) (F.O."H"))
Main Armament: six 15-inch guns
Captain G. E. B. Simeon

Ark Royal
Main Armament: sixteen 4.5-inch guns (60 aircraft)
Captain C. S. Holland

Sheffield
Main Armament twelve 6-inch guns
Captain C. A. A. Larcom

Despatch (Broad pendant)
Main Armament: six 6-inch guns
Commodore C. E. Douglas-Pennant, D.S.C. (Comre. W.I.)

Faulknor
Main Armament: five 4.7-inch guns
(D.8) Captain A. F. De Salis

Firedrake
Main Armament: four 4.7-inch guns
Lieutenant-Commander S. H. Norris

Forester
Main Armament: four 4.7-inch guns
Lieutenant-Commander E. B. Tancock

Fury
Main Armament: four 4.7-inch guns
Lieutenant-Commander T. C. Robinson

Wishart
Main Armament: four 4.7-inch guns
Commander E. T. Cooper

Encounter
Main Armament: four 4.7-inch guns
Lieutenant-Commander E. V. St. J. Morgan

Kelvin
Main Armament: six 4.7-inch guns
Commander J. H. Allison, D.S.O.

Jaguar
Main Armament: six 4.7-inch guns
Lieutenant-Commander J. F. W. Hine

Force "F"
Manchester (Flag, Vice-Admiral L. E. Holland, C.B. (C.S.18))
Main Armament: twelve 6-inch guns
Captain H. A. Packer

Southampton
Main Armament: twelve 6-inch guns
Captain B. C. B. Brooke

Duncan (D.13)
Main Armament: four 4.7-inch guns
Captain A. D. B. James

Hotspur
Main Armament: four 4.7-inch guns
Commander H. F. H. Layman, D.S.O.

Vidette
Main Armament: four 4-inch guns
Lieutenant E. N. Walmsley

Peony
Main Armament: one 4-inch gun
Lieutenant-Commander M. B. Sherwood, D.S.O. (retired)

Salvia
Main Armament: one 4-inch gun
Lieutenant-Commander J. I. Miller, D.S.O., R.N.R.

Gloxinia
Main Armament: one 4-inch gun
Lieutenant-Commander A. Pomeroy, R.N.V.R.

Hyacinth
Main Armament: one 4-inch gun
Lieutenant J. I. Jones, R.N.R.

Force "D"
Ramillies
Main Armament: eight 15-inch guns
Captain A. D. Read

Newcastle
Main Armament: twelve 6-inch guns
Captain E. A. Aylmer, D.S.C.

Coventry
Main Armament: ten 4-inch A/A guns
Captain D. Gilmour

Berwick
Main Armament: eight 8-inch guns
Captain G. L. Warren

Defender
Main Armament: four 4.7-inch guns
Lieutenant-Commander G. L. Farnfield

Greyhound
Main Armament: four 4.7-inch guns
Commander W. R. Marshall-A'Deane, D.S.C.

Gallant
Main Armament: four 4.7-inch guns
Lieutenant-Commander G. P. F. Brown

Hereward
Main Armament: four 4.7-inch guns
Lieutenant-Commander C. W. Greening

Diamond
Main Armament: four 4.7-inch guns
Lieutenant-Commander P. A. Cartwright

Appendix H

Italian Naval Forces: Action off Cape Spartivento

Commander-in-Chief, and Commanding First Squadron: Admiral I. Campioni

First Squadron

(Two Battleships, eight Destroyers) Admiral Campioni, C.-in-C.

Vittorio Vento (Flag, C.-in-C.)
Main Armament: nine 15-inch, twelve 6-inch
Speed: 29 knots

Giulio Cesare
Main Armament: ten 12.6-inch, twelve 4.7-inch
Speed: 26 knots

7th Destroyer Flotilla
Freccia
Main Armament: four 4-inch, six 21-inch torp. tubes
Speed: 36 knots

Dardo
Main Armament: four 4-inch, six 21-inch torp. tubes
Speed: 36 knots

Saetta
Main Armament: four 4-inch, six 21-inch torp. tubes
Speed: 36 knots

Strale
Main Armament: four 4-inch, six 21-inch torp. tubes
Speed: 36 knots

13th Destroyer Flotilla
Granatiere
Main Armament: four 4-inch, six 21-inch torp. tubes
Speed: 39 knots

Fuciliere
Main Armament: four 4-inch, six 21-inch torp. tubes
Speed: 39 knots

Bersagliere
Main Armament: four 4-inch, six 21-inch torp. tubes
Speed: 39 knots

Alpino
Main Armament: four 4-inch, six 21-inch torp. tubes,
Speed: 39 knots

Second Squadron
(Six 8-inch Cruisers, eight Destroyers) Vice-Admiral A. Iachino

1st Cruiser Division
Pola (Flag, Vice-Admiral A. Iachino)
Main Armament: eight 8-inch, twelve 4-inch A.A.
Speed: 33 knots

Gorizia
Main Armament: eight 8-inch, twelve 4-inch A.A.
Speed: 33 knots

Fiume
Main Armament: eight 8-inch, twelve 4-inch A.A.
Speed: 33 knots

9th Destroyer Flotilla
Alfieri
Main Armament: four 4.7-inch, six 21-inch torp. tubes
Speed: 39 knots

Oriani

Main Armament: four 4.7-inch, six 21-inch torp. tubes

Speed: 39 knots

Carducci

Main Armament: four 4.7-inch, six 21-inch torp. tubes

Speed: 39 knots

Gioberti

Main Armament: four 4.7-inch, six 21-inch torp. tubes,

Speed: 39 knots

3rd Cruiser Division

Trieste (Flag, Vice-Admiral Bolzano)

Main Armament: eight 8-inch, twelve 4-inch A.A.

Speed: 36 knots

Trento

Main Armament: eight 8-inch, twelve 4-inch A.A.

Speed: 36 knots

Bolzano

Main Armament: eight 8-inch, twelve 4-inch A.A.

Speed: 36 knots

12th Destroyer Flotilla

Lanciere (Damaged in action)

Main Armament: four 4.7-inch, six 21-inch torp. tubes

Speed: 39 knots

Corazziere

Main Armament: four 4.7-inch, six 21-inch torp. tubes

Speed: 39 knots

Ascari

Main Armament: four 4.7-inch, six 21-inch torp. tubes

Speed: 39 knots

Libeccio
Main Armament: four 4.7-inch, six 21-inch torp. tubes
Speed: 39 knots

Appendix I

Action off Cape Spartivento: Admiral Somerville's Reasons for Decision to Abandon Chase

Vice-Admiral Somerville summarised the reasons for and against continuing the chase as follows: –

For continuing the chase –
- The possibility that the speed of the enemy might be reduced by some unforeseen eventuality.
- He might appreciate that his force was superior to mine and decide to turn and fight.

Against continuing the chase –
- There was no sign that any of the enemy ships, and especially his battleships, had suffered damage, nor was there reasonable prospect of inflicting damage by gunfire, in view of their superior speed. Unless the speed of the enemy battleships was reduced very materially he could enter Cagliari before I could bring him to action with *Renown* and *Ramillies.*
- I was being led towards the enemy air and submarine base at Cagliari, and this might well prove a trap. His appearance in this area appeared to be premeditated, since it was unlikely that this was occasioned solely by the information he had received the previous night of Force "D" 's presence in the Narrows.
- The extrication of one of my ships damaged by air or submarine attack from my present position would certainly require the whole of my force and must involve leaving the convoy uncovered and insufficiently escorted during the passage of the Narrows.
- The enemy main units had been driven off sufficiently far to ensure they could no longer interfere with the passage of the convoy.
- A second T/B attack could not take place until 1530 to 1600, by which time the convoy would be entirely uncovered and the enemy fleet could be under

the cover of the A.A. batteries and fighters at Cagliari. I entertained little hope that the attack would prove effective, as I knew that the second flight was even less experienced than the first.

- I had no assurance that the cruisers reported to the north-west might not be working round towards the convoy and the *Ark Royal.*
- It was necessary for contact to be made with the convoy before dark, to ensure the cruisers and destroyers required for escort through the Narrows should be properly formed up. It was also necessary to provide the fullest possible scale of defence against T /B and light surface force attack at dusk. To effect this a retirement between 1300 and 1400 was necessary.

Appendix J

Details of British Naval Aircraft

I. Fighter Aircraft Capable of Deck Landing

Remarks

The climb of these aircraft varied; for Gladiator and Fulmar it was 3½ to 4½ minutes to 10,000 feet; for the Skua 12½ minutes.

Sea Gladiator

Crew: 1

Armament: four .303 Fixed front gun; one .303 Rear free gun; one 500 lb. or one 250 lb. bomb

Whether dive bomber: No

Fitted for observer navigation, W/T, and folding: No

Maximum speed: 213 knots

Endurance at maximum (approx.): ¾ hour

Maximum endurance at economical speed: 2¼ hours

Skua

Crew: 2

Armament: four .303 Fixed front gun; one .303 Rear free gun; one 500 lb. or one 250 lb. bomb

Whether dive bomber: Yes

Fitted for observer navigation, W/T, and folding: Yes

Maximum speed: 195 knots

Endurance at maximum (approx.): 2 hours

Maximum endurance at economical speed: 6 hours

Fulmar

Crew: 2

Armament: eight .303 Fixed front gun; one 500 lb. or one 250 lb. bomb

Whether dive bomber: No
Fitted for observer navigation, W/T, and folding: No
Maximum speed: 230 knots
Endurance at maximum (approx.): 2 hours
Maximum endurance at economical speed: 6 hours (with extra tank)

II. Reconnaissance and Strike Aircraft

Swordfish
Crew: 3 reconnaissance; 3 strike
Armament: one .303 (or .3) Fixed front gun; one .303 (or .3) Rear Gun; Torpedo or bombs, 1,500 lbs.
Capable of dive bombing: Yes
Capable of torpedo attack: Yes
Maximum speed: 125 knots
Maximum endurance and range without extra tankage:–
Reconnaissance Strike Force: 5½ hours, 450 miles
Whether extra tankage: Yes

Albacore
Crew: 3 reconn: 2 strike
Armament: one .303 (or .3) Fixed front gun; one .303 (or .3) Rear Gun; Torpedo or bombs, 1,500 lbs.
Capable of dive bombing: Yes
Capable of torpedo attack: Yes
Maximum speed: 155 knots
Maximum endurance and range without extra tankage:–
Reconnaissance Strike Force: 6 hours, 630 miles
Whether extra tankage: Yes

Walrus (Catapult ship aircraft)
Crew: 3 reconnaissance
Armament: one .303 (or .3) Fixed front gun, one .303 (or .3) Rear Gun; Bombs, 500 lbs.
Capable of dive bombing: Limited
Capable of torpedo attack: No
Maximum speed: 110 knots

Maximum endurance and range without extra tankage:–
Reconnaissance Strike Force: 3½ hours, 300 miles
Whether extra tankage: No

Endnotes

1 See Naval Staff History, *Battle Summary No. 1*, and *Mediterranean, Vol. 1*.

2 *El Nil, Rodi, Knight of Malta.*

3 *Zeeland, Kirkland, Masirah, Norasli.*

4 Zone minus 2 Time is used throughout.   .

5 D1 being the date of commencement of the operation, i.e. when the covering force left Alexandria.

6 The *Warspite* had been modernised in 1937. Maximum range of her 15-inch guns was 32,200 yards, as against 23,400 for the *Malaya* and *Royal Sovereign*. The *Warspite* and *Malaya* could steam at 23 knots, the *Royal Sovereign* at only 20 – a serious disadvantage compared with the 26-knot Italian battleships.

7 A relief force consisting of the battleship *Ramillies* and the 4th Cruiser Squadron and four destroyers was to leave Alexandria (as soon as the four destroyers which were to be drawn from Force "C" could be fuelled on arrival in the evening of D6) and cover the arrival of Convoy M.S.1.

8 Force "H"

Hood. (Flag, F.O. Force "H") (eight 15-inch) - Vice-Admiral Sir James F. Somerville, K.C.B., D.S.O., Captain I. G. Glennie.

Valiant (eight 15-inch) - Captain H. B. Rawlings, O.B.E.

Resolution (eight 15-inch) - Captain O. Bevir.

Arethusa - Captain Q. D. Graham.

Enterprise - Captain J. C. Annesley, D.S.O.

Delhi - Captain A. S. Russell.

Ark Royal. (Flag, V.A.(A)) (30 T.S.R., 24 Fighters) - Vice-Admiral L. V. Wells, C.B., D.S.O., Captain G. S. Holland.

18 Destroyers, S.O., Capt.(D) 8 (*Faulknor*) - Captain A. F. de Salis.

9 This plan shows the actual movements of the Italian forces, which closely adhered to the original plan until after they had left the convoys off the North African coast.

10 *Banda Nere, Colleoni* (2ⁿᵈ Division).

11 *Pola* (flag, Vice-Admiral R. Paladini); *a, Gorizia, Fiume* (1ˢᵗ Division); *Trento, Bolzano* (3ʳᵈ Division).

12 *Eugenio di Savoia, Duca d'Aosta, Attendolo, Montecuccoli* (7ᵗʰ Division).

13 *Da Barbiano, Cadorna, da Giussano, Diaz* (4ᵗʰ Division); *Duca degli Abruzzi, Garibaldi* (8ᵗʰ Division).

14 **Force "A"** (7ᵗʰ Cruiser Squadron)

Orion (Flag of V.A.(D) (eight 6-inch, eight 4-inch H.A.) - Vice-Admiral J. C. Tovey, C.B., D.S.O., Captain G. R. B. Back.

Neptune (eight 6-inch, eight 4-inch H.A.) - Captain R. C. O'Connor.

Sydney (eight 6-inch, eight 4-inch H.A.) - Captain J. A. Collins, R.A.N.

Liverpool (twelve 6-inch, eight 4-inch H.A.) - Captain A. D. Read (joined from Port Said a.m. 9ᵗʰ July).

Gloucester (twelve 6-inch, eight 4-inch H.A.) - Captain F. R. Garside, C.B.E.

Stuart (five 4 7-inch, one 3-inch H.A.) - Commander H. M. L. Waller, R.A.N. (Capt. (D). 10ᵗʰ D.F.).

Force "B"

Warspite (Flag of C.-inC.), (eight 15-inch, eight 6-inch, eight 4-inch H. A.) - Admiral Sir A. B. Cunningham, K.C.B., D.S.O., Captain D. B. Fisher, O.B.E.

Nubian (eight 4.7-inch) - Captain P. J. Mack (Capt. (D) 14ᵗʰ D.F.)

Mohawk (eight 4.7-inch) - Commander J. W. M. Eaton.

Hero (four 4.7-inch) - Commander H. W. Biggs, D.S.O.

Hereward (four 4.7-inch) - Lieut.-Commander C. W. Greening.

Decoy (four 4.7-inch, one 3-inch H.A.) - Commander E. G. McGregor.

Force "C"

Royal Sovereign (Flag R.A.1) (eight 15-inch, 12 6-inch, eight 4-inch H.A.) - Rear-Admiral H. D. Pridham-Wippell, C.B., C.V.O., Captain H. B. Jacomb.

Malaya (eight 15-inch, twelve 6-inch, eight 4-inch H.A.) - Captain A. F. E. Palliser, D.S.C.

Eagle (Aircraft Carrier) (nine 6-inch, four 4-inch H.A.), (17 T.S.R.: 3 Fighters) - Captain A. R. M. Bridge.

Hyperion (four 4. 7-inch) - Commander H. St. L. Nicolson (Capt. (D) 2nd D.F.).

Hostile (four 4.7-inch) - Commander J. P. Wright.

Hasty (four 4.7-inch) - Lieut.-Commander L. R. K. Tyrwhitt.

Ilex (four 4.7-inch) - Lieut.-Commander P. L. Saumarez, D.S.C.

Imperial (four 4.7inch) - Lieut.-Commander C. A. de W. Kitcat.

Dainty (four 4.7-inch, one 3-inch H.A.) - Commander M. S. Thomas.

Defender (four 4. 7-inch, one 3-inch H.A.) - Lieut.-Commander St. J. R. J. Tyrwhitt.

Juno (six 4.7 inch) - Commander W. E. Wilson.

Janus (six 4. 7-inch) - Commander J. A. W. Tothill.

Vampire (four 4-inch) - Lieut.-Commander J. A. Walsh, R.A.N.

Voyager (four 4-inch) - Commander J. C. Morrow, R.A.N

15 For this occasion, in addition to her normal complement of two T.S.R. Squadrons, the *Eagle* embarked three spare F.A.A. Gladiators (fighters) from Alexandria, which proved their value in the ensuing operations, by shooting down a shadower and two or three bombers. They were flown by Commander (Flying) Keighly-Peach, an old fighter pilot and another officer.

16 Except the *Liverpool*, which was at Port Said, having just arrived there after transporting troops to Aden. She sailed to rendezvous direct with Vice-Admiral Tovey.

17 It is now known that neither of these submarines was sunk.

18 Vice-Admiral Sir Wilbraham T. R. Ford, K.B.E., C.B.

19 There are discrepancies in the reports of this position which cannot be reconciled,

(a) In the C.-in-C.'s report on the operation it is stated to be 33° 35' N. 19° 40' E. at 1510.

(b) In the C.-in-C.'s War Diary, 33° 18' N.,19° 45' E. at 1510.

(c) The actual signal made by F/B L5803 (quoted in an enclosure to the C.-in-C.'s report) puts it as 10 miles 180° from 33° 18' N.,19° 45' E., i.e. 33° 08' N., 19° 45' E. at 1500. This latter position is within 20 miles of the actual position of the Italian 8-inch cruisers (to which it undoubtedly refers) at the time.

20 Sunrise, 0520; Beginning of nautical twilight (sun 6° below horizon), 0450, Zone minus 2.

21 It is not known on what information these positions were based. Actually, no British forces from Alexandria were so far west till nearly 24 hours later.

22 See Section 4.

23 The 8th, 15th and 16th Destroyer Flotillas (nine destroyers) had been sent into harbour to re-fuel at 0600, 9th, and did not rejoin the fleet till 1930 that evening. Three other destroyers and two light cruisers (the *Cadorna* and *Diaz*) had been detached with engine trouble or defects in the course of the day.

24 This manoeuvre anticipated the wishes of the Commander-in-Chief who at 1506 (time of receipt 1520) signalled: – "Do not get too far ahead of me. I am dropping back on battlefleet. Air striking force will not be ready till 1530." Throughout the action, Admiral Tovey manoeuvred his squadron by blue pendant only.

25 The 6-inch cruisers *Garibaldi* and *Abruzzi*. According to Italian records their time of opening fire was 1518.

26 Actually a 6-inch cruiser, the *Abruzzi* or *Garibaldi* (8th Division).

27 According to the Italians, no hit was scored.

28 The Italian 4th Division, *Barbiano* and *Giussano*. Neither was hit. The two ships altered right round to port and after steering to the southward for a few minutes passed astern of their battleships on a north-westerly course and took no further part in the action. The other two ships of the division, the *Cadorna* and *Diaz*, had been detached a couple of hours earlier to Messina, suffering from engine trouble.

29 3rd Division, *Trento, Bolzano*.

30 "The 3rd Division was attacked by torpedo aircraft, three of which were shot down; the torpedoes were avoided by manoeuvring". *Italian Official History*.

31 It is difficult to reconcile this relative position with the Italian movements as shown on their plan.

32 If the impressions of the *Eagle*'s striking force are correct, the fleet was in considerably greater disorder than the parade ground precision of their movements, shown in the plan subsequently produced by them, would imply (see Plan 4).

33 About this time the *Orion* thought she scored a hit on the bridge of a destroyer of the *Maestrale* class, bearing 303°, range 17,100 yards; but the Italians state that no such hit was obtained.

34 This is not confirmed by Italian sources.

35 C.-in-C.'s Report (in M.05369/41).

36 14th D.F. in the centre, 2nd D.F., to port, and 10th D.F. to starboard.

37 *Warspite* at 1641, 1715, 1735, 1823, I911; *Eagle* at 1743, 1809, 1826, 1842, 1900. No records of times or numbers of attacks on other ships are available.

38 An interesting decision as illustrating the considerations which should govern the acceptance of risks. The *Ark Royal*, our only large modern carrier in the Mediterranean, was of unique importance. Already a major attack on Italian battleships (subsequently carried out at Taranto in November 1940) was under consideration. Under these circumstances, Admiral Somerville declined to accept the risk to her for the sake of a subsidiary operation. It is to be noted that he had no hesitation in accepting a greater risk to her in connection with the bombardment of Genoa the following February. In war, risks must often be accepted, but the object should always be adequate.

39 Between 1643 and 1750, 12 attacks were carried out by formations of varying strength, usually three at a time. After a pause of about an hour, the attacks recommenced and between 1844 and 2110 a further 11 attacks – the last in the Messina Strait – were carried out.

40 *Italian Official History of the War at Sea.*

41 The *Stuart* had only 15 tons of oil remaining on arrival.

42 Cunningham of Hyndhope, *A Sailor's Odyssey*, English edition, p. 263

43 Less *Decoy*.

44 Less *Vampire* and *Voyager*.

45 The *Warspite* was shadowed during the day by aircraft which transmitted "longs" by W/T at intervals to direct the attacking aircraft.

46 The Commander-in-Chief's report (in M.05369) puts this number as 300. The number 160 is taken from the *Warspite*'s detailed return of the attack, enclosed in the C.-in-C.'s

report.

47 The Commander-in-Chief subsequently remarked that "the most unpleasant attack on *Warspite* at 1530, 12th July, resulted in 24 bombs along port side and 12 across starboard bow simultaneously, all within 1 cable but slightly out of line" (Mediterranean War Diary).

48 Actually no torpedo hit was obtained by the F.A.A. According to the Italians, three 6-inch shell hits on the *Bolzano* was the only damage suffered by the 8-inch cruisers.

49 See Appendix C.

50 C.-in-C.'s report, in M.05369/41.

51 The operation orders were contained in the two signals from Vice-Admiral Tovey (V.A.(D)) following: –

(i) To: D(2), repeated to C.-in-C., C.S.3, R.A.(L), *Hero, Havock, Hasty, Ilex, Sydney*. IMPORTANT. Carry out following operation. Object destruction of U-boats. Leave Alexandria 0001 tomorrow, Thursday, with *Hyperion, Ilex, Hero, Hasty*. Sweep to Kaso Strait to pass through about 2130, then along north coast Crete to pass through Antikithera Channel about 0600C, 19th July, then to Alexandria to arrive 0800C, 20th July. *Sydney* and *Havock* will support as in my **1451/17. (T.O.O.1447/17.)**

(ii) To: *Sydney*, repeated to *Ilex, Havock*, R.A.(L), C.S.3, *Hero*, C.-in-C., D(2), *Hasty*. IMPORTANT. My 1447. Carry out following operation. Objects support of force under

D.(2) and interception of Italian shipping in Gulf of Athens. Leave Alexandria with *Havock* at 0430, tomorrow Thursday. Pass through Kaso Strait at about 2200C thence to Gulf of Athens to search for enemy shipping, then pass through Antikithera Channel to arrive in Alexandria 1400C, 20th July. **(T.O.O. 1451/17.)**

The operations ordered in the above signals were preliminary to a further submarine hunt starting on 20th July between Crete and Cyrenaica by eight destroyers, which were afterwards to sweep into the Aegean to cover a convoy for Aegean ports sailing from Alexandria on the 19th.

52 Zone minus 3 Time is used throughout.

53 One of the Dodecanese, at that time Italian.

54 Report by C.O., H.M.A.S. *Sydney* (M.020932/40).

55 *Bande Nere, Colleoni* armament:—eight 6-inch, six 4-inch A.A.: speed 34 knots.

56 North-west extremity of Ganea Bay, Crete.

57 Island off C. Busa, north-west extremity of Crete.

58 N.I.D. 1900/48. Report of Admiral Casardi to Ministry of Marine.

59 "I realised that I was placing Commander ... Nicolson ... in an awkward position and running a certain degree of risk of non-contact by not informing him of my position, course and speed by W/T on getting his enemy report. I was however determined to make full use of surprise ... I appreciated that, if I made a wireless signal, the enemy would learn that other forces were in the vicinity and make away back through the Straits" (Report by C.O., H.M.A.S. *Sydney*).

60 From 0747 to 0832 all alterations of course by the destroyer division were made by White pendant, i.e. leaders together the rest in succession. (This is not shown in Plan 6).

61 It is now known that the *Bande Nere* had already been hit by a 6-inch shell which passing through the foremost funnel and exploding near the after part of the aircraft discharge machinery killed four ratings and wounded four more.

62 Report by C.O., H.M.A.S. *Sydney*.

63 The purpose of these manoeuvres gave rise to some speculation at the time, but Admiral Casardi's report states that they were merely "to lessen the effect of the enemy's fire."

64 Captain Umberto Novaro died from his wounds on board the hospital ship Maine at Alexandria on 23rd July.

65 Vice-Admiral Tovey subsequently remarked that "it was an unfortunate and serious mistake that all destroyers did not continue the pursuit of the second cruiser without delay" – an opinion concurred in by the Commander-in-Chief (see Appendix D).

66 This signal did not surprise Captain Collins, who since 0845 – from the *Bande Nere*'s determination to escape to the southward, instead of to the westward (which would have been easier) and later her desertion of the *Colleoni* – had suspected she was leading him on to superior forces. There is, however, no confirmation from Italian sources that any such support had been contemplated.

67 The Commander-in-Chief also postponed the movements of convoy Aegean North 2, and the ships which had sailed from Port Said were ordered to return. An oiler convoy from Alexandria to Port Said was ordered to proceed unescorted.

68 Up till then Captain Collins had supposed that the *Havock* was with the *Hyperion* and *Ilex* a few miles astern and catching him up.

69 An Italian report on 25th July, 1940 stated the crew was safe. They had swum ashore from their scuttled aircraft and been made prisoners.

70 At a later date additional awards included: Officers, two D.S.O.s, two D.S.C.s, four Mentions in Despatches. Ratings, six D.S.M.s, eight Mentions.

71 Admiral Casardi was presumably well aware of the advantage of speed he possessed over the British heavy ships of the Mediterranean Fleet.

72 "*Sydney's* gunnery narrative ... shows the results obtainable by an efficient control team backed by good material, and it should be given the weight due to the experience of a ship which has had the unique opportunity of firing 2,200 main armament rounds in action in 6 weeks." – C.-in-C., Med., 0903/0710/30/2 of 21st September 1940 (M.020932/40).

73 C.-in-C., Med., 0903/0710/30/2 of 21st September 1940.

74 "The manner in which Commander (D) brought his Division into action, after having heard nothing of me until I made my first enemy report at 0827, was most reassuring. The division appeared on my disengaged bow, steering a course to pass ahead of me and practically at right angles to the enemy's course. It was evident that Commander Nicolson had on sighting me anticipated my order to close and attack the enemy with torpedoes". Report by C.O., H.M.A.S. *Sydney* (in M.020932/40).

75 Report by C.O., H.M.A.S. *Sydney* (in M.020932/40).

76 "In convoy defence there is only one object, namely THE SAFE AND TIMELY ARRIVAL OF THE CONVOY AT ITS DESTINATION" – *Fighting Instructions*, 1939, Art. 625. In mid-1941, the Section on "Convoy Defence" was amended. In this and later versions, including *Fighting Instructions*, 1947, "the safe and timely arrival of the convoy at its destination" remains the primary object or aim of the escort Commander but it is not so strongly emphasised, the words "there is only one object" being omitted.

77 See Appendix M.

Force "B"

Renown (F.O.H.), *Ark Royal, Sheffield, Despatch* (Commodore) [West Indies], *Faulknor* (D.8), *Forester, Fury, Duncan* (D.13), *Wishart, Encounter, Kelvin, Jaguar*

Force "F"

Manchester, Southampton, Hotspur, Peony, Salvia, Gloxinia, Hyacinth, Clan Forbes, New Zealand Star

Force "D"

Ramillies, Newcastle, Coventry, Berwick, Defender, Firedrake, Greyhound, Gallant, Hereward, Clan Fraser, Diamond

Note. For the sake of clarity, the composition of these forces is repeated in abbreviated form throughout the narrative, e.g. Force "F" (2 cr. 1 dr., etc.).

78 For measures and movements in the Eastern Mediterranean, see *Naval Staff History, Mediterranean, Vol. II*, Chapter I.

79 Zone minus 2 Time is used throughout.

80 In this connection it is interesting to note the constant changes which circumstances had imposed on the composition of Force "H" Between 1st July and 27th November 1940, the following different ships were at one time or another included in the Force: – 7 capital ships, 3 aircraft carriers, 13 cruisers, 33 destroyers.

81 At Vice-Admiral Holland's request, the Commander-in-Chief, Mediterranean, was asked whether the safe passage of personnel or M.T. ships should receive priority if circumstances were to arise which made a decision necessary, after Force "F" had parted company for the passage of the Narrows. The Commander-in-Chief replied, "Personnel" but subsequent instructions were received from the Admiralty that this must be subject to the overriding consideration that if Italian forces were in sight, the action taken by the cruisers must be the same as if personnel were not embarked.

82 Air reconnaissance from Malta, on 24th November, gave the following disposition of Italian forces: –

Taranto Outer harbour, two battleships, five cruisers, nine merchant vessels. Inner harbour (not seen).

Messina – Three cruisers, five destroyers, six submarines.

Catania – Nil.

Augusta – A few small vessels.

Syracuse – Possibly one destroyer and a few smaller vessels.

83 Attack by torpedo bombers on Italian Fleet, 11th November 1940.

84 Reliance was apparently placed entirely on reconnaissance by shore-based aircraft to locate enemy units in the Western Mediterranean during the days immediately preceding the battle (24th/27th November), a task for which Vice-Admiral Somerville subsequently stated they proved entirely inadequate.

No information was received from any special sources, and the first report received by the Admiral of enemy ships being at sea in the Western Mediterranean was provided by carrier reconnaissance a few hours before the action commenced.

85 See Appendix N.

86 Sunrise was at 0824, Zone minus 2.

87 A signal from the Chief of Staff, Alexandria, timed 0330/27, indicated that the presence of Force "D" might be known to the enemy.

88 Owing to faults in the receiver the *Renown* failed to receive the first 11 aircraft reports made on the reconnaissance wave.

89 Exclusive of the *Hotspur*. The *Coventry* and destroyers *Wishart* and *Duncan* did not make contact till 1300.

90 An observer who witnessed this alteration of course reported that the eastern group of cruisers appeared to be thrown into confusion. The leading ship turned 180°, while the following ships turned only 90°. Collisions appeared to have been narrowly averted, and at one time all three ships seemed to be stopped with their bows nearly touching each other.

91 In Admiral Somerville's report, time of sighting is given as 1128, but in the Chronological Appendix to the report it is given as 1120. From other evidence, this latter time appears to be the correct one.

92 See Section 53.

93 No further report of this group was received during the action, and the Admiral consequently remained in doubt as to its whereabouts and intentions. The *Ark Royal* was, however, between his main forces and the convoy, and he considered that her returning aircraft would sight and report this group should it attempt to work round to a position from which to attack the latter.

94 This report almost certainly referred to Force "B."

95 In the matter of actual numbers and strength the Admiral's statement about the "English being numerically superior" was incorrect, for there were two capital ships on each side, seven Italian 8-inch cruisers compared with one 8-inch and four 6-inch on our side, and 16 Italian destroyers to our ten (i.e. not counting the two destroyers with the *Ark Royal*).

96 Presumably Admiral Campioni had in mind the action off Calabria, 9th July 1940, when the Italian Air Force, although well within range, failed to inflict any damage on

the British Fleet, and, in addition, bombed their own.

97 The *Newcastle* could not maintain the speed of the remainder and never quite reached her station.

The *Berwick* had signalled at 1158 that as her speed was limited to 27 knots she proposed to join the *Renown*. This she turned to do, thereby losing ground. She subsequently took station on the starboard bow of the *Manchester*, but owing to her lack of speed, dropped back during the action.

98 The destroyers maintained a distance of five cables apart throughout the action. Vice-Admiral Somerville remarks that when the number of destroyers present or on a flank is limited to approximately one flotilla, this is a very suitable distance. It relieves the commanding officers of the necessity to maintain accurate station, and reduces the damage likely to be caused by gunfire.

99 Evidence as to the movements of the western group immediately prior to the action was conflicting. It appeared probable that this group was in line ahead on a southerly course until 1210, when course was altered together to the northward. Between 1210 and 1220 further alterations might have been made. When first observed from the *Renown* the ships appeared to have a fairly broad inclination to the eastward. Actually, this group – the 3rd Division (*Trieste, Trento, Bolzano*) – was making two 180° turns to starboard, in order to take station 270° from the 1st Division. (See Plan 10).

100 Third Division (*Trieste, Trento, Bolzano*).

101 First Division, *Pola* (flag, Vice-Admiral Iachino), *Fiume, Gorizia*.

102 The Vice-Admiral, 18th Cruiser Squadron, was doubtful what the results of an attempt at concentration would have been, as the ships of the 18th Cruiser Squadron had not been in company for a considerable time, and had come from Rosyth, Reykjavik (Iceland), Malta and the vicinity of the Azores.

103 This shell entered "Y" gun barbette about 15 inches above the quarter deck, and, travelling down through the training pump space, burst on the starboard side of the barbette above the main deck, and expended itself in the cabin flat, killing Surgeon-Lieutenant W. W. Wildman, R.N.V.R., and six ratings, and wounding nine others. A considerable fire was started inside the turret training space, which spread to the gunhouse and was not subdued for over an hour.

104 The 35 officers and 623 other ranks of the Army and R.A.F. taking passage in the *Manchester* were dispersed between decks throughout the ship. All bathrooms were filled with troops. A number of officers and men were formed into willing parties to

transfer ammunition from "X" and "Y" turrets to "A" and "B" turrets. "To carry a shipload of passengers into battle," wrote Vice-Admiral Holland, "is an unenviable lot, but their presence had perforce to be dismissed from my mind. They themselves were exhilarated at having been in a sea battle."

105 On this decision Admiral Holland wrote: – "It was reasonable to suppose that the smoke screen enveloping Group A (the western group) was hiding some damage, and this group was believed to be the weaker of the two. By closing Group A it seemed that some immediate tactical achievement might result. Against this, however, it has to be appreciated that the object of the whole enterprise was to pass a convoy through the Narrows, and that if our cruisers sheered off to the westward the field would be left clear for Group B (the eastern group), to turn to the south-eastward and attack the convoy. I therefore decided that Group B should be our future target ..."

106 The destroyer *Lanciere* was hit at 1235 by a 6-inch shell in the after boiler-room. She continued to steam at 23 knots, but at 1240 a second shell struck her amidships, port side, penetrating a petrol tank without exploding. A third shell struck her under the water line, starboard side, without exploding. About 1300 she came to a stop, and at 1440 was taken in tow by the *Ascari* at 7 knots for Cagliari.

107 Vice-Admiral Iachino was not impressed by the British gunnery. "The English," he wrote, "as usual, fired rapid salvoes with a limited spread, making frequent turns to disturb our fire and so as to bring all their guns to bear. The general result was ineffective and not well directed. The fire from our cruisers was appreciably better and more efficacious, since two enemy cruisers were certainly hit."

108 This was observed by the *Manchester, Newcastle* and *Southampton*, but no report of it reached Vice-Admiral Somerville until after the action.

109 According to Italian sources this hit did not occur.

110 The Italians claimed to have shot down two aircraft, but this was not the case.

111 Course was altered in order to close Vice-Admiral Iachino's cruisers.

112 At 1308 Vice-Admiral Somerville had signalled to Vice-Admiral Holland: "Is there any hope of catching cruisers?" to which the latter had replied "No." A later message from Vice-Admiral Holland estimated that the enemy had three knots excess of speed.

113 Sunset was at 1807; nautical twilight ended 1908, Zone minus 2.

114 See Appendix O.

115 It was, obviously undesirable to use the *Manchester* and *Southampton* for this purpose

on account of the R.A.F. personnel embarked in these two ships for passage.

The *Sheffield's* radar was required to deal with the bombing attacks which would inevitably develop.

116 A subsequent air search failed to locate the damaged ship, so the stoppage was apparently only temporary.

117 The signal ran "Striking Force report that Italian battleship, *Cavour* class, damaged and speed reduced." The groups for "damaged and speed reduced" were received in corrupt form in *Renown*. The first part of the signal gave no indication that it was a report of damage inflicted by the striking force.

118 Vice-Admiral Holland remarked that he was in a good position to observe the British A.A. fire-at the formation, which attacked at 1645. The gunfire was intense, but he estimated the bursts to have been 1,000 feet low and about 1,000 yards short.

119 When it had become clear that an action was in progress south of Sardinia, Commodore Douglas-Pennant had decided to take the convoy south of Galita Island, keeping in the narrow deep water channel to minimise the risk from mines. Several French aircraft sighted the convoy in the course of the day. A submarine contact – afterwards believed to have been "non-sub" – enforced an alteration of 180° in the narrow part of the channel; this caused a delay of some 45 minutes. Apart from this the passage was uneventful.

120 Both Vice-Admiral Somerville and the Captain of the *Ark Royal* suspected that the original enemy reports by aircraft referred in actual fact to Force "D." Taking all things into consideration, the Admiral considered that the crews of the reconnaissance aircraft acquitted themselves with credit.

121 On this occasion the *Manchester* did not open fire at extreme range.

122 Force "H" 215/12 of 19th December 1940.

123 *A Sailor's Odyssey* (English edition), pp.292-294.

PART III

Supplements to the London Gazette

SUPPLEMENT

TO

The London Gazette

Of TUESDAY, the 27th of APRIL, 1948

Published by Authority

Registered as a newspaper

WEDNESDAY, 28 APRIL, 1948

REPORT OF AN ACTION WITH THE ITALIAN FLEET OFF CALABRIA, 9th JULY, 1940.

The following Despatch was submitted to the Lords Commissioners of the Admiralty on the 29th January, 1941, by Admiral Sir Andrew B. Cunningham, K.C.B., D.S.O., Commander-in-Chief, Mediterranean Station.

H.M.S. WARSPITE
29th January, 1941.

Be pleased to lay before Their Lordships the accompanying narrative of operations by the Mediterranean Fleet during the period 7th to 13th July, 1940 (Operation M.A.5)*, which included the brief engagement which took place with the Italian Fleet off the Calabrian Coast on the afternoon of 9th July.

2. It was during these operations that the Fleet first received serious attention from the Italian Air Force, and Calabria was the first time contact was made with Italian surface forces, other than destroyers.

3. It is still not clear what brought the enemy fleet to sea on this occasion, but it seems probable that it was engaged on an operation designed to cover the movement of a convoy to Libya. When our Fleet was reported South of Crete, it seems that the enemy retired close to his bases, fuelled his destroyers by relays, and then waited, hoping to draw us into an engagement in his own waters (under cover of his Air Force and possibly with a submarine concentration to the Southward of him) whence he could use his superior speed to withdraw at his own time.

Admiralty footnote:—
* Operation M A 5—an operation in the form of a sweep by the Fleet in the Central Mediterranean designed to give cover to two convoys on passage from Malta to Alexandria

58152

4. If these were, in fact, the enemy's intentions, he was not altogether disappointed, but the submarines, if there were any in the vicinity of the action, did not materialise, and fortunately for us, his air attacks failed to synchronise with the gun action.

5. From an examination of enemy reports it appears that the enemy forces consisted of two battleships, 16 (possibly 17 or 18) cruisers, of which 6 (and possibly 7) were 8-inch, and 25 to 30 destroyers.

6. It will be noted that the whole action took place at very long range and that WARSPITE was the only capital ship which got within range of the enemy battleships. MALAYA fired a few salvos which fell some 3,000 yards short. ROYAL SOVEREIGN, owing to her lack of speed, never got into action at all.

7. WARSPITE's hit on one of the enemy battleships at 26,000 yards range might perhaps be described as a lucky one. Its tactical effect was to induce the enemy to turn away and break off the action, which was unfortunate, but strategically it probably has had an important effect on the Italian mentality.

8. The torpedo attacks by the Fleet Air Arm were disappointing, one hit on a cruiser being all that can be claimed, but in fairness it must be recorded that the pilots had had very little practice, and none at high speed targets, EAGLE having only recently joined the Fleet after having been employed on the Indian Ocean trade routes.

9. The enemy's gunnery seemed good at first and he straddled quickly, but accuracy soon fell off as his ships came under our fire.

10. Our cruisers—there were only four in action—were badly outnumbered and at times came under a very heavy fire. They were superbly handled by Vice-Admiral J. C. Tovey,

C.B., D.S.O., who by his skilful manoeuvring managed to maintain a position in the van and to hold the enemy cruiser squadrons, and at the same time avoid damage to his own force. WARSPITE was able to assist him with her fire in the early stages of the action.

11. The enemy's smoke tactics were impressive and the smoke screens laid by his destroyers were very effective in completely covering his high speed retirement. With his excess speed of at least 5 knots there was little hope of catching him once he had decided to break off the action. An aircraft torpedo hit on one of his battleships was the only chance and this unfortunately did not occur.

12. The chase was continued under exceedingly heavy bombing attacks until the British Fleet was 25 miles from the Calabrian Coast, and was then reluctantly abandoned, the destroyers being very short of fuel and the enemy fleet well below the horizon.

13. A feature of the action was the value, and in some cases the amusement, derived from intercepted plain language enemy signals.

14. My remarks on the bombing attacks experienced by the Fleet during the course of these operations have already been forwarded.

15. I cannot conclude these remarks without a reference to H.M.S. EAGLE. This obsolescent aircraft carrier, with only 17 Swordfish embarked, found and kept touch with the enemy fleet, flew off two striking forces of 9 torpedo bombers within the space of 4 hours, both of which attacked, and all aircraft returned. 24 hours later a torpedo striking force was launched on shipping in Augusta and throughout the 5 days operations EAGLE maintained constant A/S patrols in daylight and carried out several searches. Much of EAGLE's aircraft operating work was done in the fleeting intervals between, and even during, bombing attacks and I consider her performance reflects great credit on Captain A. M. Bridge, Royal Navy, her Commanding Officer.

Individual pilots and observers have already been rewarded for their work during these operations.

16. The meagre material results derived from this brief meeting with the Italian Fleet were naturally very disappointing to me and all under my command, but the action was not without value. It must have shown the Italians that their Air Force and submarines cannot stop our Fleet penetrating into the Central Mediterranean and that only their main fleet can seriously interfere with our operating there. It established, I think, a certain degree of moral ascendency, since although superior in battleships, our Fleet was heavily outnumbered in cruisers and destroyers, and the Italians had strong shore based air forces within easy range, compared to our few carrier borne aircraft.

On our side the action has shown those without previous war experience how difficult it is to hit with the gun at long range, and therefore the necessity of closing in, when this can be done, in order to get decisive results. It showed that high level bombing, even on the heavy and accurate scale experienced during these operations, yields few hits and that it is more alarming than dangerous.

Finally, these operations and the action off Calabria produced throughout the Fleet a determination to overcome the air menace and not to let it interfere with our freedom of manoeuvre and hence our control of the Mediterranean.

(Signed) A. B. CUNNINGHAM.

Admiral.
Commander-in-Chief,
Mediterranean.

NARRATIVE

FLEET OPERATIONS—PERIOD, 7TH TO 13TH JULY, 1940.

The Mediterranean Fleet, less RAMILLIES and the 3rd Cruiser Squadron, left Alexandria on 7th July to carry out Operation M.A.5, the object being the safe and timely arrival at Alexandria of two convoys from Malta with evacuees and Fleet stores.

2. It was intended that the Fleet should reach a position of cover East of Cape Passero p.m. on 9th July, detaching destroyers to Malta, which with JERVIS and DIAMOND, who were already at Malta, would sail p.m. escorting the convoys. It was also intended to carry out operations against the Sicilian Coast on the 9th.

3. The fast convoy, M.F.One, consisted of the Egyptian ship EL NIL, the ex-Italian ship RODI and the British ship KNIGHT OF MALTA. The slow convoy, M.S.One, consisted of the British ships ZEELAND, KIRKLAND and MASIRAH and the Norwegian ship NOVASLI.

4. The Fleet sailed from Alexandria in three groups:—

Force A—7th Cruiser Squadron* and destroyer STUART.

Force B—Commander-in-Chief in WARSPITE, with destroyers NUBIAN, MOHAWK, HERO, HEREWARD and DECOY.

Force C—Rear-Admiral, 1st Battle Squadron† in ROYAL SOVEREIGN, with MALAYA, EAGLE and destroyers HYPERION, HOSTILE, HASTY, ILEX, IMPERIAL, DAINTY, DEFENDER, JUNO, JANUS, VAMPIRE and VOYAGER.

5. All forces were clear of the harbour by 0001 on 8th July and proceeded as follows:—

Force A—To pass through position 35° 00′ N, 21° 30′ E.

Force B—To pass through position 34° 15′ N, 24° 50′ E.

Force C—To pass through position 33° 20′ N, 27° 50′ E.

6. LIVERPOOL, who was at Port Said, having just arrived there after transporting troops to Aden, sailed to rendezvous direct with Vice-Admiral (D).‡

Flying Boat Patrols.

7. The following flying boat patrols were arranged by 201 Group (R.A.F.):—

9th, 10th and 11th July—Continuous patrol on lines Malta-Cape Spartivento and Cape Colonne-Corfu.

Admiralty footnotes
* The 7th Cruiser Squadron consisted of ORION, NEPTUNE, SYDNEY, GLOUCESTER and LIVERPOOL.)
† Rear-Admiral 1st Battle Squadron—Rear-Admiral H D. Pridham-Wippell.
‡ Vice-Admiral (D)—Vice-Admiral J. C Tovey, C B, D S O.

8th July—Flying boats on passage Malta-Zante-Malta.

12th July—Flying boats on passage Malta-Zante-Alexandria.

13th July—To a depth of 60 miles to the Westward of convoy M.S.One.

8. At 2339/7th July when in position 32° 35′ N, 28° 30′ E., HASTY sighted an Italian U-boat on passage on the surface at 1,000 yards range. A full pattern depth charge attack was made and the U-boat was probably sunk. At 0100/8 when rejoining Rear-Admiral, 1st Battle Squadron, another attack was carried out on a confirmed contact. It is considered that this attack damaged a second U-boat.

9. The night passed without incident, the Commander-in-Chief with Force B setting a mean line of advance of 305 degrees at 20 knots. At 0800/8 IMPERIAL was sighted returning to harbour with a burst feed tank.

10. At 0807 a report was received from PHOENIX of two enemy battleships and four destroyers in position 35° 36′ N, 18° 28′ E., steering 180 degrees at 0515. She attacked at extreme range but the attack was apparently unsuccessful.

As it was suspected from this report that this force might be covering an important convoy, Vice-Admiral, Malta, was ordered to arrange for a flying boat to locate and shadow this force. The course of the Fleet was maintained pending further information.

Two submarines were sighted by EAGLE's A/S patrols, one of which was attacked with bombs.

11 In the meantime all forces were subjected to heavy bombing attacks by aircraft which appeared to come from the Dodecanese. Seven attacks were delivered on WARSPITE between 1205 and 1812, about 50 bombs being dropped. There were no hits.

12. Between 0951 and 1749 six attacks were made on Force C, about 80 bombs being dropped. There were no hits.

13. Most ships experienced some very near misses but the only hit was on Force A, GLOUCESTER being hit by one bomb on the compass platform causing the following casualties:—

Officers, killed 7 (including Captain F. R Garside, C.B.E), 3 wounded.

Ratings, 11 killed and 6 wounded.

The damage caused to the bridge structure, and D C.T.* necessitated gun control and steering from aft.

14. At 1510 flying boat L.5803 reported two battleships, 6 cruisers and 7 destroyers in position 33° 35′ N, 19° 40′ E., steering 340 degrees, and at 1610 that this force had altered to 070 degrees. This flying boat had to return to Malta at 1715 and no relief was available to continue shadowing. However, the enemy Fleet was resighted by another Sunderland from Malta early the following morning.

15. At the time, it was suspected that these two battleships were in fact 8″ cruisers. The intensive bombing which had been experienced had already given the impression that the Italians had some special reason for wishing to keep us out of the Central Mediterranean.

This, in conjunction with these enemy reports, made it appear that the Italians might be covering the movement of some important convoy, probably to Benghazi, and it was decided temporarily to abandon the operations in hand and to move the fleet at best speed towards Taranto to get between the enemy and his base.

Force B maintained a mean line of advance of 310 degrees at 20 knots during the night.

16. There were no incidents during the night and at 0440 EAGLE flew off three aircraft to search to a depth of 60 miles between 180 and 300 degrees.

The Approach Period   9th July, 1940 (0600-1430).

17. At 0600 the fleet was concentrated in position 36° 55′ N, 20° 30′ E., and cruising disposition No. 1 was ordered. The 7th Cruiser Squadron and STUART were in the van 8 miles ahead of Commander-in-Chief in WARSPITE, who was screened by NUBIAN, MOHAWK, HERO, HEREWARD and DECOY. The Rear-Admiral, 1st Battle Squadron, in ROYAL SOVEREIGN, with MALAYA and EAGLE, screened by HYPERION, HOSTILE, HASTY, ILEX, DAINTY, DEFENDER, JUNO, JANUS, VAMPIRE and VOYAGER, was 8 miles to the rear of WARSPITE. The mean line of advance was 260 degrees, speed 15 knots.

18. At 0732 flying boat L.5807 reported the main enemy fleet consisting of 2 battleships, 4 cruisers and 10 destroyers in position 37° 14′ N, 16° 51′ E., steering 330 degrees at 15 knots, and at 0739 that 6 cruisers and 8 destroyers were stationed 080 degrees 20 miles from the main fleet, steering 360 degrees, and that at 0805 the main fleet had altered to 360 degrees.

At this time the main enemy fleet were about 145 miles 280 degrees from our own fleet.

At 0810, as a result of these reports, the mean line of advance of the fleet was altered to 305 degrees at 18 knots in order to work to the Northward of the enemy fleet and if possible get between him and his base.

At 0858 three aircraft from EAGLE were flown off to search a sector between 260 and 300 degrees to maximum depth.

Between 1026 and 1135 reports were received from flying boats 5807 and 9020 and EAGLE'S Duty B and Duty C, which, though they differed considerably, yet gave an indication of the movements of the enemy.

19. At 1105, EAGLE's Duty D reported 2 battleships and one cruiser in position 38° 07′ N, 16° 57′ E., with 4 other cruisers near. At 1115 flying boat L.5807 reported the enemy battlefleet in position 38° 06′ N, 17° 48′ E., steering 360°.

It is probable that if in this latter report these ships were correctly identified, the real position should have been considerably further to the Westward. Reports up to this time indicated that the enemy forces consisted of at least 2 battleships, 12 cruisers and 20 destroyers, and that during the forenoon they were dispersed over a wide area It seems probable that the cruisers and destroyers reported at 0739 took a wide sweep shortly afterwards to the Northeastward and that they were joined by other cruisers and destroyers, possibly those which had been with the main fleet.

20. Acting on reconnaissance reports received up to 1115. EAGLE's striking force was flown off at 1145 to attack the enemy fleet, which at this time was believed to be in position 295 degrees 90 miles from WARSPITE, steaming North.

This position seems to have been approximately correct but, owing to an insufficiency of aircraft in EAGLE, touch was lost at 1135 and, in the event, the enemy battlefleet altered course to the Southward about this time and the striking force failed to find them.

21. WARSPITE's noon position was 37° 30′ N, 18° 40′ E

22. At 1215 flying boat 5803 reported 6 cruisers and 10 destroyers in position 37° 56′ N, 17° 48′ E., steering 220 degrees, at 25 knots, and at 1220 three 8″ cruisers in position 37° 55′ N, 17° 55′ E., steering 225 degrees.

23 At 1252 the striking force, having missed the battlefleet, sighted a large number of enemy ships steering to the Southward and, assuming that the battlefleet last reported steering North had altered to the Southward, worked round to the Westward of this force and attacked the rear ship of the enemy line at 1330. At the time this was presumed to be a battleship, but from the high speed and rapid turning which was observed it was almost certainly a cruiser. The two battleships were by this time considerably further to the Southward. No hits were observed. Heavy A.A. fire was encountered from the cruisers and attendant destroyers but the aircraft received only superficial damage. The striking force landed on at 1434.

24. A search by EAGLE's aircraft Duty C reported no enemy ships between bearings 334 and 291 degrees to a depth of 60 miles from 38° N, 18° E., at 1330. It was now clear that at about 1200 the main enemy battlefleet had turned Southward and that the cruiser forces which had been sweeping to the North-eastward had turned South-west to effect a concentration in approximately 37° 45′ N, 17° 20′ E. (See Diagram No. 1.)

25. At 1340, flying boat 9020 reported 3 battleships and a large number of cruisers and destroyers in position 37° 58′ N, 17° 55′ E., steering 220 degrees, and at 1415 that the enemy's course and speed was 020 degrees, 18 knots. It was now clear that after concentrating the enemy had turned Northward again and that our Fleet was rapidly closing the enemy.

At this time the impression was growing that the enemy intended to stand and fight, albeit on his own ground and with more than one road of escape left open to him.

Course was maintained to the North-westward to cut him off from Taranto until it became clear at 1400 that this object had been achieved, when course was altered to 270 degrees to increase the rate of closing

26. Speed of approach was limited by the maximum speed of ROYAL SOVEREIGN, with WARSPITE acting as a battle cruiser to support the 7th Cruiser Squadron, who, being so few and lacking in 8″ ships, were very weak compared with the enemy's cruiser force. At 1430 the Commander-in-Chief in WARSPITE was in position 38° 02′ N, 18° 25′ E., steering 270 degrees at 22 knots. The 7th Cruiser Squadron were 8 miles ahead, with ROYAL SOVEREIGN, MALAYA and

EAGLE 10 miles astern. EAGLE's striking force landed on at 1434. At 1435, EAGLE's Duty C reported the enemy course and speed as 360 degrees 15 knots and at 1439 that the enemy centre was 260 degrees 30 miles from WARSPITE. This ended the approach period and surface contact was made soon afterwards.

Weather during the Approach.

27. During the forenoon the wind veered from North-west to North by West, force 5, but later back to North-west again. The sea was slight, visibility 15 to 20 miles. The sky was clear up to 0800 but was 2/10ths clouded at noon.

The Fleet Action.

28. At 1452 NEPTUNE reported two enemy vessels in sight bearing 238 degrees.

At 1455 ORION sighted 3 destroyers bearing 234 degrees, 31,000 yards.

At 1500 ORION sighted three destroyers and 4 cruisers between 240 and 270 degrees.

29. At 1500 (See Diagram No. 2) the 7th Cruiser Squadron, except the damaged GLOUCESTER who had been ordered to join EAGLE, was 10 miles 260 degrees from WARSPITE and were formed on a line of bearing 320 degrees and steering 270 degrees at 18 knots. NUBIAN and 4 destroyers were screening WARSPITE.

EAGLE, screened by VOYAGER and VAMPIRE, was proceeding to take up a position 10 miles to Eastward of WARSPITE and was shortly joined by GLOUCESTER who, by reason of her bomb hit the previous day, was unfit to engage in serious action.

30. The cruisers were then rapidly closing the enemy forces which were distant 12 to 18 miles between bearings of 235 and 270 degrees. At 1508 NEPTUNE sighted 2 enemy battleships bearing 250 degrees 15 miles, and the course of the 7th Cruiser Squadron was altered to 000 degrees and then to 045 degrees at 1510 to avoid getting too heavily engaged until WARSPITE was in a position to give support. At 1514 the 7th Cruiser Squadron's line of bearing was altered to 350 degrees and the enemy cruisers marked " C " in the diagram opened fire at a range of 23,600 yards. At 1516 the 7th Cruiser Squadron altered course to 025 degrees and at 1520 to 030 degrees to open " A " arcs.*

31. At 1512 the 7th Cruiser Squadron was ordered by Vice-Admiral (D) to engage an equal number of enemy ships. NEPTUNE and LIVERPOOL opened fire at a range of 22,100 yards and SYDNEY opened fire at the fourth cruiser from the right, thought to be of the ZARA class. ORION opened fire first on a destroyer (Z in Diagram No. 2) then on the right hand cruiser bearing 249 degrees, range 23,700 yards.

32. In the meantime the enemy advanced forces were sighted from WARSPITE who opened fire on an 8″ cruiser bearing 265 degrees at a range of 26.400 yards This was a cruiser in " C " Squadron (Diagram No. 2) which was then engaging and being engaged

Admiralty footnote —
* " A " arcs—the arcs on which *all* guns of a ship's main armament will bear, thus allowing them to fire simultaneously at the enemy.

by the 7th Cr. Squadron. Ten salvos were fired and a hit possibly obtained with the last salvo. One of the WARSPITE's aircraft was on the catapult preparing to fly off but it became so urgent that fire should be opened in support of the heavily outnumbered cruisers that delay could not be accepted. The aircraft was damaged by the blast of " X " turret and subsequently jettisoned.

33. At 1530 the enemy turned away making smoke and fire was checked. WARSPITE turned through 360 degrees and made an " S " bend to enable MALAYA, who had been ordered by the Commander-in-Chief to press on at utmost speed, to catch up. The 7th Cruiser Squadron also made a 360 degree turn to starboard to conform. The enemy fire during this time was ineffective (1514 to 1530) but our cruisers were straddled several times and at 1524 splinters from a near miss damaged NEPTUNE's catapult and aircraft. The latter was jettisoned soon after as it was leaking petrol. No hits were obtained on the enemy.

34. Between 1533 and 1536 WARSPITE fired 4 salvos at each of two 6" cruisers. These cruisers were evidently of the starboard wing column which had been coming up from the Southward, but were now steering to the Eastward apparently trying to work round to get at EAGLE. At 1545 EAGLE again flew off her striking force.

35. At 1548 WARSPITE's second aircraft was catapulted for action observation, Duty Q.

36. At 1551 the 7th Cruiser Squadron was on a course of 310 degrees to close the enemy again and WARSPITE was steering 345 degrees. Six enemy cruisers were in sight ahead of the enemy battlefleet This squadron is presumed to be the Port wing column " A " in diagram No 3.

37. At 1553 WARSPITE opened fire on the right hand of the two enemy battleships of the CAVOUR class, bearing 287 degrees, range 26,000 yards WARSPITE was under fi e from both enemy battleships and was shortly afterwards straddled. MALAYA was now in station on a bearing of 180 degrees from WARSPITE and fired 4 salvos at the enemy battleships at extreme range but these fell short. The enemy fired with moderate accuracy, the majority of the salvos falling within 1,000 yards but nearly all having a large spread. Only one closely bunched salvo was observed which fel about 2 cables on WARSPITE's port bow. At 1600 the enemy was straddled and one hit observed at the base of the foremost funnel. The enemy then started to alter course away making smoke and WARSPITE altered to 310 degrees, speed 17 knots.

38. WARSPITE ceased firing at 1604 after firing 17 salvos, the enemy being obscured in smoke. MALAYA fired 4 more salvos, all short and ceased fire at 1608.
At 1605 EAGLE's striking force attacked a cruiser of the BOLZANO class and it is believed that at least one hit was obtained. No report of this hit was received until 1715.

39. At 1609 WARSPITE opened fire on an enemy cruiser bearing 313 degrees, range 24,600 yards. This was presumably one of " A " squadron which had drawn ahead of the battleships and appeared to be working round to the Northward. Fire was checked after 6 salvos as the enemy turned away making smoke.

40. In the meantime the destroyers, who had been released from WARSPITE at 1525, MALAYA at 1545 and ROYAL SOVEREIGN at 1552, had concentrated and at 1600 were on the disengaged bow of the battlefleet and steering a similar course at 25 to 27 knots. JUNO and JANUS joined the 14th Flotilla, HERO and HEREWARD the 2nd Flotilla and DECOY the 10th Flotilla. Some of these destroyers were narrowly missed by heavy shells when passing to the Eastward of WARSPITE at 1554. At 1602 the 10th and 14th Flotillas came under heavy fire from enemy cruisers but were not hit. ROYAL SOVEREIGN in the meantime was pressing on at the maximum speed her engines could give, but never got within range at all.

41. At 1605 enemy destroyers were observed from WARSPITE to be moving across to starboard from the van of the enemy fleet and at 1610 the tracks of three or more torpedoes were seen by the 14th Flotilla passing close to them. These were evidently fired at very long range.

42. Our destroyers were ordered at 1614 to counter attack enemy destroyers and at this time were 4 miles East-north-east of WARSPITE and turning to the North-west.

43. At 1619 the 10th Flotilla opened fire on the enemy destroyers at a range of 12,600 yards. STUART's first salvo appeared to hit. At this time the three flotillas were disposed with guides on a line of bearing 220 degrees, destroyers disposed 180 degrees from guides, course 300 degrees. The 7th Cruiser Squadron were also engaging the enemy destroyers.

44 Between 1615 and 1630 a number of enemy destroyers, probably two flotillas, having worked across to starboard of their main fleet, delivered a half-hearted attack. As soon as they had (presumably) fired torpedoes they turned away Westward making smoke. It was observed that the second flotilla to attack retired through the smoke made by the first flotilla. Spasmodic firing was opened by all forces during the short intervals in which the enemy was in range and not obscured by smoke. No hits were observed by WARSPITE's aircraft.

45. Between 1630 and 1640 enemy destroyers were dodging in and out of their smoke screens and spasmodic firing by our flotillas was opened Two torpedoes were seen to cross NUBIAN's stern at 1640. WARSPITE fired a few salvos of 6" and MALAYA one salvo, at enemy destroyers between 1639 and 1641 when they disappeared in smoke.

46. During this period of the action (i.e. between the time CAVOUR was hit and the time our own fleet approached the smoke screen) P/L signals from the enemy were intercepted saying that he was " constrained to retire," ordering his flotillas to make smoke, to attack with torpedoes, and also a warning that they were approaching the submarine line.

These signals, together with my own appreciation of the existing situation, made it appear unwise and playing the enemy's own game to plunge straight into the smoke screen.

Course was therefore altered to work round to the Northward and windward of the smoke screen, course having been altered to 340 degrees at 1635. Our destroyers were well clear of the smoke by 1700 but the enemy were out of sight, evidently having retired at high speed to the Westward and South-westward.

47. Between 1640 and 1925 a series of heavy bombing attacks were made on our fleet by enemy aircraft operating from shore bases. WARSPITE was bombed at 1641, 1715, 1735, 1823 and 1911. EAGLE was bombed at 1743, 1809, 1826, 1842 and 1900. These two ships received the most attention but the 7th Cruiser Squadron received numerous attacks and many bombs fell near the destroyers. In some cases attacks were made from a considerable height. There were no hits and the fleet suffered no damage but there were numerous near misses and a few minor casualties from splinters. MALAYA claimed to have damaged two aircraft with A.A. fire but no enemy machines were definitely seen to crash.

48. From 1700 the fleet steered 270 degrees, the destroyers forming Cruising Order No. 3 in company with the 7th Cruiser Squadron to the Northward of WARSPITE. By 1735 the fleet was within 25 miles of the coast of Calabria and course was altered to 200 degrees. When, however, it became clear that the enemy had no intention of resuming the fight and could not be intercepted before making Messina, course was altered to 160 degrees at 1830 to open the land and to 130 degrees at 1930

49. After the action, as subsequently reported by WARSPITE's aircraft, the enemy fleet was left in considerable confusion, all units making off at high speed to the South-west and Westward towards the Straits of Messina and Port Augusta. It was not until 1800 that they sorted themselves out, the cruiser squadrons taking station to the South-eastward of their battleships and destroyers to the North-west and astern of them. The last enemy report was received from WARSPITE's aircraft at 1905 and the enemy fleet was then in position 37° 54′ N, 16° 21′ E, i.e about 10 miles off Cape Spartivento, steering 230 degrees at 18 knots.

They were attacked by their own bombers at 1705 and again at 1857. No hits were observed.

50. At 2115 course was altered to 220 degrees for a position South of Malta. There were no incidents during the night.

51. The following destroyers were detached so as to arrive at Malta at 0500 —STUART. DAINTY, DEFENDER, HYPERION, HOS. TILE, HASTY, ILEX, JUNO. (STUART arrived with only 15 tons of fuel remaining).

52. At 0800 the fleet was in position 35° 24′ N, 15° 27′ E., steering West, and remained cruising to the South of Malta throughout the day while destroyers were fuelled.

53. An air raid took place on Malta at 0855 but no destroyers were hit. Three or four enemy aircraft were shot down.

54. The first batch of destroyers completed fuelling at 1115 and rejoined the Commander-in-Chief at 1525. HERO, HEREWARD, DECOY, VAMPIRE and VOYAGER were then sent in, the last three to sail with convoy M.S. One after refuelling. At 2030 ROYAL SOVEREIGN with NUBIAN, MOHAWK and JANUS were sent in, and GLOUCESTER and STUART were detached to join convoy M.F. One which had been sailed from Malta by the Vice-Admiral, Malta, at 2300 on 9th July escorted by DIAMOND, JERVIS, and VENDETTA.

55. Flying boat reconnaissance of Augusta had located 3 cruisers and 8 destroyers in harbour and at 1850 EAGLE's striking force was flown off to carry out a dusk attack. Unfortunately these forces had left harbour before the striking force arrived. One flight, however, located a destroyer of the NAVIGATORI class in a small bay to the Northward and sank it. The other flight returned without having dropped torpedoes. The striking force landed at Malta on completion of the operation.

56. At 2000 the 7th Cruiser Squadron was detached to search to the Eastward in the wake of convoy M.F. One.

57. At 2100 the fleet was in position 35° 28′ N, 14° 30′ E., steering 180 degrees. There were no incidents during the night.

Thursday, 11th July.

58. At 0130 course was altered to 000 degrees so as to be in position 35° 10′ N, 15° 00′ E., at 0800. ROYAL SOVEREIGN, with HERO, HEREWARD, NUBIAN, MOHAWK and JANUS, rejoined from Malta at this time and EAGLE landed on the striking force from Malta.

59. At 0900 the Commander-in-Chief in WARSPITE screened by NUBIAN, MOHAWK, JUNO and JANUS, proceeded ahead at 19 knots to return to Alexandria. The Rear-Admiral, 1st Battle Squadron, in ROYAL SOVEREIGN, with EAGLE and MALAYA and remaining destroyers, proceeded on a mean line of advance of 080 degrees at 12 knots to cover the passage of the convoys.

60. The fleet was again subjected to heavy bombing attacks. Between 1248 and 1815 five attacks were made on WARSPITE and attendant destroyers, 66 bombs being dropped. Between 1112 and 1804, twelve attacks were carried out on the forces in company with the Rear-Admiral, 1st Battle Squadron, about 120 bombs being dropped, and four bombing attacks were carried out on convoy M S. One. There was no damage and no casualties. It was noted that the ship was shadowed by aircraft who transmitted " longs " by W/T at intervals in order to direct attacking aircraft.

61. At 1500 convoy M.S. One was passed and VAMPIRE relieved JANUS on WARSPITE's screen, JANUS remaining with the convoy.

62. WARSPITE was in position 34° 22′ N, 19° 17′ E., steering 110 degrees at 2100.

Friday, 12th July.

63. There were no incidents during the night. Course was altered from time to time during the day to throw off shadowing and attacking aircraft. At 0700, Vice-Admiral (D) with the 7th Cruiser Squadron rejoined the Commander-in-Chief and was then detached with ORION and NEPTUNE to join convoy M.F. One, LIVERPOOL and SYDNEY remaining in company with WARSPITE.

64. The following bombing attacks took place during the day: —

Between 0850 and 1150 seventeen attacks were made on WARSPITE, about 300 bombs being dropped.

Between 1110 and 1804 three attacks were made on the 1st Battle Squadron and EAGLE, 25 bombs being dropped.

There were no hits but several near misses.

As a result of these attacks a course was set, to close the Egyptian coast and No. 252 Wing requested to send fighters. Fighters were sent later in the afternoon but no more attacks developed.

65. The Rear-Admiral, 3rd Cruiser Squadron in CAPETOWN, and CALEDON, sailed from Alexandria to rendezvous with convoy M.S. One at 1000/13th in the vicinity of position 33° 50′ N, 23° 00′ E

Saturday, 13th July.

66. The Commander-in-Chief in WARSPITE, with the 7th Cruiser Squadron and escorting destroyers, arrived Alexandria at 0600 and convoy M.F. One and escort at 0900. RAMILLIES, screened by HAVOCK, IMPERIAL, DIAMOND and VENDETTA, was then sailed to escort convoy M.S. One.

67. The force with Rear-Admiral, 1st Battle Squadron, was subjected to bombing attacks between 1056 and 1623. During this time EAGLE's three Gladiators shot down a shadowing aircraft and 2 bombers and another was so severely damaged that it probably did not reach home. Blenheim fighters were sent out during the afternoon to provide protection.

68. Force C entered harbour at Alexandria at 0815 on 14th July, and the 3rd Cruiser Squadron, convoy M.S. One and escort, and RAMILLIES, at 0900 on the 15th.

LONDON
PRINTED AND PUBLISHED BY HIS MAJESTY'S STATIONERY OFFICE
To be purchased directly from H.M. Stationery Office at the following addresses:
York House, Kingsway, London, W.C.2; 13a Castle Street, Edinburgh, 2;
39–41 King Street, Manchester, 2, 1 St. Andrew's Crescent, Cardiff;
Tower Lane, Bristol, 1; 80 Chichester Street, Belfast
OR THROUGH ANY BOOKSELLER
1948
Price 1s. 0d. net

S.O. Code No 65-38273

Numb. 38281

SUPPLEMENT

TO

The London Gazette

Of TUESDAY, the 4th of MAY, 1948

Published by Authority

Registered as a newspaper

2799

WEDNESDAY, 5 MAY, 1948

ACTION BETWEEN BRITISH AND ITALIAN FORCES OFF CAPE SPARTIVENTO ON 27th NOVEMBER, 1940.

The following Despatch was submitted to the Lords Commissioners of the Admiralty on the 18th December, 1940, by Vice-Admiral Sir James F. Somerville, K.C.B., D.S.O., Flag Officer Commanding, Force " H ".

H.M.S. RENOWN.
18th December, 1940.

Be pleased to lay before Their Lordships the attached narrative of an engagement which took place on 27th November, 1940, during the execution of Operation " Collar ", between forces under my command and an Italian Naval force in the area to the South of Sardinia.

Object of Operation " Collar ".

2. The object of this operation was to secure the safe and timely passage through the Mediterranean of the following:—

1,400 Royal Air Force and Military personnel.

Two SOUTHAMPTON Class Cruisers,

Three M.T. ships,

Four Corvettes.

Composition of British Force.

3. The British force was composed as follows:—

Force " B ". Battleship:—
RENOWN (Flag Officer Commanding, Force " H ").

Aircraft Carrier:—
ARK ROYAL.

Force " B "—continued.
Cruisers:—
SHEFFIELD.
DESPATCH.

Destroyers:—
FAULKNOR.
FIREDRAKE.
FORESTER.
FURY.
DUNCAN.
WISHART.
ENCOUNTER.
KELVIN.
JAGUAR

Force " F ". Cruisers:—
MANCHESTER (C.S.18)*
SOUTHAMPTON.
(Carrying approximately 700 R.A.F. and Military personnel each.)

Destroyer:—
HOTSPUR.
(With no asdics and speed limited.)

Corvettes:—
PEONY.
SALVIA.
GLOXINIA.
HYACINTH.
(Corvettes fitted with L.L. sweeps† and a s d i c s. Maximum speed—16 knots.)

Admiralty footnotes:—
* C.S. 18—Vice Admiral Commanding, 18th Cruiser Squadron.
† L.L. sweep—anti-magnetic mine sweep.

58153

A

Force " F ".—continued.

S.S. CLAN FORBES.
S.S. CLAN FRAZER.
S.S. NEW ZEALAND
STAR.
(M.T. ships carrying
mechanical transport,
etc., maximum speed
16 knots.)

Force " D ". Battleship:—
RAMILLIES.

Cruisers:—
NEWCASTLE.
COVENTRY.
BERWICK.

Destroyers:—
DEFENDER.
GREYHOUND.
GRIFFIN.
HEREWARD.

Method of Execution.

4. Forces " B " and " F " to escort and cover the passage of the M.T. ships and corvettes through the Western Mediterranean, being met to the South of Sardinia at approximately noon on 27th November by Force " D " proceeding from the Eastern Mediterranean. Forces " B ", " F " and " D " then to proceed in company to a position West of Skerki Bank, which would be reached at dusk. After dark, Force " F ", the corvettes and COVENTRY with destroyers of Force " D " to part company and proceed through the Narrows to the Eastern Mediterranean, Force " B ", with RAMILLIES, NEWCASTLE and BERWICK, proceeding to Gibraltar.

Condition of Ships taking part.

5. RENOWN, ARK ROYAL and SHEFFIELD were in good fighting condition with the exception that ARK ROYAL had an unduly high percentage of inexperienced pilots and observers, and the efficiency of her torpedo striking force was low, owing to lack of opportunity for exercise.

6. MANCHESTER and SOUTHAMPTON would each be carrying some 700 Royal Air Force and Military personnel.

7. BERWICK (so I had been informed by her Commanding Officer) was not capable of more than 27 knots owing to the removal of some rows of turbine blades and to the higher water temperature in the Mediterranean affecting her vacuum.

8. NEWCASTLE's boilers had developed defects, and judging from signals received, could not be considered entirely reliable.

9. The destroyers of the 8th and 13th Flotillas had been running very hard, but there was no reason to anticipate any definite defects developing during the operation. HOTSPUR was without asdics, had been temporarily repaired and her speed was limited, though in fine weather it was hoped she could reach 20 knots or possibly more.

10. The condition of RAMILLIES, COVENTRY and the Mediterranean Fleet destroyers was satisfactory so far as was known.

11. The corvettes were incapable of making a speed of advance of 14 knots except in fair weather.

12. With the exception of RENOWN, SHEFFIELD, ARK ROYAL and the destroyers of the 8th and 13th Flotillas, the ships taking part in this operation had not worked together as a squadron.

13. Doubts had been expressed by Vice Admiral L. E. Holland, C.B. (Vice Admiral Commanding, 18th Cruiser Squadron) concerning the advisability of MANCHESTER and SOUTHAMPTON being included in Force " F ", for the following reasons:—

(i) Extreme importance was attached to the safe and timely arrival of the R.A.F. personnel at Alexandria. The best way to ensure this was for the cruisers to proceed independently and rely upon their high speed and mobility for the achievement of their object;

(ii) With so many additional on board, the ships were not in a fit condition to fight. If obliged to engage, casualties amongst the R.A.F. personnel might be heavy and the object of this part of the operation compromised.

14. I agreed that these ships would not be in a satisfactory state to fight an action and that the achievement of part of our object, namely, the safe arrival of the personnel, would be assured with greater certainty if the cruisers proceeded independently.

On the other hand, achievement of our complete object, which included the safe passage of the M.T. ships and corvettes, was more likely to be accomplished if we made a show of force, since this might deter the Italians from attempting to interfere with the operation.

15. At Admiral Holland's request I asked the Commander-in-Chief, Mediterranean, whether the safe passage of personnel or the M.T. ships should receive priority, if circumstances arose which made a decision necessary after Force " F " had parted company for the passage of the Narrows. The Commander-in-Chief, Mediterranean, replied " Personnel," but subsequent instructions were received from the Admiralty that this must be subject to the overriding consideration that if Italian forces were in sight action taken by the cruisers must be the same as if personnel were not embarked.

ESTIMATE OF ENEMY FORCES LIKELY TO
BE ENCOUNTERED AND NEED FOR
REINFORCEMENT.

16. Prior to the commencement of Operation " Collar " I informed the Admiralty that I considered the inclusion of ROYAL SOVEREIGN (undergoing repairs in Gibraltar) in my force was desirable in view of a possible Italian concentration in the Western Mediterranean which I estimated could reach a total of

Three battleships,

Five to seven 8" cruisers,

Several 6" cruisers and other light forces.

The Admiralty reply indicated that some doubt was entertained concerning the necessity for this reinforcement, but approval was eventually given for the inclusion of ROYAL

SOVEREIGN in Force " B " if I considered this essential.

The Commander-in-Chief, Mediterranean, was frankly sceptical and considered I was unduly pessimistic. In his opinion, the probability of an Italian concentration in the Western Mediterranean was more remote now than at any time since Operation " Hats " (30th August—5th September).

Since defects in ROYAL SOVEREIGN could not be completed in time she was unable to take part in the operation.

EXECUTION OF OPERATION " COLLAR."

17. The M.T. ships included in Force " F " passed through the Straits of Gibraltar during the night of 24th/25th November and were joined by the corvettes to the East of Gibraltar a.m. 25th November. The remainder of Forces " B " and " F " sailed at 0800 on 25th November.

The operation proceeded according to plan and without incident until the morning of 27th November. The corvettes had been detached on the evening of 26th November, as they were unable to keep up with the convoy. A detailed account of the situation at 0800 on 27th November and subsequent events on that day are given in the attached narrative.

POINTS OF INTEREST.

Enemy Intelligence prior to 27th November.

18. So far as I am aware, reliance was placed entirely on shore based air reconnaissance to locate the position of enemy units in the Western Mediterranean prior to 27th November. This reconnaissance proved quite inadequate for the purpose and there was insufficient information concerning the location of Italian naval forces prior to the 27th November and no report of enemy ships being at sea in the Western Mediterranean until they were sighted by carrier reconnaissance a.m. 27th November.

Enemy Intelligence on 27th November.

19. With the exception of a Sunderland flying boat operating from Malta to cover the area in which our forces would be operating on 27th November, air reconnaissance was limited to that furnished by ARK ROYAL's aircraft.

ARK ROYAL has a high proportion of young and inexperienced pilots and observers. Some of these had to be employed on the initial dawn reconnaissance, since it was necessary to hold the first air striking force in readiness to attack any enemy force attempting to interfere with the concentration of Forces " B " and " F " with Force " D ".

Not only had many of these young observers little or no experience of reporting enemy formations, but the need for maintaining wireless silence, except in the immediate neighbourhood of Gibraltar provides little opportunity to exercise communications in the air.

These factors, coupled with variable visibility and the similarity of Italian warships' silhouettes, made their tasks difficult.

Taking the above into consideration, I consider the crews of the reconnaissance aircraft acquitted themselves with credit.

Results obtained by Air Striking Force Torpedo Attacks.

20. The results obtained by torpedo bomber attacks on high speed targets during the present war have fallen far short of the estimates based on peacetime practices adjusted for " opposition."

So far as ARK ROYAL is concerned, this is attributed entirely to lack of initial training and subsequent runner practices.[*] Skilful, unobserved approaches were made in each case and the attacks pressed home with courage and resolution, but the results obtained were disappointing.

Delay in reporting Result of first Striking Force Attack.

21. It is not always appreciated that sustained observation on enemy ships by the crews of aircraft in the striking force is impracticable. Observations of " own drop " even in peacetime practices, is very difficult, and under action conditions, quite fortuitous. Succeeding attackers may, or may not, be able to observe hits from preceding attacks, but in general the only definite evidence is the subsequent behaviour of the target. On this occasion it was not until the return of the striking force to ARK ROYAL had afforded an opportunity for the interrogation of all aircraft crews, that the probability of one hit on the Littorio class was established. Subsequent observation of the target indicated that her speed had not been reduced to an extent which prevented her keeping in company with the Cavour class, at about 25 knots, but does not disprove the estimate that one hit was obtained.

Fighting Efficiency.

22. With the exception of RENOWN, ARK ROYAL, SHEFFIELD and the destroyers of the 8th Destroyer Flotilla (the permanent nucleus of Force " H "), the remaining ships taking part in the engagement had been drawn from various stations and in certain cases, met for the first time just before the action opened.

23. To illustrate the constant changes that have taken place in the composition of Force " H " since 1st of July, it is of interest to note that the following different ships have at some time or other been included in this force for operations, viz. :—

Seven capital ships,
Three aircraft carriers,
Thirteen cruisers,
Thirty three destroyers.

24. The fact that ships carried out their action duties correctly and with the minimum of signalled instructions is a tribute to the soundness of our tactical training in peace and to the " Fighting Instructions."

Decision to discontinue the Chase.

25. My reasons for deciding that a continuance of the chase offered no reasonable prospect of inflicting damage on the enemy and was not justified are contained in the Narrative. Had I received timely information before breaking off the action that some of the enemy ships appeared to have sustained damage, I should have felt justified in continuing the action for a short period. But I was not prepared to hazard the achievement of my main objective, the safe passage of the convoy, unless there was substantial assurance. I could inflict material

---

Admiralty footnote:—
[*] Runner practices—practice firings with torpedoes not fitted with warheads. ... ..

damage on the enemy by the destruction of one or more of his battleships. The policy I followed was in general accordance with the accepted principles of war and the "Fighting Instructions." I do not suggest that a rigid adherence to these principles and instructions is either necessary or desirable, but on the other hand I consider that the interests of the country are best served by general adherence to established principles, and instructions based on those principles.

Conduct of Officers and Men.

26. Both from personal observation and reports I have received, I am able to state that the conduct of officers and men taking part in this engagement left nothing to be desired. It was a pleasure to observe the enthusiasm with which the ship's company of RENOWN closed up at their action stations on hearing that enemy forces were in the vicinity and their subsequent disappointment when it was clear that the enemy did not intend to stand and fight was obvious.

(Signed) J. F. SOMERVILLE.
Vice-Admiral,
Flag Officer Commanding,
Force " H ".

NARRATIVE OF THE ACTION BETWEEN BRITISH AND ITALIAN FORCES ON 27TH NOVEMBER, 1940.

Movements Prior to the Action.

Sunrise on the 27th November was at 0824 (zone — 2) and at 0800 the situation was as follows:—

(a) RENOWN in company with ARK ROYAL, SHEFFIELD and 4 destroyers (Group I) were in position at 37° 48' N, 07° 24' E, steering at 083° at 16 knots, a position of cover, 10 to 20 miles ahead and to the North Eastward of the convoy having been maintained throughout the night;

(b) Vice Admiral Commanding, 18th Cruiser Squadron in MANCHESTER with SOUTHAMPTON, DESPATCH and 5 destroyers (Group II) were in company with the M.T. convoy in position 37° 37' N, 06° 54' E. The 4 corvettes were about 10 miles to the Westward of the convoy, having been unable to keep up with the latter.

2. At this time ARK ROYAL flew off a section of fighters, one A/S patrol, one meteorological machine and a reconnaissance of 7 T.S.R.s* designed to cover the area to the West of Sardinia, and between Sardinia and Africa; the depth of this reconnaissance to the Eastward being just sufficient to cover Force " D " which was approaching from Skerki Bank. The fighter section on their return to ARK ROYAL reported that they had shot down a Cant. Z.506—10 miles North West of Bona at 0930.

3. Group I continued to the Eastward so as to be ready to concentrate with Force " D " should air reconnaissance reveal the presence of important enemy units in the vicinity of that Force. C.O.S. Alexandria's signal timed 0330/27 indicated that the presence of Force " D " might be known to the enemy.

4. At 0900, in the absence of any report from air reconnaissance, which by that time was expected to have reached a depth of 90 miles from Group I, course was shaped to the South West to join the convoy in accordance with the prearranged plan and provide additional A.A. defence by the time the first bombing attack was likely to develop.

5. The first sighting of the enemy from the air took place at 0852 when one of ARK ROYAL's reconnaissance aircraft sighted a group of warships and closed to investigate. At 0906 an Alarm Report was made of four cruisers and six destroyers but this report was not received by any ship.

6. At 0920, Group I sighted the convoy and course was adjusted to pass astern of it in order to place Group I to the South of the convoy, and up sun from the latter, whilst carrying out flying operations and thus in the probable direction of air attack.

7. At 0956, whilst Group I was still on the Port quarter of the convoy, an aircraft report (T.O.O.* 0920) of the presence of 5 cruisers and 5 destroyers was received by V/S† from ARK ROYAL.

8. It seemed possible that this might be a report of Force " D," and ARK ROYAL was asked to confirm that this was an enemy report. Steam for full speed was, however, at once ordered and Captain (D), 8th Destroyer Flotilla, directed to detail 2 destroyers to screen ARK ROYAL and 2 to screen the convoy.

9. By 1016, as a result of further reports from aircraft, and confirmation from ARK ROYAL, the presence of enemy Battleships and Cruisers was established. RENOWN altered course to 075° to join RAMILLIES and speed was increased as rapidly as possible to 28 knots.

10. The composition and relative position of the enemy forces was far from clear, the situation as viewed on the Plot at 1035 being shown in Diagram 1.

11. I decided:—

(i) That the convoy should continue towards its destination but on a South Easterly course in order to keep well clear of any action that might develop;

(ii) To limit the escort of the convoy to DESPATCH, COVENTRY and 2 destroyers;

(iii) To proceed with all remaining forces to concentrate with Force " D " and then attack and drive off the enemy.

12. To implement these decisions ARK ROYAL was instructed to prepare and fly off a T/B‡ striking force and to act independently under cover of the battle fleet. DESPATCH was placed in charge of the convoy which was ordered to steer 120° at full speed. Cruisers and destroyers of Force " F " were ordered to join Flag Officer Commanding, Force " H "; COVENTRY was ordered to join the convoy, and RAMILLIES was informed of Flag Officer Commanding, Force " H " 's position, course and speed.

Admiralty footnote:—
* T.S.R.—Torpedo/Spotter/Reconnaissance aircraft.

Admiralty footnotes:—
* T.O.O.—time of origin.
† V/S—visual signal.
‡ T/B—Torpedo Bomber.

13. MANCHESTER, SHEFFIELD and SOUTHAMPTON were now concentrating in the van, cruisers and destroyers being stationed 050° 5 miles from RENOWN, i.e. on the estimated bearing of the enemy. This position was subsequently adjusted as requisite.

14. At 1032 I made a signal to Malta W/T reporting the position of 2 enemy battleships.

15. At 1058 a Sunderland flying-boat closed RENOWN and reported the position of Force "D" as being 34 miles, 070°. The flying-boat was ordered to shadow and report the composition of the enemy bearing 025°, 50 miles.

16. Reconnaissance aircraft from ARK ROYAL had meanwhile sighted and reported two groups of cruisers and 2 battleships. There were, however, a number of discrepancies between the reports both as to position and composition so that it was not possible to get a clear picture of the situation. It seemed certain that five or six enemy cruisers were present but it was doubtful whether the number of battleships was one, two or three. But, whatever the composition of the enemy force, it was clear to me that in order to achieve my object —the safe and timely arrival of the convoy at its destination—it was essential to show a bold front and attack the enemy as soon as possible.

17. The enemy who had originally been reported as steering to the Westward, were now reported as altering course to the Eastward at 1115.

18. An Observer who witnessed this alteration of course reported that the Eastern group of cruisers appeared to be thrown into a state of confusion. The leading ship turned 180° whilst the two following ships turned only 90°. Collisions appeared to have been narrowly averted and at one time all three ships appeared to be stopped with their bows nearly touching each other.

19. Based on the Sunderland's report of the position of Force "D", junction with that Force now appeared to be assured. Speed was therefore reduced to 24 knots to maintain a position between the estimated position of the enemy battle fleet and the convoy.

20. At 1128 Force "D" was sighted bearing 073° approximately 24 miles. Shortly after this ARK ROYAL flew off the first T/B Striking Force.

21. Aircraft reports now available appeared to show that the enemy's force consisted of 2 battleships, about 6 or more cruisers and a considerable number of destroyers. RAMILLIES was therefore ordered to steer 045° so as not to lose ground as the action appeared likely to develop into a chase. BERWICK and NEWCASTLE joined Vice Admiral Commanding, 18th Cruiser Squadron, who had been placed in command of all cruisers in the van.

The Approach.

22. At 1134, acting on the latest estimate of the enemy's bearing and distance, speed was increased to 28 knots and at 1140 course altered to 050° to close the enemy.

23. At this time MANCHESTER, SOUTHAMPTON and SHEFFIELD were in single line ahead about five miles fine on the Port bow of RENOWN with BERWICK and NEWCASTLE joining Vice Admiral Commanding, 18th Cruiser Squadron, from the Eastward.

24. Two miles astern of the cruisers, Captain (D), 8th Destroyer Flotilla in FAULKNOR was gradually collecting the Eighth Flotilla and ENCOUNTER, some of whom had been screening the convoy. The four destroyers of Force "D" were also joining Captain (D), 8th Destroyer Flotilla, and were eventually stationed 3 miles, 270° from FAULKNOR. Ten miles fine on the Starboard bow of RENOWN, RAMILLIES was just turning up to a parallel course. ARK ROYAL had dropped well astern and was between our main force and the convoy carrying out flying operations.

25. At 1154 the Sunderland flying-boat returned and reported 6 cruisers and 8 destroyers bearing 330° 30 miles from RENOWN, and that no battleships had been sighted. Unfortunately her report gave no course or speed of the cruisers and she had disappeared from sight before this information could be obtained. This report which was the first visual link received appeared to show that one group of the enemy forces was considerably further to the West than the groups previously reported by aircraft and that it was in a position to work round astern to attack ARK ROYAL and the convoy if the course of our forces to the North East was maintained.

26. No further report of this group was received during the action and I was consequently in doubts as to its whereabouts and intentions. ARK ROYAL was however between my main forces and the convoy and I considered that returning aircraft would sight and report this group should they attempt to work round to a position from which to attack the convoy.

27. Course was however altered to North so as not to get too far to the Eastward.

28. The situation as it appeared to me from the Plot just before noon is shown in Diagram 2. The number of enemy battleships and cruisers present was still not definitely established, but I judged that in all probability only two battleships were present.

29. At this time the prospects of bringing the enemy to action appeared favourable.

(i) We had effected our concentration of which the enemy appeared to be unaware, since no shadowers had been sighted or reported by R.D/F, and his speed had been reported as between 14 and 18 knots, which suggested he was still awaiting the reports of reconnaissance.

(ii) The sun was immediately astern and if remaining unclouded would give us the advantage of light.

(iii) There seemed every possibility of a synchronised surface and T/B attack if the nearest position of the enemy was correct, and providing he did not retire at once at high speed.

30. My intentions at this time and throughout the ensuing chase were as follows:—

(i) To drive off the enemy from any position from which he could attack the convoy.

(ii) To accept some risk to the convoy providing there was a reasonable prospect of sinking one or more of the enemy battleships.

To achieve (ii) I considered the following conditions must be fulfilled:—

(a) A reduction of speed of the enemy to 20 knots or less by T/B attack.

(b) Engagement of enemy battleships by RENOWN and RAMILLIES in concert.

31. At 1207 RENOWN was reported as having a hot bearing on one shaft. Revolutions on this shaft had to be reduced. This, combined with a dirty bottom and paravanes, limited her speed to 27½ knots.

32. At the same time as this report was received puffs of smoke were observed on the horizon bearing 006° and cruisers in the van sighted masts and ships between the bearings of 346° and 006°.

33. At 1213 ARK ROYAL's signal timed 1147 was received reporting the composition of the enemy as 2 battleships and 6 cruisers accompanied by destroyers. This however did not disprove the Sunderland's information that a further group of 6 cruisers and destroyers was still further to the Westward.

34. By this time our cruisers were concentrated in the van and had formed a line of bearing 075°—255°, in sequence from West to East, SHEFFIELD, SOUTHAMPTON, NEWCASTLE, MANCHESTER and BERWICK. NEWCASTLE could not maintain the speed of the remainder and never quite reached her ordered station.

35. At 1158 BERWICK signalled that as his speed was limited to 27 knots he proposed to join RENOWN. Vice Admiral Commanding, 18th Cruiser Squadron ordered BERWICK to join him but by that time the BERWICK had already turned to implement his proposal and consequently lost ground. BERWICK took station on the Starboard bow of MANCHESTER but owing to lack of speed dropped back during the action.

36. During the approach the 9 destroyers in company (three being detachable with the convoy and two with ARK ROYAL) were moving up to a position 5 miles 040° from RENOWN. This position was selected so that they would be available to counter attack any destroyers attempting to launch an attack on RENOWN or RAMILLIES.

37. The situation as seen from the cruisers immediately before the action commenced was as follows:—

(i) 3 enemy cruisers and some destroyers—hereafter referred to as the Western group—were visible between the bearings of approximately 340° and 350°, at a range of about 11 miles hull down and steering a Northerly course.

(ii) A second group of cruisers also accompanied by destroyers—hereafter referred to as the Eastern group—to the right of the Western group, were further away and steering approximately 100°.

Evidence as to the movements of the Western group immediately before action was joined is conflicting. It appears probable however that the Western group was in line ahead on a Southerly course until 1210 when they turned together to a Northerly course. Between 1210 and 1220 further alterations of course may have been made, as, when first observed from RENOWN they appeared to have a fairly broad inclination to the Eastwards.

The Action.

38. At 1220 the enemy opened fire and immediately afterwards our advanced forces replied. The enemy's first salvo fell close to MANCHESTER being exact for range but a hundred yards out for line.

39. At 1223 I informed Commander-in-Chief, Mediterranean, that I was engaging the enemy.

40. Immediately fire was opened by our advanced forces on ships of the Western group, they made smoke and retired on courses varying between N.W. and N.E. Behind their smoke screen they appeared to make large and frequent alterations of course becoming visible at intervals—sometimes almost end on, and sometimes at quite a broad inclination—remaining in sight for a few minutes before again becoming lost in their smoke.

41. Just before opening fire at the Western group, who were already wreathed in smoke, RENOWN sighted two ships, who were not making smoke, at extreme visibility, bearing 020°. It was thought at the time that these might be the enemy battleships but they later proved to be cruisers of the Eastern group.

42. At 1224 RENOWN opened fire at the right hand ship of the Western group at a mean range of 26,500 yards. Six salvos were fired before the latter was lost in smoke.

43. At 1226, RAMILLIES fired two salvos at maximum elevation to test the range. Thereafter RAMILLIES—proceeding at 20.7 knots—dropped astern and followed in the wake of RENOWN throughout the action.

44. When RENOWN's target became obscured, course was altered to Starboard to close the supposed battleships and to bring the Western group of cruisers broader on the bow. Shortly afterwards two salvos were fired at a fleeting glimpse of the centre cruiser of the Western group.

45. Course was then further altered to Starboard to open " A " arcs* on the left hand ship of the Western group which now bore 356°. Eight salvos were fired at her when she next appeared, but at 1245 she too was lost to sight in smoke.

46. During this time our cruisers had been hotly engaged with the Western group at ranges varying between 23,000 and 16,000 yards. Many straddles were obtained but smoke rendered spotting and observation generally extremely difficult.

47. MANCHESTER, SHEFFIELD and NEWCASTLE all opened fire initially on the right hand ship of the Western group,

Admiralty footnote:—
* " A " arcs—the arcs on which *all* guns of a ship's main armament will bear, thus allowing them to fire simultaneously at the enemy.

BERWICK engaged the left hand ship of the same group whilst SOUTHAMPTON engaged the left hand ship of the Eastern group.

48. No concentration of fire was ordered owing to the speed with which the situation changed and to the large selection of targets available. Moreover, as Vice Admiral Commanding, 18th Cruiser Squadron, states in his report, it is doubtful what the results of an attempt at concentration would have been, as ships of the 18th Cruiser Squadron had not been in company for a considerable time and assembled on the battleground from Rosyth, Reykjavik, Malta and the vicinity of the Azores.

49. MANCHESTER and SHEFFIELD continued firing at the same cruiser until 1236 and 1240 respectively but NEWCASTLE after 18 broadsides shifted to BERWICK's target, whilst SOUTHAMPTON, after 5 salvos at her original target engaged a destroyer for eleven minutes. This destroyer was seen to be hit. At least one other destroyer is believed to have been hit during this phase and FAULKNOR at 1227 and NEWCASTLE at 1233½ report seeing a hit on a cruiser—in the case of NEWCASTLE the left hand ship of the Western group—by what appeared to be a large calibre shell. These hits were not observed in RENOWN.

50. The enemy's fire was accurate, particularly in the early stages, and MANCHESTER was exceptionally lucky not to have received damage. His rate of fire was however extremely slow and when he was fully engaged his spread became ragged and his accuracy deteriorated rapidly. BERWICK was hit at 1222 by an 8-inch shell, Y turret was put out of action and some casualties were incurred.

51. By 1234 the Western group were almost lost in smoke and Vice Admiral Commanding, 18th Cruiser Squadron, decided that the Eastern group should in future form his target. MANCHESTER accordingly shifted to the left hand ship of the Eastern group, 30 degrees on his Starboard bow at a range of 21,000 yards. This ship was identified as an 8-inch cruiser, probably of the Zara class.

52. Between 1233 and 1240 all ships of the 18th Cruiser Squadron shifted target on to the Eastern group of the enemy. BERWICK was again hit at 1235, officers' cabins being damaged and the Port After Breaker Room wrecked, but without further casualties. At this time she had just started to engage a ship of the Eastern group which was thought to be an 8-inch cruiser of the Pola class. 47 salvos were fired at this target between 1238 and 1308.

53. In order to ensure that the Eastern group should not be able to work round ahead and attack the convoy, Vice Admiral Commanding, 18th Cruiser Squadron altered the course of the Squadron from North to 090° bringing the Eastern group on to his Port bow. To counter what appeared to be an attempt of the Eastern group to cross the T of the 18th Cruiser Squadron, the course of the latter was altered to the Southward. The enemy however immediately resumed their North Easterly course and the 18th Cruiser Squadron led back to 070° at 1256 and to 030° at 1258.

54. During this period the rear ship of the enemy line was observed by MANCHESTER,

NEWCASTLE and SOUTHAMPTON to be heavily on fire aft. Between 1252 and 1259 this ship appeared to lose speed, but thereafter picked up again and drew away with her consorts. No report of this damage to the enemy was received by Flag Officer Commanding, Force "H" until after the action. Subsequent reports indicate that at least one enemy destroyer with the Eastern group was frequently straddled and possibly hit.

55. Whilst the action between the 18th Cruiser Squadron and the Eastern group was starting, the first T/B Striking Force was nearing its objective. On their way they had first sighted the Western group retiring in a rather scattered state to the N.E., and then the Eastern group steaming to the South East at high speed in line ahead. Shortly after this, 2 battleships were observed 20 to 30 miles further to the Eastward and steering a South Easterly course. As the Striking Force manoeuvred to get up sun from the enemy the latter were seen to turn in succession to S.W. and then a few minutes later they turned together into line ahead on a North Easterly course.

56. Shortly after this last turn had been completed, the Striking Force attacked the enemy battle fleet. They dropped their torpedoes inside the screen of 7 destroyers at a range between 700 and 800 yards. The leader of this Striking Force slightly overshot his target—the leading battleship which was of the Littorio class—and therefore swung away and attacked the second ship which was of the Cavour class. The remaining ten pilots attacked the leading ship. Immediately after the attack the leading ship hauled round to the Northward and it was thought that the Cavour class ship went ahead of her, but there was no apparent loss of speed. As a result of careful comparison of notes on return to ARK ROYAL it was considered that one hit had probably been obtained on the Littorio class battleship. As the Striking Force turned away from their "drop" they machine-gunned the bridges of the capital ships and destroyers. The Eastern group of cruisers had tried to attract the attention of the battle fleet to the impending attack by firing at the Striking Force—though well out of range—as they approached. These bursts were seen in RENOWN. Nevertheless the attack was not observed in the battleships until the leading aircraft had dropped to about 1,500 feet, when an intense but mainly ill directed fire was opened.

57. As the Striking Force completed their attack at about 1245 the Eastern group of cruisers coming up at high speed from the Westwards opened a heavy and accurate fire on them, but fortunately without success, and all returned safely to ARK ROYAL.

58. At the same time as the Striking Force made their attack on the enemy battle fleet RENOWN had lost sight of her final target of the Western group in the smoke and was looking for a further target. At this moment two large ships steering to the Westward emerged out of the smoke cloud left by the Western group. Turrets were trained on to the new targets but fortunately before fire was opened they were identified as three-funnelled French liners.

59. As RENOWN was no longer engaged, and with the information then available it appeared that action with the battleships might be imminent, I decided to concentrate on RAMILLIES. Shortly after starting to turn however, the Eastern group of cruisers was seen to present a possible target and as the Plot indicated that the enemy battleships were heading North East, course was steadied on 070° to engage these new targets.

60. At 1300, after a swing to Starboard to avoid a reported submarine, course was altered to close the position of two battleships which had just been reported on that bearing by Vice Admiral Commanding, 18th Cruiser Squadron.

61. At 1311 RENOWN fired two ranging salvos at the left hand of the two ships believed at the time to be battleships. It is now considered that they were more probably two of the Eastern group of cruisers. Both salvos fell well short and the range was opening rapidly.

62. When sighted by Vice Admiral Commanding, 18th Cruiser Squadron at 1300 the two enemy battleships were steering to the South West and closing the range rapidly. At 1305 the 18th Cruiser Squadron therefore turned to work round the flank of the enemy battleships and to close the gap on RENOWN, but, at the same time the battleships altered course to the North Eastward and appeared to be retiring at high speed, whereupon the 18th Cruiser Squadron was turned back to a course of 050°.

63. During this short phase of the action large splashes, confirming the presence of capital ships, fell in the vicinity of BERWICK and MANCHESTER.

64. The relative position of my forces and those of the enemy as given by the Plot at 1315 is shown in Diagram 3. The situation was as follows:—

(i) Firing had practically ceased owing to the enemy drawing out of range.

(ii) The heavy smoke made by the enemy had prevented accurate fire during the chase and so far as could be ascertained, no damage had been inflicted.

(iii) In reply to a signal from me to C.S.18 at 1308 " Is there any hope of catching cruisers? " I was informed " No ". (A later message from C.S.18 estimated the enemy had three knots excess speed.)

(iv) It was known that the Striking Force had attacked. No report of results had been received, but it was evident that the speed of the enemy had not been materially reduced and was certainly not as low as 20 knots. It was presumed that the attack had been unsuccessful and this was not unexpected.

65. In view of our rapid approach to the enemy coast I had to decide whether a continuance of the chase was justified and likely to be profitable. The arguments for and against continuing the chase appeared to be:—

For Continuing the Chase.

(i) The possibility that the speed of the enemy might be reduced by some unforeseen eventuality.

(ii) He might appreciate that his force was superior to mine and decide to turn and fight.

Against Continuing the Chase.

(i) There was no sign that any of the enemy ships and especially his battleships had suffered damage, nor was there reasonable prospect of inflicting damage by gunfire in view of their superior speed. Unless the speed of the enemy battleships was reduced very materially he could enter Cagliari before I could bring him to action with RENOWN and RAMILLIES.

(ii) I was being led towards the enemy air and submarine base at Cagliari and this might well prove a trap. His appearance in this area appeared to be premeditated since it was unlikely that this was occasioned solely by the information he had received the previous night of Force " D's " presence in the Narrows.

(iii) The extrication of one of my ships damaged by air or submarine attack from my present position would certainly require the whole of my force and must involve leaving the convoy uncovered and insufficiently escorted during the passage of the Narrows.

(iv) The enemy main units had been driven off sufficiently far to ensure they could no longer interfere with the passage of the convoy.

(v) A second T/B attack could not take place until 1530 to 1600 by which time the convoy would be entirely uncovered and the enemy fleet could be under the cover of the A/A batteries and fighters at Cagliari. I entertained little hope that the attack would prove effective as I knew that the second flight was even less experienced than the first.

(vi) I had no assurance that the cruisers reported to the North West might not be working round towards the convoy and ARK ROYAL.

(vii) It was necessary for contact to be made with the convoy before dark to ensure the cruisers and destroyers required for escort through the Narrows should be properly formed up. It was also necessary to provide the fullest possible scale defence against T/B and light surface force attack at dusk. To effect this a retirement between 1300 and 1400 was necessary.

Decision to Break Off the Chase.

66. After reviewing these pros and cons I had no doubt in my mind whatsoever that the correct course was to break off the chase and rejoin the convoy as soon as possible. I consequently ordered a course of 130° to be steered.

67. At approximately 1335 I received a report of an enemy damaged cruiser in position about 30 miles from me and ten miles from the enemy coast. I considered the desirability of detaching two cruisers to search for and attack this cruiser. It was obviously undesirable to use MANCHESTER or SOUTHAMPTON. SHEFFIELD's R.D/F was required to deal with the bombing attacks which would inevitably develop and this left BERWICK and NEWCASTLE.

68. I considered this most carefully but decided against such a detachment for the following reasons: —

(i) It would involve my main forces remaining in a position to support these cruisers and prevent them from being cut off by enemy forces.

(ii) Action as in (i) would cause an unacceptable delay in rejoining the convoy.

(iii) Isolated ships in such close proximity to the enemy coast would be singled out for air attack. BERWICK was most vulnerable to this form of attack and her disablement would have involved all my force to effect her extrication.

(iv) There was no evidence to indicate that the damaged ship would remain stopped and she might well effect an escape before she could be overtaken.

A subsequent air search failed to locate this cruiser, so it appears that the stoppage was, in fact, only temporary.

69. I therefore ordered Vice Admiral Commanding, 18th Cruiser Squadron, to join the convoy with MANCHESTER and SOUTHAMPTON and instructed ARK ROYAL to attack the damaged cruiser if he considered it feasible.

70. At 1410 ARK ROYAL flew off the second T/B Striking Force. This Force consisted of the T.S.R.s who had carried out the morning reconnaissance. The Squadron Leader was given the enemy battlefleet as his objective but with full liberty to change the objective if a successful attack was impracticable and if by so doing he considered he had more chance of achieving successful results.

71. The second T/B Striking Force located three cruisers screened by four destroyers 12 miles off the S.E. coast of Sardinia and steering to the Eastward at high speed. Some 8 miles ahead of the cruisers the two battleships were also seen now heavily screened by ten destroyers.

72. In view of the total absence of cloud cover it was considered essential to attack out of the sun if any surprise was to be achieved. An attempt to reach such a position on the battleships would inevitably have led to the cruisers sighting and reporting the position of the Striking Force. It was therefore decided to attack the cruisers.

73. As the first aircraft reached the dropping position the cruisers turned together to Starboard. This caused several of the following flights, who were already committed to their drop, to miss their targets, but one hit was observed on the rear cruiser and another possible hit on the leading cruiser.

74. The attack was unobserved until very late, only two salvos being fired before the first torpedo was dropped. After this the gunfire was intense but appeared to be quite regardless of direction or danger to their own ships. One large projectile was seen to hit the water close to the rear cruiser and shells from close range weapons were seen to burst close alongside all ships.

75. Two of our aircraft were hit by shrapnel but neither was unserviceable and all returned safely to ARK ROYAL.

76. A striking force of 7 Skuas which flew off from ARK ROYAL at 1500 failed to locate the damaged cruiser but attacked 3 cruisers of the Condottieri class steering North off the South West corner of Sardinia. An unobserved attack was carried out on the rear cruiser and two near misses may have caused some damage. On the way back to the carrier an Italian R.O.43 was shot down.

Enemy Air Attacks.

77. At 1407 whilst our surface forces were proceeding at 19 knots to rejoin the convoy R.D/F gave indications of enemy bomber formations in the vicinity. The line was staggered.

78. The first visual indication of the attack was bomb splash on the horizon. This was the result of an attack by the Fulmar Fighter Patrol which caused several of the enemy formation to jettison their bombs.

79. As soon as the enemy aircraft, which consisted of 10 S.79 in V formation, were sighted a Blue Turn* was executed to bring all guns to bear. The enemy maintained a steady course and dropped their bombs well clear of the heavy ships, their bombs falling close to the screening destroyers.

80. Two further attacks were made, each by squadrons of 5 aircraft. In both cases ARK ROYAL who had been engaged in flying operations and was not actually in the line, was the objective. In these attacks, apart from a few bombs which were jettisoned as a result of interception by our fighters, most accurate bombing was carried out. ARK ROYAL was completely obscured by bomb splashes two at least of which fell within 10 yards of the ship. No hits were however obtained and no damage resulted.

81. The complete failure of either fighter attack or gunfire to break up the formation flying of the Italian squadrons was most noteworthy.

82. No further bombing attacks took place, and the convoy was sighted at 1700.

Remarks on the Movements of Enemy Forces after the Action.

83. The movements of enemy units from the time when surface action ceased at 1312 until he was finally lost to sight by air reconnaissance at 1655 are not fully established. From analysis of various reports the following appear most probable: —

(a) Immediately after surface action ceased the enemy battlefleet, which consisted of 1 Littorio and 1 Cavour class screened by 7 destroyers, steered for Cagliari at about 25 knots. At about 1500 they turned to the Eastward and at about 1520 to the North Eastward round Cape Carbonira. When last seen at 1655 they were steering North up the East coast of Sardinia. At some time between the attacks of the first and second T/B Striking Forces they are reported to have increased their destroyer screen from 7 to 10 destroyers. There is no indication that their speed was ever materially reduced below 25 knots.

(b) The Eastern group of cruisers had closed to about 8 miles from the battlefleet at 1240 and thereafter probably followed astern of them. When attacked by the second T/B Striking Force at 1520 they were on an Easterly course South of Sardinia and at that time were screened by 4 destroyers. After the attack it seemed probable that one cruiser became detached and may have proceeded to Cagliari. One ship of this group had been heavily hit aft by 6-inch fire.

(c) When the action ceased the Western group were a considerable distance to the North and West of their own battlefleet and the Eastern group, due to the direction of their retirement. It is probable that they then turned towards Cagliari and rejoined their battlefleet, but their movements are very uncertain.

LONDON

PRINTED AND PUBLISHED BY HIS MAJESTY'S STATIONERY OFFICE

To be purchased directly from H.M. Stationery Office at the following addresses:
York House, Kingsway, London, W.C.2; 13a Castle Street, Edinburgh, 2;
39–41 King Street, Manchester, 2; 1 St. Andrew's Crescent, Cardiff;
Tower Lane, Bristol, 1; 80 Chichester Street, Belfast
OR THROUGH ANY BOOKSELLER

1948

Price 1s. 0d. net

S.O. Code No. 65-38281

Admiral Sir Jock Slater

GCB LVO DL

Sir Jock Slater is a former First Sea Lord and great-nephew of Admiral Sir Andrew Cunningham, Commander-in-Chief of the Mediterranean Fleet during the period when the actions covered in this volume took place. He acknowledges that the Admiral inspired him to join the Navy. As a young Naval Officer, he spent many weekends with the Cunninghams at their home in Hampshire and remembers well his wide ranging discussions with his great-uncle, by then Admiral of the Fleet the Viscount Cunningham of Hyndhope,

Sir Jock joined the Royal Navy in 1956 at Britannia Royal Naval College, passing out in 1958 with the Sword of Honour and a Queen's Telescope. During his early career he served in the frigate HMS *Troubridge*, the inshore minesweeper HMS *Yaxham*, the Royal Yacht *Britannia* and the destroyer HMS *Cassandra*. In 1965 he was given brief command of the coastal minesweeper HMS *Soberton*, which he took on fishery protection duties, before specialising in navigation at HMS *Dryad*. He then served in the aircraft carrier HMS *Victorious* in the Far East and subsequently the frigate HMS *Scarborough* as Squadron Navigating Officer of the Dartmouth Training Squadron. He became Equerry to HM The Queen in 1968 and, after three years of Royal Duty, was appointed a Lieutenant of the Royal Victorian Order and promoted to Commander, taking command of the frigate HMS *Jupiter*. In 1973 he was appointed to the Directorate of Naval Operations and – on promotion to captain in 1976 – he commanded the destroyer HMS *Kent*. In 1978 he spent a year at the Royal College of Defence Studies and then became Assistant Director of Naval Warfare. He went on to become the first Captain of the aircraft carrier HMS *Illustrious*, bringing her out in record time from the shipbuilders for duty in the South Atlantic at the time of the Falklands conflict. He then became the Captain of the School of Maritime Operations at HMS Dryad.

In 1985 Sir Jock was promoted to Rear Admiral and became Assistant Chief of the Defence Staff (Policy and Nuclear). Further promotion to Vice Admiral followed in October 1987 on appointment as Flag Officer Scotland and Northern Ireland and Naval Base Commander, Rosyth. He was knighted in 1988 and went on to be Chief of Fleet Support and a Member of the Admiralty Board. He was promoted to full admiral in 1991 on appointment as Commander-in-Chief Fleet and a Major NATO Commander. Advanced to Knight Grand Cross of the Order of the Bath in 1992, he became Vice Chief of the Defence Staff in January 1993.

In July 1995 Sir Jock became First Sea Lord and Chief of the Naval Staff and played a key role in the Strategic Defence Review of 1997-98, not least arguing the case for the new generation of Aircraft Carriers. He stood down in October 1998, remaining on the Active List for life.

In retirement, Sir Jock has served as a non-executive director of the Vosper Thorneycroft Group and of Lockheed Martin UK. He is an Elder Brother of Trinity House and has also been Chairman of the Imperial War Museum and of the Royal National Lifeboat Institution and Prime Warden of the Worshipful Company of Shipwrights.

Michael Pearce

Mike Pearce served with the Ministry of Defence (Navy) for nearly 40 years and was on the staff of the Britannia Royal Naval College, Dartmouth for 12 years. Closely connected with the Royal Navy throughout his career, he held management and planning roles within many different fields of MoD activity and on numerous projects for the Royal Navy in London, Hampshire and at the Naval Base at Devonport. As a naval historian, he has been a trustee of the Britannia Museum since its inception in 2008 and is a series editor for the Britannia Naval Histories of World War II; in 2012 he co-authored, with Dr Richard Porter, the introduction to *Fight for the Fjords*, and in 2013 wrote the introduction to *Between Hostile Shores*, both in the series. His particular area of expertise is the period 1860-1960 and he continues to undertake research, both on behalf of the Trust and in his own areas of interest.

He traces his first spark of interest in naval matters back to the age of four, when his father lifted him shoulder-high on the Isle of Wight ferry so that he could see HMS *Vanguard*, the last British battleship. His interest in naval history took off in his teens when he started reading and buying naval history books—he has never stopped. At school he was often found tucked away in corners, avidly reading naval history and he counts himself fortunate that his career enabled him to put his knowledge to effective use.

Married to Anne, they have two grown-up children and live in South Devon where Mike is a qualified watchkeeper with the National Coastwatch Institution at Prawle Point.

Britannia Naval Histories of World War II

Britannia Naval Histories of World War II is a series containing reproduced historical material, newly commissioned commentary, maps, plans and first-hand accounts of specific battles. Each foreword is written by naval veterans of the highest order, including HRH Prince Philip, Duke of Edinburgh.

Never previously published in this format, World War II Battle Summaries are documents once stamped 'restricted' or 'classified' and held in the archive of Britannia Royal Naval College in Dartmouth, South West England. They are unique records written up by naval officers during the cinflict, and soon after 1945. Events are recorded in minute detail, accompanied by maps and plans drawn up during the period by serving officers. Where Führer Conferences are featured, these contain Hitler's words as they were mintued and typed at the time. These historical texts have been recognised in a contemporary format. The first-hand accounts are from worldwide sources and contain invididuals' reactions, emotions and descriptions, making fascinating reading 70 years on.

Introduction by
G H Bennett

Hitler's Ghost Ships
Graf Spee, Scharnhorst and Disguised German Raiders

Paperback
ISBN 978-184102-308-3 | **£17**
Hardback
ISBN 978-184102-307-6 | **£35**
Extent
224 pages
Format
156 x 234 mm
Category
JWMV2 Military and Naval Ships

Foreword
Admiral Sir Jonathon Band,
former First Sea Lord and Chief
of Naval Staff

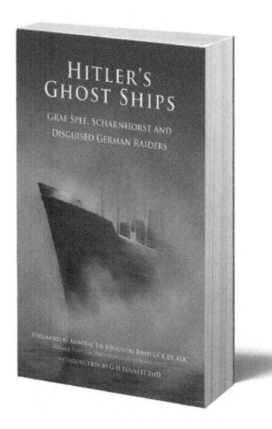

- The German Navy's tactics of disguise to oust the British fleet and isolate island Britain.
- Includes tracking maps drawn when the Battle Summary was compiled.

Disguised Auxiliary cruisers could sidle up to merchant vessels undetected as they were flying a neutral flag, similar to 17th century pirate ships. Completion of the disguised ships was difficult and took its toll on the German dockyard workers and crews, sailing in waters dominated by the Royal Navy. The Battle Summaries chart how the Royal Navy dealt with the threat of these raiders of 70 years ago.

Introduction by
M J Pearce and R Porter

Fight for the Fjords
The Battle for Norway 1940

Paperback
ISBN 978–184102–306–9 | **£17**
Hardback
ISBN 978–184102–305–2 | **£35**
Extent
408 pages
Format
156 x 234 mm
Category
JWMV2 Military and Naval Ships

Foreword
Admiral Lord Alan West, a
former First Sea Lord and
Parliamentary Under–Secretary
of State at the Home Office

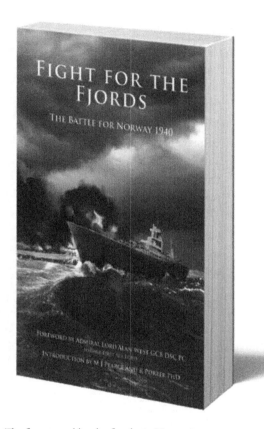

- Contains the wartime British and German documents that detail this famous sea battle.
- Includes tracking maps drawn when the Battle Summary was compiled.

The fierce naval battles fought in Norwegian waters during the spring of 1940 were recorded in documents that were once subject to restrictions under the Official Secrets Act. Fight for the Fjords includes the German account, written within three years of the end of World War II, and the British report, which compiled previously unavailable Royal Navy records to produce one complete account. The combination of these two summaries forms a unique record.

Introduction by
J E Harrold

Dark Seas
The Battle of Cape Matapan

Paperback
ISBN 978–184102–304–5 | **£17**
Hardback
ISBN 978–184102–303–8 | **£35**
Extent
160 pages
Format
156 x 234 mm
Category
JWMV2 Military and Naval Ships

Foreword
Written by HRH Prince Philip
who served in the action

※ The only publication to have a first-hand account of the battle by HRH Prince Philip.

※ Includes original hand-drawn maps and diagrams.

Written shortly after World War II, the summary of the Battle of Cape Matapan draws on first-hand accounts of action on both sides. Unearthed from archives, the vivid and compelling detail is reproduced and newly published as Dark Seas. During the battle, the enemy was hunted, trailed, avoided and engaged. Accurate intelligence combined with the inaccurate and misleading in the 'fog of war'. This is a unique insight into one of the last fleet engagements in naval history.

Introduction by
G H Bennett

Hunting Tirpitz
Naval Operations Against Bismarck's Sister Ship

Paperback
ISBN 978–184102–310–6 | **£17**
Hardback
ISBN 978–184102–309–0 | **£35**
Extent
304 pages
Format
156 x 234 mm
Category
JWMV2 Military and Naval Ships

Foreword
Admiral Sir Mark Stanhope,
First Sea Lord and Chief of
Naval Staff

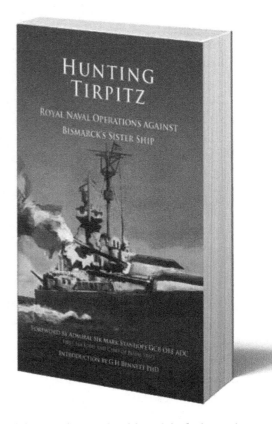

// Operation Chariot, Operation Source, Operation Tungsten are detailed and analysed.

// Includes original hand-drawn maps and diagrams.

// Contains newly translated first hand accounts by German crew members of Tirpitz.

While it was the RAF that delivered the final coup de grâce, it was the Royal Navy, from 1942 to 1944, that had contained, crippled and neutralised the German battleship in a series of actions marked by innovation, boldness and bravery. From daring commando raids on the coast of France, to the use of midget submarines in the fjords of Norway and devastating aerial attacks by the Fleet Air Arm, the Royal Navy pursued Tirpitz to her eventual destruction.

Introduction by
P D Grove

Turning the Tide
The Battles of Coral Sea and Midway

Paperback
ISBN 978-1-84102-333-5
Hardback
ISBN 978-1-84102-334-2
Number of Pages
240 pages

Foreword

Capt. John Rodgaard USN
During his 41 years with the
US Navy, Captain Rodgaard
also served on navy and joint
intelligence tours including
Submarine Group 8, Carrier
Group 4 and the J2 Defense
Intelligence Agency. He is an
author and has contributed
to the Discovery Channel's
Unsolved History series. He is
a graduate of the United States
Naval War College.

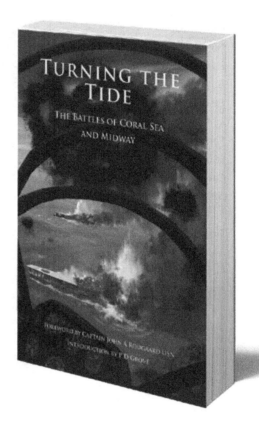

- ⫻ Includes tracking maps drawn when the Battle Summaries were compiled.
- ⫻ Explains the turning point of the Pacific War.

The Battles of Coral Sea and Midway in 1942 were the conflicts which resulted in the first naval victories for the United States. The tide turned for the US, following their amphibious landings on Guadalcanal. Japanese losses were devastating and many of the Japanese airmen who had carried out the attacks at Pearl Harbor would meet their end at the Battle of Midway.

Introduction by
G H Bennett, R Bennett
and E Bennet

Bismarck
The Chase and Sinking of Hitler's Goliath

Paperback
ISBN 978-1-84102-326-7
Hardback
ISBN 978-1-84102-327-4
Number of Pages
160 pages

Foreword
Commander 'Sharkey' Ward
DSC Author of *Sea Harrier over the Falklands*, Sharkey Ward is known as something of a maverick who led 801 Naval Air Squadron during the Falklands War in 1982. Ward retired from the Royal Navy in 1989 and lives in Grenada.

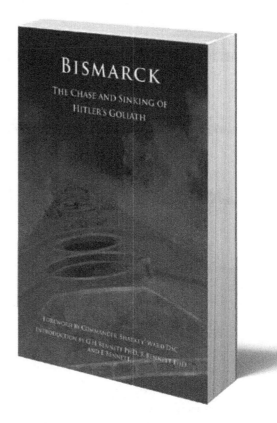

※ Contains both a German and British first-hand account.
※ Includes tracking maps drawn when the Battle Summary was compiled.
※ Quotes from the minutes of Führer Conferences, alongside signals sent to and from *Bismarck*.

Bismark – the most formidable surface ship in Hitler's fleet – was chased and finally sunk by the Royal Navy. This news, relayed at the time, later became a matter of speculation: did the mighty battleship sink during action or was she scuttled by her crew in a final act of defiance? Containing extraordinary detail from 1941 Führer Conferences on Naval Affairs and the Battle Summary from the Admiralty, this new title is an essential addition to the series.

Special Edition

Warships at a Glance, 1914: A Naval Cadet goes to War Foreword is by Capatain Henry Duffy, RN, Captain, Britannia Royal Naval College 2014.
Cloth bound ISBN 978-1-84102-376-2

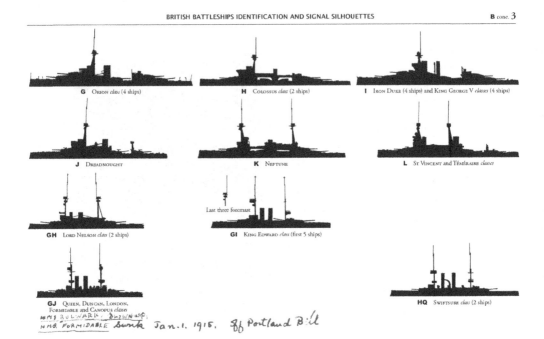

G Orion *class* (4 ships)   **H** Colossus *class* (2 ships)   **I** Iron Duke (4 ships) and King George V *classes* (4 ships)

J Dreadnought   **K** Neptune   **L** St Vincent and Téméraire *classes*

GH Lord Nelson *class* (2 ships)   Last three foremast   **GI** King Edward *class* (first 5 ships)

GJ Queen, Duncan, London, Formidable and Canopus *classes*   **HQ** Swiftsure *class* (2 ships)

HMS BULWARK. Blown up,
HMS FORMIDABLE Sunk, Jan. 1. 1915. off Portland Bill

This special edition of Warships At A Glance has been reproduced to mark the centenary of the outbreak of the First World War. It is a tribute to the cadets and midshipmen of the Royal Navy, some of them very young, who fought and died for their country in that conflict.

One copy in the Archive at BRNC, Dartmouth bears the name 'A L Tidd', written in the immature hand of a 14 year-old. Alec Lister Tidd was born on 12th April 1900 in Guildford, Surrey, and joined Osborne in Drake Term, in January 1914, leaving in April 1915 to join St Vincent Term of Britannia Royal Naval College at Dartmouth. Christmas 1916, he passed out from Dartmouth and was commissioned as a Midshipman with a seniority of 1st January 1917, joining the battleship HMS Neptune in the Grand Fleet at Scapa Flow, where he served until after the end of the First World War, being given the acting rank of Sub Lieutenant on 15th November 1918 and witnessing the surrender of Germany's High Seas Fleet seven days later. HMS Neptune was the only ship of her class and her silhouette is prominent in *Warships At A Glance*, among the newer battleships of the Royal Navy.

Made in the USA
Coppell, TX
18 March 2020

17070739R00109